D1600750

MARIE DE MÉDICIS

AN · QVID · HABENT · VERI · PRÆSAGIA · LOETA · FVTVRI
HOC · DOCET · HENRICI · CONIVGIALIS · AMOR ·
SCILICET · VT · CAPIVNT · MEDICES · GENTILIA · SIGNA
FRANCICA; SIC · CAPTVS · REX · IN · AMORE · TVO · EST ·

· IOHAN · WIRICX · EXCVE · 1601 ·

MARIE DE MEDICIS
AND THE FRENCH COURT IN THE XVIITH CENTURY:
TRANSLATED FROM THE FRENCH OF LOUIS BATIFFOL BY MARY KING EDITED BY H. W. CARLESS DAVIS

BOOKS FOR LIBRARIES PRESS
FREEPORT, NEW YORK

First Published 1908
Reprinted 1970

DC
122.9
M3
B3
1970

INTERNATIONAL STANDARD BOOK NUMBER:
0-8369-5569-2

LIBRARY OF CONGRESS CATALOG CARD NUMBER:
72-137368

PRINTED IN THE UNITED STATES OF AMERICA

AUTHOR'S PREFACE

THE particular endeavour of this volume is not to present the complete " psychology " of Marie de Médicis—a task which would entail the consideration of the Queen's public life and of her later history, after her fall from power in 1617. As its title shows, this work aims at presenting the picture of a French Queen surrounded by her Court, between the years 1600 and 1617, when Marie de Médicis was Queen and Queen-Regent—a period of particular interest, because one in which a new dynasty, but recently emerged from the throes of civil war, had not yet suffered the fate which buries the individuality of princes beneath the artificiality of courts and courtly etiquette. Under Henry IV., and for some years after his reign, the Court of France offers the picturesque spectacle of a great lord's household—royal in outward show, internally the home of a burgher. The King's peculiar character invested him with a manner and habit very different from the old world Valois elegance, and the future pomposity of Louis XIV. While part of the interest of this study lies, therefore, in its picture of real and original social conditions, certain less special conditions will also be brought upon the scene. We shall see that, however gradually the general scheme of the French Court was built up, and continued during

199369

successive centuries—and this scheme was preserved until the fall of the *ancien régime*, allowing only for developments arising from the continually increasing veneer of ceremonial—the scrupulous conservation of tradition was a passion with the men of that age ; that, amidst all the troubles and disorder of the sixteenth century, the administrative machine proper remained all-powerful with its spirit of narrow regulation, its tendency toward formalism, and meticulous and peremptory "functionalism." We shall thus see that the throne, in France in the early seventeenth century, was so far from wielding the absolute power claimed for it by contemporary jurists, as to be circumscribed on all sides by a series of passive forces, more masters of the State indeed than the King's self, and invoking principles of immemorial usage and the "fundamental laws of the Realm." Studies of the kind the issue of which now follows have, for this reason, a deeper interest than depends upon reconstructions of a vanished mode of life through its least details. They are essentially a contribution to the knowledge of institutions, ideas and customs, and it is by means of inquiries having for object the reconstitution of historic scenes that history will conduct us to a clearer understanding of past events.

L. B.

CONTENTS

CONTENTS

CHAPTER III

THE QUEEN'S HOUSEHOLD

CHAPTER IV

PALACE LIFE

CONTENTS

CHAPTER V

THE ROYAL FAMILY AND ITS ITALIAN CONNECTIONS

CONTENTS

CONTENTS

CHAPTER VI

THE QUEEN'S FRIENDS—LÉONORA GALIGAÏ

CHAPTER VII

ARTS AND ARTISTS

Marie de Médicis a patron of the arts rather as a lover of luxury than as connoisseur—Her patronage of, but total failure to influence, contemporary artists—Passion for jewels and favourite jewellers—Ruinous purchases of diamonds: her varied and splendid ornaments—Nicolas Roger and the Queen's patronage of the goldsmiths—Her relations with the architects—Salomon de Brosse, chief of these, works on the Château de Montceaux and builds the Luxembourg—Palace of the Luxembourg, a purely French work—The Queen as patron of the painters—Numerous orders for pictures and portraits—The Queen's painters—François Porbus—Many portraits of children—Tapestries—Marie de Médicis retains Decomans and La Planche—The Queen's *tapissier*, Antoine Mesnillet, commissioned to search out valuable textiles for her—The sculptors—Patronage of

CONTENTS

CHAPTER VIII

THE QUEEN'S PURSE

MARIE DE MÉDICIS

CHAPTER I

Sad childhood of Marie de Médicis—Death of her mother, brother, and sister—Remarriage of her father—Her companion in solitude, Léonora Galigaï—Severe education of Marie—Her beauty and health at seventeen—The marriage question—Numerous and brilliant pretenders rejected—The Princess, influenced by a prediction, will be Queen of France—Continual applications for loans by the Kings of France to the Grand Dukes of Tuscany at this time—Henry IV. would marry Marie for a dowry—The bargain—Ceremony and journey into France—Character and consequences of the temperament of the new Queen at this time —Her gaiety and graciousness, moderate intellect and variable temper—Neurotic tendencies—Purity, passion for magnificence, liberality—Formal religiosity—Gifts and alms—Impersonal and obligatory good works.

THE little Princess of Tuscany, Marie de Médicis, was brought up in that Pitti Palace which Ammanati had recently made so beautiful. Yet, amidst all the treasures of art accumulated by her family, and the luxurious life affected by her father, her childhood was a sad one, for she was barely five years old when, in 1578, her mother died. This pale and delicate Archduchess, Joan of Austria, grand-daughter of the Emperor Ferdinand, the brother of Charles V., had been a woman of no great intelligence. Her death, due to the brutality of the hard man whom she had married, left four young children alone—one son, Philip, and three daughters, Eleanor, Anne, and Marie.[1] The father, Francesco

---

[1] Historians variously ascribe Marie's birth to 1573 and 1574. The date of 1573 is assumed in these pages. P. Matthieu relates that owing to an error under which the child was believed a boy, the people loudly

A

Maria de' Medici—who, in 1574, succeeded Cosimo I. as Grand Duke of Tuscany—was a vigorous, violent prince, endowed with brilliant mental gifts and refined tastes, but egotistical, proud, and passionate to the point of cruelty. His vain, false, and ugly nature was entirely given over to passions which he knew neither how to resist nor to control, and his connection with the notorious Bianca Capello had long been the talk of Italy and all the foreign Courts. Two months after his wife's death he married this woman, and too impatient to endure the presence of his children who recalled unwelcome memories, installed them in the Pitti, and retired with Bianca to the solitude of Pratolino. Immured in this place, and abjuring all company, he busied himself in supervising the increase of his fortune, which was assured by galleons laden with merchandise, banking-houses in all the principal cities of Italy, and shops through which he trafficked in grain and diamonds. Their stepmother was a cause of shame and sorrow to the children.   Marie de Médicis avowed later that, " in seeing the widow of a Florentine burgher " take her mother's place, " she found the burden of shame from this disgraceful alliance almost intolerable."   Duke Gonzaga of Mantua wrote to the Archduke Ferdinand : " The Grand Duke has not feared, if not to abandon his daughters entirely to this debased woman, at least to permit them publicly to accompany her through Florence." [1]

Less than a year after Joan of Austria's death, Bianca Capello was giving brilliant entertainments— balls, banquets, tourneys, plays, country parties, and hunting the bull or wild beasts with nets.   She had persuaded the Grand Duke that a certain Antonio was their son, and the Prince, becoming passionately fond of this child, loaded him with favours, settled upon him sixty

acclaimed the birth. On hearing that his child was a girl, the Grand Duke consoled himself with the remark " that he believed she would be a big one."

[1] For those who would study the history of Florence or the Medici at this time, no work will be found more useful than R. Galluzzi's " History of the Grand Duchy of Tuscany."

thousand crowns, a palace in Florence, and a country house at Magia. For the rest, Bianca's frequent " hopes " of motherhood were far more interesting to him than thoughts of his daughters in the Pitti.

Child as she was, Marie de Médicis retained only painful impressions of this period of her life. Whether they were chance or omen, the terrible accidents of the time remained graven upon her memory, and sixty years later she still spoke of them with terror. Thrice lightning struck her room ; once it broke the windows, the second time injured her tire-woman, and the third time burned the curtains of a bed ; and twice earthquakes shook Florence, and rocked the ducal palace. Finally, walking one day by the sea near Pisa, the little Princess was all but drowned. She was to suffer other and yet greater troubles.

Her brother Philip, always puny and delicate, died in 1583. Their sister Anne, five years her senior, a gay and lively girl who contributed some gaiety to their little group, died suddenly, on February 19, 1584, from fever following long-continued bleeding at the nose. She was fifteen years old. In the same year Eleanor married the Duke of Mantua. Marie de Médicis, a child of eleven years, was thus left alone, motherless and almost fatherless, subject to an etiquette which required her to remain confined as much as possible to the great palace, and surrounded almost entirely by strangers.

Seeing her thus isolated, those about her obtained the Duke's sanction to the idea of providing her with a young companion, and chose for the purpose Léonora Dori, afterwards called Galigaï, a child her junior by three years. Léonora was not a pretty child, being thin, dark, small, and nervous ; but she was very intelligent, full of spirits, and of an infectious gaiety, described later by her secretary as " a pleasing and droll humour." On the point of her origin contemporary gossip of twenty or thirty years later than this date was ill-natured, alleging her now daughter of a cabinetmaker, now of a carpenter and a fallen

woman, and in any case stigmatising her as "a girl of low
birth," also " as devoid of education as she was lacking in
the graces of her sex." Her extreme unpopularity must
put us on our guard against these statements. When
questioned during her trial, in 1617, as to her social
position, Léonora declared her mother's name as Caterina
Dori, and that her father, whom she had never known, was
a Florentine gentleman. The Court of Henry IV., when,
in 1600, there was question of accepting Léonora Galigaï
as Mistress of the Robes at Paris, made inquiries as to
whether she were fitted by birth to enter the Queen's
coach, and received for reply that the friend of Marie
de Médicis was of good burgher blood, the which was,
in Florence, equivalent to noble rank.

The two little girls agreed very well, for Léonora,
who was shrewd, clever, and prudent, attached herself to
her mistress, taking the greatest pains to oblige and
amuse—" very diligent to follow and to do her will."
Marie, alone as she was, and otherwise surrounded only
by older, rather austere persons, became very fond of
the devoted companion who sought only to please her—
" who beguiled her time and took counsel with her ";
and thus was founded that regard which habit was only to
strengthen, and which was to last until death.

The Grand Duke Francis, seized by a violent fever,
died suddenly, on October 9, 1587, at the early age of
forty-seven, and when Bianca Capello followed him next
day, within a few hours, the mysterious double fatality
excited the suspicions of the Florentines, mortal enemies
of their Grand Duke. Her father's death greatly im-
proved Marie's position. In default of heirs male, the
Grand Duchy of Tuscany passed to her uncle, Ferdinand,
Cardinal-Deacon of the Holy Roman Church, who forthwith renounced the purple to assume this secular
dignity. Heavily built and stout like his brother,
although but thirty-eight years of age, and without distinction of manner, Ferdinand was good and liberal—as
moderate and benevolent as Francis had been hard and

unfeeling—" of genial disposition and kindly ways, and loved his niece as if she were his daughter." On April 30, 1589, he married Christine, Princess of Lorraine—a niece of Catarina de' Medici, who herself brought about this marriage—a girl of sixteen, just the age of Marie de Médicis. With the arrival of this young Archduchess at Florence, the Pitti resumed the air of gaiety and of festivity long unknown to it. The parity in age of the aunt and niece was an advantage but also an inconvenience, making it very difficult for the princesses to maintain the conventional distance between them. During the early part of Christine's residence at the Pitti, signalised by sumptuous festivities—celebrations such as Marie de Médicis had never known—Ferdinand was full of kindness for Marie, and Christine very gracious. Her children, two sons and a daughter, were soon, however, to absorb the latter's affections.

The Grand Duke Francis had confided Marie's education to Madame Orsini, a Roman lady, of severe and narrow ideas, who kept her in the most complete retirement, allowed her to see no one, and took care that she should know nothing either of politics or affairs—" keeping constant watch over her." By this method the little Princess of Tuscany was kept in effectual ignorance of the world, but, on the other hand, learned docility and respect for her father, and, after his death, for her uncle and aunt. By order of her father, also, Antonio, Bianca's son, was associated with her in her studies, since rivalry is a spur, and later a cousin, Virginio Orsino, son of the Duke of Bracciano and of Isabella de' Medici. Antonio, on account of his origin, was too much hated to produce any impression upon Marie de Médicis, but with Virginio it was otherwise. Their early comradeship presently ripened into a warmer affection, mutual it seems, but one which never amounted to love, at all events in the girl's case. Probably it was no serious matter, and but for an indiscretion of Christine, Marie's youthful aunt, the bitter jealousy of Henry IV., and the frivolous conversation of the French Court at a later date, nothing would have come down to us of the vague idyl of two young people.

Although her father ordained that his daughter should receive all the instruction considered desirable at that day, Marie was not taught French. The arts, on the other hand, were taught her in a very practical manner. The Grand Duke was a scholar and an artist, a botanist, chemist, and lapidary; he painted, and made porcelain in imitation of the Chinese. He was also no mean connoisseur of precious stones. Marie inherited these tastes, and applied herself with zest to painting, architecture, music, sculpture, and engraving. Thus Philippe de Champaigne was afterwards to receive a design of her own engraving, probably a work of this period and still extant in the Cabinet des Estampes—too finished, however, to be a child's work, so that we must believe that the Princess's skill owed much to the zeal of her master.

In the matter of precious stones, Marie was her father's zealous disciple and quickly learned to distinguish the real from the false, thus unfortunately acquiring an extravagant taste which was to prove her bane through life. She had also a pronounced liking for mathematics, and delighted in the theatre and music which were in high favour at her uncle's Court. Jacopo Peri and Julio Caccini were now composing their operas, and Ottavio Rinuccini setting to music the pastoral *Daphne*.

Marie de Médicis was, at seventeen, a tall, blonde girl, eminently healthy though inclined to stoutness, of a fresh and brilliant complexion, and possessed of regular features which, without laying positive claim to beauty, still made her a lively and wholesome person to behold. Her looks, indeed, bore witness to her mixed origin. From her Austrian mother she inherited the lower part of her face—the prominent chin of the Hapsburgs, their sufficiently pure oval, somewhat full lips and not very distinguished mouth, and their delicate and well-shaped nose. From the Medici side she inherited her father's broad and beautiful forehead, his firm and direct glance, and the assured bearing of the monied burgher class. Intellectually this mixed inheritance was less profitable, for, with her mother's insufficient intellect, she had her father's tenacious will, a combination of characteristics which makes only for obstinacy. Gracious, amiable, and smiling, Marie was none the less a woman whose glance and brow betrayed a rather limited and stubborn personality, and of this she early proved herself the possessor.

The heiress of those great merchants and bankers, the Medici, was a " royal " match, and the question of Marie's marriage was not long to be delayed. Her uncle Ferdinand, intent upon following the policy most likely to secure him the greatest profit, had no intention of disposing of her except under the most advantageous conditions, or of giving her up unless in return for large and sure political hopes. At one moment Virginio was thus a cause of some anxiety, for had he not, Sully was afterwards to write, " dared to conceive hopes above his station " ? Christine had been obliged to forbid the young man any communication with Marie, and to keep him under surveillance. But Marie had no fancy for him, and seems to have troubled herself very little about the matter.

Many were the negotiations projected, studied, and given up. Already in 1587, Marie being then fourteen, Ferdinand, newly come to his throne and yet uncertain as to potentialities, entertained thoughts of a match with the son of the Duke of Ferrara. The idea did not proceed much further, for the foreign Courts became uneasy on learning that the Grand Duke was considering this question. Spain was particularly agitated, it being of the first importance to that country that the accumulated treasures of Florence should not, by means of a dangerous alliance, pass into the control of some political adversary. With tireless perseverance, therefore, did this country keep watch upon, and employ itself in thwarting, all projects; and having once assured the failure of the combination with Ferrara, insinuated the advantages of a marriage with the Farnese of Parma. Here, however, His Catholic Majesty reckoned without the suitor. The Prince of Parma had his own reasons for declining the suggestion. Nothing abashed, the King presented a new candidate in the Duke of Braganza, ready enough to press his suit, but this time rejected by Ferdinand. Next, the Grand Duchess Christine suggested a French Prince—Monsieur de Vaudémont, of the house of Lorraine—and was greatly surprised to encounter an energetic resistance from Marie herself. This needed explanation. Léonora, the Princess's little confidant, was accused of giving bad advice. Explanations were difficult, a scene followed, and Léonora was threatened with dismissal.

At this juncture Ferdinand himself conceived the brilliant idea of marrying his niece to the Archduke Matthias, heir and brother of the Emperor, Rudolf II. Having recently lost his Archduchess, Maximilienne Grégoire, this pretender had no objection to marrying a second time. The Grand Duke, therefore, essayed the impossible to compass his end—insinuation, artifice, flattery, presents to the Prince's governor, the Marquis of Denia; and even condescended to baser intrigues, but to no avail. Thereupon the King of Spain reappeared, putting Braganza forward for the second time. But Braganza was not a reigning Prince, and the Grand Duke declared that he could not accept for his niece a person in the condition of a private individual. He aspired to place her " in a higher position than that in which she was born, and to make a more advantageous match for her." The Emperor, thus put upon his mettle, reconsidered possibilities, demanded Marie de Médicis either for himself or for his brother the Archduke, and despatched one of his councillors, Corradino, to Florence.

Ferdinand, enchanted, agreed upon the dowry. His niece should have six hundred thousand crowns if she married the Emperor, four hundred thousand if her husband were the Archduke. Corradino, however, found it impossible to fix a date. The peace must come first—and other things. After much absurd manœuvring Ferdinand at last understood that he was being mocked. He was to be kept in suspense as long as the Emperor was concerned that the Princess of Tuscany should not marry an adversary; that danger over, the contract would be broken. Highly incensed, he retracted his promises.

For herself Marie de Médicis was unmoved, having her own ideas. She had chanced to meet a Capuchin nun, then famous throughout Italy for her holiness, who had founded a great monastery at Siena with the alms showered upon her, and this woman had predicted that she should be Queen of France. Such a prediction greatly impressed her, and Léonora, with ambitions and intelligence for the pair of them, had no difficulty in convincing her that she must wait for this crown. Whether she also counselled Marie against all the other matches remains a debatable point. Florence of course believed it, and long afterwards reproached her with it at her trial. She defended herself clumsily then, but the point is really of no account; such advice certainly accorded with Marie's own ideas.

Relations between France and the Grand Duchy of Tuscany were extremely close at this moment. The Most Christian Kings, when in straits for money, had long been in the habit of applying to the enormously rich Florentine banker, and interest and policy were alike wont to claim his attention to their pleas. Between the years 1562 and 1569, Charles IX. had thus borrowed one hundred and ninety-two thousand eight hundred and fifty-seven gold ducats. Fighting inch by inch, single handed and without resources, Henry IV. was obliged to draw still more heavily upon the wealth of Florence in order to conquer the realm left him by Henry III.'s death. The Grand Duke was credited with the enormous income of twenty millions, almost the amount of the entire revenue of France. With a commercial instinct as strong as his brother's, Ferdinand had continued all his predecessor's business affairs, selling grain, maintaining a fleet for the transport and coasting-trade, and pushing the enormous exchange and banking interests of his house. Having a share in almost all the principal houses of Florence, he was even said to have organised a contraband trade in the Spanish colonies, under the Dutch and English flags, and to have shared the profitable piracies of these two nations upon the subjects of the King of Spain. The bankruptcy of Philip II. ruined many of the Florentine houses, but left their astute ruler untouched—witness the immense fortune of which he died possessed.

The transport of a hundred thousand crowns from the banks of the Arno to Paris required seventeen waggons, escorted by five companies of cavalry and two hundred foot-soldiers, and as the loans made by Florence to Henry IV. grew in number, a singular situation came to pass. To justify his requests and to obtain his end, Henry IV. humbled himself, spoke of protection, multiplied respectful expressions and evidences of a submissive spirit, and allowed it to be understood that he sought advice. Florence, on the other hand, became angry; complaints and reproaches were heard on all sides, and the city adopted a tone of singular liberty and remonstrance. The King spent too much. Florence would not ruin herself for him. "How comes it that the kingdom of France, which is richer than we are, does not suffice for you?" Pressed by necessity, Henry IV. proceeded yet further. He proposed to become Catholic, thinking thus to please the Grand Duke. He was ready to promise anything.

In 1592, Cardinal de Gondi, entrusted with the negotiation of another loan, and expatiating to Ferdinand upon the projects of the King of France, explained these intentions and hazarded the remark that Henry might procure from Rome an annulment of his marriage with

Marguerite de Valois. When free, might he not marry Marie de Médicis? Gondi, a prudent man, added that the Grand Duke would undoubtedly give his niece the dowry of a million gold crowns. Ferdinand seized upon this scheme with alacrity, and since he raised no immediate objection to the sum named, the Cardinal assumed his consent. Henry IV., notified of the result of the interview, was delighted. There was, after all, time in which to reflect, for the annulment of his marriage was yet to be. He, therefore, hastened to send La Clielle to Florence to confirm Gondi's statements. Promises passed in his name. Meanwhile, loans were more easily raised.

Here the affair almost fell through. Henry IV. was too occupied in securing his kingdom; his heart wandered elsewhere, and Florence, well informed as to what passed at Paris, considered that the King's passion for Gabrielle d'Estrées made the marriage impossible. Ferdinand's hopes were dimmed, and the search for a husband for his niece proceeded in other quarters. A year or two passed thus, when the King's councillors, ready to eliminate the alarming prospect of his marrying Gabrielle d'Estrées at any cost, determined to reopen the question of an alliance with Marie de Médicis. The sentiment of the whole kingdom was for Henry's remarriage, and fears of a scandalous union with the mistress were no less universal. In 1597, the Legate mentioned the Princess of Tuscany to Cardinal de Gondi. The Pope strongly favoured the annulment of the King's marriage with Marguerite, the removal of Gabrielle, and the Florentine scheme. The King was in overwhelming need of money. Financial necessity and concern for his dignity moved his ministers : he himself at last bowed to the former.

The debts owed by France to the Medici had become more and more considerable. With the sums which he had himself borrowed added to the still unpaid debt inherited from his predecessors, Henry IV. found himself indebted to an amount greater than he could possibly repay—

by common report two hundred millions, in fact something less. To Claude Groulart, the King acknowledged a debt of five hundred thousand crowns ; in fact, he owed one million, one hundred and seventy-four thousand, one hundred and forty-seven gold crowns—a sum which he could never hope to find ? Out of all patience at last, and full of wrath, the Grand Duke finally seized as security Château d'If and the Pomègues Islands, opposite Marseilles. The King, obliged to pocket his shame in silence, fell a prey to the threats and arguments of his advisers who averred that the single act of marrying Marie de Médicis might wipe out his debts, obtain " great store of monies for his own affairs, and free his kingdom of its excessive debts," and, in the person of his new uncle, secure a banker easy of access. Thus compelled, Henry IV. did not act by halves. " I am of those," he gaily wrote to Monsieur de Chatte, " who believe that a good marriage should aid them in the paying part of their debts." Yet, refractory as ever where inclination and interest clashed, Gabrielle d'Estrées, and afterwards Henriette d'Entraigues, Marquise de Verneuil, were retained at his side—each under promise of marriage.

Florence was, as usual, well informed by its agents, and Geronimo Gondi found the Grand Duke ready when he arrived to reopen negotiations. Rome, obstinate where there was question of divorcing Marguerite de Valois that a mistress might take her place and so legitimise her bastards, had few scruples should the supplanter be Marie de Médicis. Gondi, therefore, found little difficulty in agreement upon the principal point of marriage, but a dowry of a million crowns was quite another matter. Plead as he might that Ferdinand had accepted this but a few brief years before, the Florentine's indignation overflowed. Such exorbitant demands were not to be entertained for a moment, and Villeroy and Rosny had perforce to recall their envoy.

The venue was now changed, Baccio Giovannini journeying to the Louvre on behalf of the Grand Duke.

There, Henry IV. began by demanding nothing less than one and a half millions—the million to be remitted from his debts, the remainder to be paid cash down. Giovannini must realise that, in 1592, when Henry's throne was not assured, Florence had consented for a million. He was undisputed king now, and so worth a half the more. The envoy replied that he had orders not to follow the French Court upon this ground, that he could offer five hundred thousand crowns, and that the Emperor would have been contented with four hundred thousand for his heir, the Archduke. Secretly, however, the Florentine entreated his master to compromise since " if the King do not marry Marie, he will marry either a mistress or not at all, the kingdom be ruined, and Florence lose the entirety of her loans." On the other side, the ministers no less urgently pressed reason on the King. Let him be content with eight hundred thousand crowns. Papal influence was invoked with the Duke of Tuscany, the annulment of Marguerite de Valois's marriage was pressed at Rome, and when Ferdinand at length consented to six hundred thousand crowns, the King's ministers, more and more disturbed by his passion for Henriette d'Entraigues, decided that he must accept that sum. Truly, Sully declared, no Queen of France brought ever yet such a portion, and to Henry IV. he added, with no intention of irony, " It is not fitting that your Majesty marry a wife for money, nor yet that the Grand Duke buy your alliance with the like." Thus, partly for weariness, partly through indifference—his mind being elsewhere—Henry IV. yielded. Marie de Médicis should bring to France six hundred thousand crowns ; of these, three hundred and fifty thousand were to come in cash, the remaining quarter of a million to be written off the royal account.

The poor Princess Marie counted for little in this argument, her tastes or her happiness being clearly of quite secondary consideration. The King of France knew almost nothing of his future bride, and he asked less. Hearing " of the virtues, the graces, the Christian piety, and the beauty of this accomplished Princess," he was content to accept these crude facts, and not until six months after the decision was made did he inquire of Monsieur d'Alincourt, newly returned from Florence, what might be that courtier's opinion of his bride to be. Monsieur d'Alincourt, good courtier as he was, could but give " an honourable account both of the person and the worth of the Princess." Henry IV. declared himself " very well satisfied," adding, it is true, " as I am with the tenor of the clauses in the marriage-contract." He was pleased to satisfy himself of her good health, and that she seemed likely to bear him children, also that she was accustomed to ride on horse-back, for he proposed that she should travel a good deal during the first year, in which he would show her the kingdom. Among other things, he would take her to Pau, there to inspect the paternal mansion of the old Kings of Navarre, and the garden planted by himself in his child-hood. The two Courts exchanged portraits of the consorts to be.

For Marie, now in her twenty-seventh year, the debate was well ended, for after so many abortive plans for her marriage, she had well-nigh come to despair. When, after the first retreat of the King of France, Archduke Matthias, a deformed and violent man, was presented to her, she had declared retirement to a convent prefer-able to such an alliance. At this time deep melancholy preyed upon her, undermining her health so much that the freshness and brilliancy of her beauty began to fade. The conclusion of the French arrangement restored her. Concerning herself little with the man himself, she took no objection to the number of his mistresses, nor yet to his open preference for Henriette d'Entraigues. All Florence exulted with her in the event which was to place her upon the most important throne of Europe, and the dreams of the little Princess were realised.

The marriage compact was concluded late in December

of the year 1599. Early in the following spring, Sillery arrived in Florence with his son d'Alincourt, and the contract was signed upon April the twenty-fifth. The actual marriage did not, however, take place until six months later. It was decided, for many reasons, that Marie should not enter France until September, and that the ceremony should take place at Florence, Henry IV. there to be represented by his master of the horse, the Duc de Bellegarde. Thanks, however, to the war with the Duke of Savoy, the King's intrigue, more violent than ever, with Henriette d'Entraigues, and a thousand other pretexts, September wore out and the actual ceremony was not performed until the fifth day of October.

The Tuscan capital then devoted itself to ten whole days of sumptuous festivities. Monsieur de Bellegarde came accompanied by thirty French gentlemen and a brilliant suite. The papal legate, Cardinal Aldobrandini, who was to give the nuptial benediction, entered Florence under a canopy, escorted by five hundred horsemen, to the sound of cannon and the acclamations of the crowd. The celebration thus proceeded in the midst of the greatest splendour. The artists Giovanni di Bologna and Buontalenti designed the triumphal arches, decorations for the theatres, and dances and costumes. On the thirteenth of the month Marie de Médicis finally left Florence, and her journey into France began. At Pisa there were renewed rejoicings, banquets, combats on the Arno, and illuminations in her honour. She then embarked at Leghorn, where awaited her a little squadron of ships, furnished by Henry IV., the Grand Duke, the Pope, and the Order of Malta. The galley which was to transport the Queen and her dowry was magnificent, sparkling with gold and silver, and richly inlaid, but its passage was long. Touching at Portofino, and lying for eight days at Genoa on account of bad weather, the ships were again delayed at Antibes and Toulon, and not until the twenty-third day of an interminable voyage, " the weariness and annoyances " of which were with difficulty beguiled by concerts and games, did the party land at Marseilles [1] on November 9th at five o'clock in the evening.

Henry IV. did not receive his wife, being still engaged in the mountains of Savoy, but the reception was magnificent. From Paris came a large number of important personages, ministers, nobles, prelates, and the Ladies-in-waiting of the new Queen—so great a company that the Court, charged with its maintenance, provided for the victualling of seven thousand mouths, including the ships' crew. The Grand Duchess of Tuscany, having accompanied her niece as far as Marseilles and there solemnly delivered her and her dowry into the hands of the French, tearfully took leave of Marie de Médicis and re-embarked. During her slow progress towards Lyon, in order that the King might conclude his war and join her, the Queen held festival at Avignon, tarried here and there, and finally ended her fifteen days' journey by entering Lyon on December 3rd. Here the customary welcome of the Queens of France awaited her, as, under a canopy, the streets hung with tapestries, she was greeted by a procession of magistrates, clergy, and nobility, by the firing of artillery, the ringing of bells, and the acclamations of the people. The King's arrival, fixed for the tenth, really took place on the evening of the ninth, when he arrived incognito. Proceeding to the Queen's hotel, and being directed to the room where she sat at supper, he there watched her, concealed behind Monsieur de Bellegarde, nor would he disclose his presence until Marie had retired to her chamber. Having knocked at the door of this, Henry made himself known to his wife, overwhelmed her with caresses, and even embraced Léonora-Galigaï *à la française*.

[1] From various authorities we learn that the mixed character of the Queen's escorting squadron was due to the French King's total lack of vessels of war. He was therefore reduced to borrowing and even hiring. Further, the squadron was not collected to do honour to the new Queen, but to assure her safety against possible attacks by the Corsairs, who then ravaged these coasts almost as they pleased.

This done, however, he declared that there was for him neither chamber nor bed in the Queen's hotel, of which she signified her understanding. Then, on the morrow, in the cathedral, Henry IV. solemnly repeated in person that nuptial ceremony which was before performed by proxy in Florence, and at this, as at that, Cardinal Aldobrandini officiated. Marie, clad sumptuously in a blue mantle wrought with the fleur-de-lis, bore upon her head the royal crown. Subsequently, several matters, including the peace with Savoy, having kept them at Lyon for yet some days, the King saw his consort set out towards Paris, where she was not to arrive until two months later, whilst he himself rode full speed to rejoin his cherished Henriette d'Entraigues at the Château de Verneuil. Of the marriage-day at Lyon it was reported to the Grand Duke Ferdinand that his niece, "instead of showing joy at her joining unto so great a man, did nothing but weep and lament." What may have thus moved the young Queen—regret for the past, apprehension of the future, sudden emotion, or unforeseen disenchantment—we cannot tell. But, be this as it may, a year was not passed before there were born to Henry IV., at an interval of a few days, the Dauphin, son of Marie de Médicis, and Gaston, Duc de Verneuil, son of Henriette d'Entraigues.

During the days following his marriage, Henry IV. seemed very happy, and was continually heard to say that the Queen was beautiful—more beautiful than he had been told or than he would have believed from her portraits. He averred that he loved her not only as his wife but also as his mistress, and that she was above all others that one woman whom he could have desired for his consort. And, truly, the Queen was resplendent in her new grandeur. So also, once again, was she to appear to her contemporaries as the most beautiful woman of the Court, on the day after the King's death, when her sombre robes of mourning, throwing into relief her beautiful fair complexion, ill concealed the satisfaction with which she knew herself Queen-Regent of the kingdom. " For albeit there were at this season certain exceeding fair ladies at Court, to wit, and in especial, Mademoiselle d'Urfé that was to be wed with the Duc de Crouy, and Mademoiselle de Bains—ladies of the Household both, and in first flower of their age—yet might none of all compare for beauty with the Queen who was doubtless more beautiful by far than in the days of the King's life, having her blood as it were refreshed by virtue of those powers which were now come between her hands."

Marie de Médicis, a healthy and fresh girl, had certainly become a beautiful young woman, radiant with health, by the time of her marriage. A contemporary who saw her at this time in Paris describes her " fine figure, full and well developed, a little coarse, perhaps, but with beautiful eyes and complexion, and that unmarred by paint, powder, or other vain devices." The King himself described her as " by nature terribly robust and strong," while " As for myself," she wrote daily to her friends, " I was never better in my life." Henry had once sent her the gay command to " be always well and blooming." The latter epithet pleased her, and she continued to use it of herself.

In order to preserve this good health, of which he declared his need " in order to have of you as beautiful children as Gabrielle has given me," Henry IV. submitted her to a special course of hygiene, beginning with physic and bleeding. Under his urgent advice, others, such as the Florentine envoy, purged themselves thrice in three days to " expel all waste and superfluities, that nature suffer not thereby." Copious blood-letting completed the cure. Hélie Bardin, the surgeon, was now commanded to bleed the Queen at regular intervals " to refresh her, and keep her in condition," an operation that cost the treasury one hundred and fifty livres each time, and from which Marie was convinced that she received much benefit. Thus " they have drawn me such bad blood," she once wrote to Concini " that the letting of it must indeed have been necessary." Henry IV. was also a believer in the high efficacy of the waters of Pougues and Spa. These he drank in quantities at all times, causing them to be carried wherever he might be, and sometimes further betook himself to such quiet spots as Montceaux or Fontainebleau to take a regular cure. He prescribed the habit for his wife. " I take these waters," she wrote to Léonora, " not that I am ill, but to lay in a supply of good health," and in pursuance of this system she drank " sometimes as many as nine glasses of water within a few hours." As the treatment continued for eight days, we need not be surprised that the Queen found it prolific in results, but rather, perhaps, that she was never ill. From Italy she had brought with her a trouble of the stomach, which the Italian doctors never cured " because they have never understood the cause of the trouble, and prescribed for me only hot things," while the French doctors cured her, recognising " that it originated in the heat of the liver, and so ordering me only cold and refreshing things." Thus, although on principle she kept the chest of medicines sent to her by the Grand Duke of Tuscany, " remedies for many kinds of dangerous maladies," and maintained in her household the distiller, Charles Huart, to prepare for her " good and salutary remedies," she never needed to have recourse whether to the one or the other. Her greatest ill was a toothache, and then, mistrusting the French doctors, although by her own confession " both numerous and expert," she summoned one Geronimo, " operator," commanding him to come from Italy, " in all haste, and with all his recipes and medicaments for this same affliction good, therewith likewise engines for the drawing out of teeth, if haply of such there be need."

Marie's physical health was uneventful save at the times of her pregnancy, when she sometimes suffered acutely from the painful and violent scenes caused by her jealousy of the Marquise de Verneuil. She bore the birth of the Dauphin very well, though " for some time

considered in great danger," because, as she thought, she
had partaken of too much fruit ; but her other children
entered life less easily. In 1605, leaving Tours for
Amboise, she dictated, in a letter to a friend, " the state
of my health is such that I cannot use my hand to
write." Endless and violent disorders disturbed the
doctors. " A troublesome hemorrhage of the stomach,"
she informed the Grand Duchess of Tuscany, two years
later and under the like circumstances, "has tormented
me for ten or twelve days, obliges me to keep my bed,
and wears me out." With her second son, a Duke of
Orleans, who died young, the extreme fatigues, combined
with the anxiety caused her by Henriette d'Entraigues,
resulted in the infant's coming in the most pitiable state,
with water on the brain, subject to convulsions, and little
likely to live. Prior, again, to the birth of Henriette, it
was necessary to suspend all the gaieties of the Court.
Marie wasted terribly, and was tortured by violent attacks
of colic. After this confinement, which left her in a very
dangerous state, the Queen wrote to the Duchess of
Mantua that " I was racked with great pains, colics, and
internal suffocations, from which I suffered terribly."
Her prostration and weakness were so prolonged on this
occasion that Henry IV. was himself much disturbed.

The Queen's troubles were not due to want of care for
her, for, having desired to give birth to all her children
at Fontainebleau—of which she was very fond, and
where all but Henriette were born—the oval room in
that palace, now called Louis XIII.'s room, was prepared
with a " fair bed of red velvet cramoisy and adorned
with gold," and covered by a canopy of Holland cloth.
Her attendant was a midwife of repute, Louise Bourgeois,
wife to the surgeon-barber, Martin Boursier. This matron
was not only a woman of experience, but was also well
versed in medicine and able to write technical treatises—
witness that still extant on *Les Six Couches de Marie
de Médicis*. Marie was further attended by a surgeon-
accoucheur, much sought after at this time and famous

for his skill, Monsieur Honoré—" very expert," the Queen declares when recommending him to the Duchess of Lorraine, " and I am very glad to have him with me when in your predicament." Finally, the King's Physician-in-Ordinary, Monsieur Petit, was always present.

Heavenly aid was still the most important remedy with Henry IV.'s contemporaries, and it was eagerly solicited on the Queen's behalf. In all the churches of Paris, and all over the kingdom, prayers were said during forty hours ; Marie de Médicis " began a course of prayer " called " that of the Three Thursdays " ; the Treasurer-General of her household, Monsieur Florent d'Argouges, liberated the prisoners and distributed abundant alms ; finally, and above all, everybody invoked Saint Margaret. Prayer to Saint Margaret for the happy delivery of women in childbed was much the fashion, and Marie de Médicis, who firmly believed in it, caused the life of the Saint to be read aloud to her. There was at Saint Germain des Prés a piece of Saint Margaret's girdle, credited with many virtues, and in much request even by private in-dividuals who were wont to obtain a temporary use of it. The Abbey held a solemn festival yearly in its honour " to render fruitful the women who were sterile," and to ease the labour of those who were not so. Marie de Médicis sent to the Prior at Fontainebleau for this precious frag-ment, which, being brought to her by two monks, reposed upon a velvet-covered table in the oval chamber while the Queen suffered, the pious priests remaining on their knees in a neighbouring room.

Marie de Médicis' death was attributed, in 1642, to hypertrophy of the heart, and if this was true, the cardiac affection may have been due to the many emotions and deceptions of the second half of her life. There was no sign of such weakness in the time of her glory and power, but her " nervous and sanguine nature," mentioned by the Florentine envoy, Guidi, may have predisposed her to it. A " nervous and sanguine nature," at all events, best explains the moral character of Marie de Médicis.

Marie de Médicis has left upon history a most un-favourable impression. Summing up this judgment of posterity, Saint-Simon sketched an extremely severe portrait of her, and looking upon the curious drawing—now at Munich—in which Van Dyck depicts her as she was in her later days, one is tempted to lend credence to the rude author of the *Parallèle des Trois Premiers Bourbons.* This, truly, is the face of an ill-natured and jealous woman, whose repellent physiognomy proclaims " a mind extremely limited, always governed by the worst element at Court, without knowledge and without judgment, hard, haughty, imperious. . . ." Between her fall from power in 1617 and her death at Cologne in 1642, the Queen certainly spent her days in miserable intrigue, apparently set on little else than to muddle the affairs of her kingdom, to provoke trouble, and to overthrow Richelieu. A fair verdict upon the character of the mother of Louis XIII. must, however, take many things into consideration : what she was like on entering France in 1600, the impression produced upon her by her private life with Henry IV.—a life of humiliations and of tears—the changes wrought in her character by the exercise of absolute power from 1610 to 1617—a period of satisfied vanity, an unthwarted will, and tastes indulged. Finally, the measure of her fall in the *coup d'état* of April 24, 1617, must not be ignored, for by this the all-powerful queen was reduced to the level of a private person, now prisoner at Blois, now flying and in revolt—from the position of a sovereign surrounded by adulation to that of a base intriguer, discontented, quarrelsome, a spendthrift destitute of money, a woman of ambitions but without influence. Death at the close of 1616 would not have thus lowered her reputation, and might have left room to justify the policy of her Regency on the grounds that, without experience or moral authority, she could not do better than follow the counsels of old and circumspect ministers, temporise, conciliate, and yield. The year of Concini's fall was fatal to her. Disgrace and misfortune developed her faults in a lamentable degree, and entirely destroyed whatever good qualities she did possess. History has judged her conduct as a whole ; contemporary opinion in 1601 was perhaps less stern.

Marie de Médicis, indeed, created an excellent impression upon her first arrival in France, and her praises were sung in the rather vague and trite manner of the time, as " this modest turtle . . . this wise and prudent Princess who is among Queens as is the lily among flowers." The poets surrounded with a charming halo a lady, " whom seemingly had God fashioned so accomplished that, already in the early dawn of her days, art, the which nature may well envy, should vainly strive to better her in any real degree." With the King she was timid and retiring—she was always somewhat timid—and resolved to be submissive and obedient ; Henry IV. showed his happiness by a thousand attentions to her. " I could not tell you," she wrote to the Grand Duke, " with what marks of honour and of favour His Majesty has surrounded me, and with what kindness he treats me upon every occasion." The public found her " beautiful and gracious," and remarked upon the " majestic and really royal gravity " of her bearing at all public ceremonies. Sully himself succumbed to the charm. " There was nothing," he wrote later in his *Économies Royales*, " more worthy of admiration than her beautiful carriage and countenance, her good looks, fine figure, grace, majestic presence, admirable gravity—witness her sweetness and skill to win the hearts and gain the affections of persons whenas she would call to use her powers of cajolery and the charm of her beautiful words, promises, caresses, and good cheer. Nor were these her devices the less efficacious and powerful to win, in that her use thereof was the less constant and usual." The Venetian ambassador found her angelic—*di qualita veramente angeliche*—and worthy l'Estoile made himself an interpreter of the popular feeling when he wrote : " The Queen's disposition will please the King, so apt is it and gay, albeit both sufficiently modest and always civil." " Likewise," continues the

Venetian, " bears she the King in such love as toucheth on jealousy. . . . *Che sono piu proprie di donne private*," he adds—a nice side-light, whether reflecting on burgher Florentines or contemporary ethics.

It is significant that, amidst all their faint eulogies, no critic ventured to laud Marie's intelligence. Henry IV. was indeed to find that he had misjudged her upon this point at their first interviews in Lyon. The Grand Duke of Tuscany, better informed as befitted his better opportunities, owned to Monsieur d'Alincourt, ambassador of the King of France, that his niece was far from being the intellectual equal of her sister, the Duchess of Mantua. This became only too evident when the King her husband, anxious about the future, endeavoured to induct her into the management of affairs. Having, for this purpose, caused the Queen to attend the Council, she manifested such surprising incapacity and appalling indifference that he was obliged to abandon the attempt. Ignorance of the French language may have had much to do with this early repugnance to affairs of State, for the same Venetian ambassador already quoted considered the Queen *veramente di gran spirito*. Cardinal Richelieu, nevertheless, judged her later at much the same value, but discreetly attributed her insufficiency " to her small knowledge of affairs in general, the indolent habit of her mind, which disliked all effort, and finally to perpetual irresolution." This irresolution, to which the hesitating policy of the Regency bore witness, might then have been attributed to the temporising advice of over prudent counsellors but for the patent fact that Marie could never clearly see the reasons for and against alternative courses or decisions. Weakness of will is often the plea which covers a feeble intelligence, and this was incontrovertibly so in the present case.

Mention has already been made of Sully's reservation in speaking of Marie de Médicis' amiability, which he appreciated the more that it was rare. It was, indeed, most unusual. The Queen appeared to be unapproachable. " She is," wrote Richelieu, " of a rather grave and not very affectionate nature." Princesse de Conti, though her intimate friend, remarked that the sovereign was "rather cold to all," and a foreign ambassador informed his government that Marie was not at all gracious to the Princes and courtiers, in which she differed greatly from the preceding Queens of France. From a character lacking in amiability to an aggressively disagreeable character is but one step, and many considered as pride a coldness which was no more than the outward sign of a nature meagrely endowed with heart or brains. Fontenay Mareuil thus exclaimed against her "haughty bearing." Marie de Médicis was thought proud ; certainly she was obstinate. Irresolute in large affairs as she was to prove, she was already unmanageable in lesser matters—a quality very annoying to Henry IV., who "often told his friends that he had never seen a more obstinate woman, or one who held more tenaciously to her opinions." Nor did the King keep his opinions on the point a secret from his consort, for being vexed one day by the Dauphin's equally tenacious will, he was heard to say to the lad's mother : "Knowing your disposition, and foreseeing what like will be that of your son—yours, Madame, obstinate, not to say stubborn, and his opinionated—I am assured there shall be trouble between you" : a prophecy only too well fulfilled.

This apparent coldness of the Queen was none the less a cloak to her extreme nervousness. Affected by any trifle, the slightest accident would throw her into a state of agitation which might continue almost interminably. She declared to Henry IV. that "she continually tormented herself to such a degree that she was surprised that she was not thin," and violent tempers about trifles were so chronic that public opinion always attributed the first Duke of Orleans' brief and wretched life to this cause.

The extreme nervousness which shows itself by excessive sensitiveness to the chances of daily existence, often accompanies a variable disposition, prone, during calmer moments, to hardly less unbalanced gaiety. In these nervous natures, irritation and depression sometimes alternate with optimism. The temperament of Marie de Médicis was of this kind. She loved laughter and jokes, and Léonora Galigaï owed her influence to a gay humour, very ready for the balls, plays, entertainments — everything which entertained, distracted, and provoked gaiety—that suited her mistress. " We continue to live gaily, as usual," she wrote one day in 1609 to the Duchesse de Montpensier. She might have written the same on any day. Such a predisposition in an unintelligent person often leads to inconsistent levity, and the impression to be derived from considering the words and actions of Marie de Médicis during the first ten years of her residence in France is that of a woman not sure of herself, unstable, agitated, incapable of reasoning consecutively and firmly—frankly, a character both mediocre and vacillating.

The absolute change in Marie's nature consequent upon the King's death marks a contradiction frequent in characters of this class. Responsibility made of her a new woman. She who before was careless, rose late, and interested herself in nothing but the toilet and her pleasures, now applied herself to affairs with unexpected steadfastness of purpose ; held her Council every morning for hours together, and was ever ready to give audience where questions of the public interest were to be discussed. Foreign ambassadors, Contarini, Gussoni, and Nani reported their astonishment to Venice. The Queen herself avowed, in a public document, that work alone was able to diminish her profound affliction at her husband's assassination, and she had drawn from it this maxim which she recommended to all hearers : " Every sorrow becomes lighter whenas we devote our whole heart to labour for the good of the State." Did she wish to prove false the words of Gaspard de Saulx Tavannes, a writer of the sixteenth century : " Vengeance, anger, love, frivolity, and impatience unfit women for the management of affairs of state ; their rule is unstable, their enterprises are abortive, because they be fearful, irresolute, sudden, indiscreet, vain-glorious, and ambitious." In face of the numerous written documents which she received, full of advice and of " counsel to the Queen-mother upon the means proper to right conduct in the government of this Realm," and which attested the serious apprehensions of their authors as to her aptitude for the functions that chance and fortune had called upon her to discharge, was she anxious to win the esteem of all good people, and to acquit herself of her new duties with zeal ? Henry IV. was wont readily to acknowledge her discretion and ability to keep to herself such counsel as she chose not to share with others. But he added : " She is desirous of honour, and vain-glorious through excess of courage," and whereas she may often be " accused of laziness, or at least of avoiding effort," she will stay at nothing, " if so be that passion urge her thereunto." True to her blood, Marie de Médicis hungered for power, grandeur, and supreme authority. This temper explains her transformation in 1610.

The Queen's megalomania saved her, like many another, from the appeal of other passions, and whatever may have been said of them, her supposed loves must be set down as historical fictions. If she provoked feelings in others, the Queen's naturally cold nature was never sensible of this, and her imagination was too limited to supply the deficiencies of a far from ardent nature by the romantic dreams of an unemployed brain. The malicious public of her age credited her with culpable partiality for Concini, but even in contemporary ears this whisper sounded rather as a pleasantry than a conviction. If, moreover, the real relations of the Queen and the Marshal had been known— they were usually strained and unfriendly, despite appearances to the contrary—this hypothetical weakness could not have appeared so much as a thing credible. Concini largely owed his power to the two sides of a personality by which he deceived every one. Blinded by his wife's real influence, ministers believed that he held absolute sway over the Queen's mind, she that he alone controlled ministers

and princes—ideas both which, thanks to misunderstandings, were finally justified as truth. Playwrights
and novelists next linked her name with that of Cardinal
Richelieu—a late and autumnal passion, indeed, for her
who would then have been between forty-five and fifty
years old ; and for the Cardinal—so dry and highly developed in mind, so little servant of the heart and the
senses—a suggestion entirely out of keeping with his
character. The severity of Louis XIII., moreover, would
never have tolerated the bare suspicion of such a scandal
so nearly touching himself. The best informed contemporary opinion, indeed, paid homage to her moral integrity, and it need scarcely be added that the theory,
revived in our days, that Marie de Médicis, descendant
of a line of poisoners, poisoned herself, and indulged in
incantation, sorcery, and magic, is also pure legend. No
serious work lends a shadow of truth to this melodra-
matic accusation. Power was her passion, and, true scion
of a family notorious for its magnificence, the Queen sought
to adorn her exercise of the supreme authority with all the
circumstances of a truly regal ostentation. Ostentatious
liberality is one of Marie's most characteristic traits.

Contemporaries cannot sufficiently laud her kindliness. " Liberality and magnificence," cries Matthieu de
Morgues, " are our Princess's greatest virtues." Bassompierre, who knew whereof he spoke, declared that " in
magnificence and in generosity the Queen surpassed all
other princesses in the world." Richelieu found her "magnificent by nature, and, when she gave—God knows how
profusely !—she loved to say that she did it ' to show
her greatness and liberality.' " To win this reputation
was a point of honour with her, and when a suspicion
of vanity and an undoubted inclination to extravagance
complicated her feeling, her finances were presently in
perpetual straits. Donations in the name of religion were
a particular factor in this ill-considered and ostentatious
profusion.

With minds of this character, religion can be neither

strong nor enlightened, and the devotions of Marie de
Médicis were essentially formal. In conformity with the
royal protocol, she heard mass every morning, whether
at the Louvre or elsewhere; as a good parishioner she
regularly attended the church of Saint Germain l'Auxerrois at Easter, and, according to royal tradition, followed
on foot the procession of the Fête-Dieu which entered the
courtyard of the Louvre after the mass in the chapel of
the Petit Bourbon. Did the Pope declare a Jubilee, as
in 1601, the Queen must not miss it though it cost a
journey to Orleans. In the name of the Confraternity
of the Holy Sepulchre, to which she belonged, two squires
and four of her ladies made offering of consecrated bread
in several Parisian churches, that of the Cordeliers among
others, on Low Sunday, the presentation taking place
during High Mass. She had special prayers for her
favourite saints: Saint John the Baptist, protector of
Florence, Saint Francis whose girdle she wore, Saint
Dominic whose rosary she owned, Saint Theresa, Saint
Madeleine, and Saint Louis of Gonzaga. Saint Jerome,
Saint Catharine, Saint Cecilia, and Saint Ursula were
others whose cults she affected, the most of these dating
from Florentine days, but a new one, that of the King,
Saint Louis, was added to the number after her marriage,
and this with a personal end in view. Fifteen days, in
fact, after Henry IV.'s death, having removed from the
end of the long gallery of the Louvre a portrait of the
Valois, Philip VI., and replaced it by one of Louis IX.,
she announced that she desired thus to present her son
with a model in the great hero of the Middle Ages, " that
Louis XIII. might imitate the virtues, the valour, and the
piety of this saintly king, even as he did inherit his
kingdom." She " daily proposed the life of Saint Louis,
of glorious memory, as an example to the King "; but she
added, " as, for our own part, we desire to follow and to
imitate the estimable virtues of the Queen, his mother,
Blanche de Castille." To be likened to Blanche de Castille,
to suggest the comparison, was her dream, and the obliging

Mercure François did not fail to point out the points of similarity, although heretofore but external, of the two governments—like repression of factions and insurrections among the great, like founding of convents, and the same spirit of charity in two alien Queens, at one in their anxiety to preserve the State. The public, nevertheless, was unfortunately not to be convinced of the resemblance.

After the manner of a true devotee, the Queen made pilgrimages and vows. On occasion also, she commissioned others to accomplish a vow made by herself—as the Bishop of Avranches at the sanctuary of the Archangel on Mont Saint Michel. Her faith in relics led to her acceptance and bestowal of many, among the latter certain fragments of the True Cross which she sent to her nieces the Duchesse de Lorraine, being then with child; "two fragments" of the relics of Saint Vincent de Vannes to the wife of a Spanish ambassador—the one to be worn in a reliquary about the neck, the other placed in an ivory box upon an altar. The relics of Saint Fiacre, acquired from the Bishop of Meaux, went to her aunt the Grand Duchess, then building a chapel in the Saint's honour for the Augustinian canons of Florence. Profuse in those facile gifts to churches and chapels by which remission of sins was easily bought, she gave lamps to the Sainte Chapelle of Notre Dame de Montserrat, to the church of Jesus at Rome, and to Notre Dame de Chartres. Still, dissatisfied, however, she decided to calm her scruples by asking the Pope, through the French ambassador, Monsieur de Béthune, for " some dispensations for the repose of my conscience, and to maintain me so far as possible amidst those occasions for sin which do so often present themselves, and the list whereof herein I do enclose." The list was very long. Marie de Médicis' easy and mechanical religion was eminently satisfied with outward forms, and next by the providing herself with concessions and indulgences sufficient to diminish the restraints of divine law.

These gifts and alms of Marie de Médicis are to be divided into four categories—those imposed upon the Queen by French custom, those to which she was prompted by Florentine tradition, to which her taste for " magnificence " inclined her, and—last, although the least numerous—such as were inspired by real piety or charity. Of these last was doubtless that motion of the heart which, while she was yet a young girl, prompted her to free one of those Turkish slaves taken in a raid upon the Barbary coast, whom she chanced to own, to baptize her by the name of Joanna Medici, and marry her to a Florentine named Montanti. Further, while still at Florence, she converted one of her tire-women of like antecedents, herself standing as god-mother and marrying her to Mattiati Vernacini. This couple she carried with her to France in 1601. The taste for conversion was evidently very strong with her, for she later conceived the idea of winning over a certain Portuguese Jew, Montalto, a doctor in whom she had great confidence, and to that end had him instructed by Cardinal Perron! Monsieur de Brèves, the French ambassador at Constantinople, was commissioned to send her from the Levant Turkish families—workers in embroidery—that she might convert them. With money sent for the purpose, the Levantines were embarked upon Venetian ships " at the least possible expense," and taken to Paris, having previously been induced to aver " that they were of a mind to become Christians, should the wherewithal to live be there provided for them." Naturally, Marie de Médicis found herself concerned in missions to the heathen, and the King's Lieutenant " for certain lands of the savages of the West Indies," having asked for some Capuchins " further to advance as may prove possible the establishment of the Christian faith," she forthwith exercised herself and obtained four from the head of the Order in France. To protect the missionaries, the Capuchins in particular, and to return home the Huguenots " if any there be," was her constant instruction to the governors of colonies. Thus she seconded the efforts of all those who set forth to found settlements in foreign lands, but especially such as were to assure the propagation of religion. Monsieur Jean de Biencourt, Sieur de Poutrin-court, proceeding to Acadia, in Canada, received in aid of his enterprise five hundred crowns and two Jesuits, Fathers Biard and Massé.

Beyond doubt, also, the Queen was moved on the occasion of her accompanying to the Carmelite convent two of her tire-women who were taking the veil, as again when, by entreaty, she obtained from Henry IV. pardon for a poor young woman under capital sentence at For l'Evêque—truly a rare action on her part. In the like spirit she wrote, and persuaded the King to write, to the Venetian government to obtain the recall of an unfortunate exile of the Republic. For these and for such acts the Queen must receive due credit, but, for the rest, her good works were nothing else than perfunctory, impersonal in the doing, and bearing on the face of them the seal of ostentation and parade. Of these were the Queen's formal donations to the poor during Holy Week and at Christmas—in Holy Week a hundred and twenty livres to the Convents of the Quatre-Mendiants, two hundred and twenty-four livres to the seven churches in which she paid her devotions on Holy Thursday, forty-two livres to the beggars who stood beside the doors of these churches, four hundred and twenty-six livres to the less importunate poor persons, a hundred and nine livres to the thirteen girls whose feet she washed on the said Thursday, and doles to sick soldiers, to boys employed in Her Majesty's household, "to a poor man of the church," and "to a poor crazy gentlewoman." At the beginning of Lent, the Grand Almoner received six hundred livres for distribution—fifteen francs for each day of the forty. On Holy Wednesday, Marie personally distributed three hundred livres. Christmas cost her two thousand four hundred livres, allotted in like manner. All these were fixed annual expenses, duly provided by the royal purse.

Every year, Marie de Médicis provided thirteen young girls with a marriage portion, a traditional custom imitated from Florence, where Lorenzo the Magnificent had

been wont thus to dower girls of small means. The
Queen's First Almoner, Cardinal Bonsi, was charged
to present the year's list of eligible applicants for this
coveted patronage in each August, and, the Queen
having signified her selection, the portions were distributed on the fifteenth of the month to a due accompaniment of ceremonial. One Madame Dujardin performed
the act of presentation—the gifts varying between one
hundred and fifty and three hundred livres, more usually
some three hundred—one hundred crowns. Under the
guidance of this lady, " the thirteen poor girls " attended
communion-service, accomplished a certain number of
devotions " in the chapel which is beneath ground within
the church of Saint Victor," and presented themselves
to Her Majesty " on the day of the festival of Notre Dame
of mid-August," personally to thank their patron and
promise prayers on her behalf.

Yearly in Holy Week, and also at the moment of her
confinements, the Queen was used to liberate prisoners
detained for debt. The number of fortunate men thus
freed varied from forty to sixty-six on each occasion ;
they came from the Conciergerie, Petit Châtelet, Grand
Châtelet, For l'Evêque, Saint Victor, Saint Martin des
Champs, and l'Evêché. Further, each one received *tes-
tons*—small sums of money in value some twenty-five
livres, and was obliged to proceed from prison to Notre
Dame de Paris there to pray God for Her Majesty and
chant a *Salve Regina*. The cost of all this to the
Queen amounted to one thousand five hundred livres—
on occasion, three thousand and even five thousand.

Among her benefactions, Marie de Médicis provided
pensions for scholars and students—six hundred livres
" to Louis Sauger, a poor student at the College of La
Flèche, to the end that he may there continue his studies
and find sustenance." She also undertook the expenses
of students of theology, instructed at the Convent of the
Augustinians of Paris, and recommended to the Duke
of Tuscany young men proceeding " to the Sapienza di

Pisa," and promoted the development of the colleges which the Jesuits were establishing on all sides. Nor did her bounties ever ignore hospitals and convents. In 1612, out of her revenue and that of Queen Marguerite, " were furnished and fitted up " three houses in the Faubourgs Saint Victor, Saint Marcel, and Saint Germain, two for men and one for women, whereinto were brought together from the Paris pavements, and in the space of eight days, " the sturdy vagabonds and ruffians which did demand alms, sword at side, with a starched collar upon the 'peccadillo.'" [1] Modern charity, not content to sweep the streets, compels such wastrels to labour at tasks. It is worth noticing, therefore, that, by ordinance of August 27, 1612, Louis XIII. laid a like compulsion on " all poor invalids " thus incarcerated.

The Hôpital de la Charité, founded in the Faubourg Saint Germain by the Frati Ignoranti, the brethren of Saint Jean de Dieu whom she had brought from Italy, also owed much to the Queen who supported it against Parliament, the Abbey of Saint Germain des Prés within whose jurisdiction the new establishment was built, and other quarrelsome neighbours. Not content with mere lavish support of this institution, Marie took sufficient interest in its management to desire to appoint the doctors. She consented to patronise the new Oratory which she thought of installing in the Hôtel des Monnaies, befriended the Carmelites who had come from Spain at the instigation of the Duchesse de Longueville, and gave them financial aid to enable them to build their priory of Notre Dame des Champs. To the Capuchins she gave a regular annuity, as also to an infinite number of convents, the nuns of the Ave Maria, the Ursulines of Faubourg Saint Jacques, and the barefooted Carmelites.

Many as were these acts of kindness and charity, however, it is sure that few were due to her personal initiative. The rest, almost the whole number, assumed shape in

[1] *Peccadillo* was the stiff lining designed to keep the collar or ruff properly extended.

response to some request which she scarcely condescended to hear out, were the act of her almoners—begged of them indeed—done in the name of their mistress, and, to all intents, without her knowledge. That they were preordained, traditions inseparable from royalty, devoid of all personal feeling or emotion—these accidents and not the acts themselves are the characteristics of the nominal author of all—the Queen.

CHAPTER II

THE QUEEN'S DAY

WHEN, late in the evening of February 9, 1601, Marie
de Médicis entered the Louvre for the first time, turn-
ing from the wretched little Rue d'Autriche into a
palace gateway, flanked by two great mediæval towers
but so narrow that the carriage could barely pass, and
so dark that a foreign ambassador exclaimed, " What
an entrance ! It would better suit a prison than the
house of so great a prince ! "—when, having traversed
its deserted courtyard, less than a quarter the size of
the courtyard of to-day, mounted the great staircase
called after Henry II., crossed, without meeting a single
person, the long dimly-lighted hall now the Lacaze room,
and, by way of the King's room, gained her own apartment where only worn furniture, faded hangings, and
dim pictures could be distinguished in the obscurity ;—

she was "astonished and frightened, believing either that it was not the Louvre, or that she was the victim of a practical joke." Soon realising, however, that "the informality and freedom of the French Court were alone responsible for this unworthy reception," her inherited family taste for all the elegances and luxuries of life was not long in transforming an interior which, during the past fifty years, had been the home of so many queens. In these apartments, then, as embellished by herself, we are now to follow the new Queen's history.

The Queen's apartments occupied the first floor of what was then called "the old part of the *hôtel*," and consisted of a suite of five rooms, to-day looking only upon the courtyard, but formerly lighted on two sides, the partition walls of which may yet be found in that part of the Musée du Louvre which lies between the Hall called of The Seven Chimneys and the middle of the wing overlooking the Seine. At the top of her private staircase, "the Queen's staircase," was the guardroom, always occupied by ten lifeguardsmen and their officer. Next to this, in the antechamber, the usher, Philippe Clément, an old servant of the royal house, passed his days before a huge sideboard. Lighted by six large candles of yellow wax, in brackets affixed to the wall, this was the Queen's dining-room.

The Queen's cabinet or reception-room, the third in the suite, was adorned by woodwork painted in delicate arabesques of light tints. A beautiful oriental carpet, ordered in Turkey by the French ambassador, Monsieur de Brèves, covered its floor, while twelve armchairs or small sofas, and twelve chairs covered in crimson velvet, studded all with large gold nails, formed its chief furniture. For other ornaments, the Queen's souvenirs and presents were arranged in ebony cabinets —a small casket of silver filigree, a gift of the Electress Palatine; an agate cup, gift of the Maréchale de Fervaques; a beautiful mirror from the Duchess of Mantua, "which I have placed in my cabinet," wrote the Queen,

" as a piece very worthy to be exhibited." Four silver chandeliers, vermilion-gilt,[1] lighted the long evening card-parties, and we may well credit their inefficiency for the purpose. In the great fireplace, under its richly sculptured mantel, shone silver andirons weighing 33 marks, 6 ounces, and 3 grains.[2]

Of the four windows of the adjoining sleeping-room, the most beautiful of the suite, two opened upon the courtyard and two upon the Seine, the last with a balcony. The woodwork of the fireplace, the ceiling, and the wainscoting, was entirely renewed by Marie and bore the royal cipher of Henry IV. On a raised platform at the back of the room stood the splendid bed of which the wooden posts were richly carved and gilded, and hung with curtains changed twice in each year. Canopy, curtains, and the coverings of the tables in this apartment were all of the same stuff—in summer silk, in winter "old-rose velvet," both designed and furnished by the upholsterers Antoine, Pierre Rousselet, and Simon Nantier. Magnificent rails of solid silver with ornaments in the same metal, twenty-four great chased silver plaques and two bowls of silver worked with a pattern of vines, isolated this bed from the rest of the chamber as though within a sanctuary to be entered by none but the two valets de chambre in whose care it was. " Four great candlesticks, also of silver," of the like design and by the same artist, Nicolas Roger, stood at the four corners of the room. The cost of all this amounted to forty thousand francs. To complete the decoration, family portraits of the Medici hung upon the walls, which were also set about with cabinets—one, " in imitation of the Chinese, with silver handles on the drawers," being the work of Laurent Septabre, " worker in ebony, dwelling in the gallery of the Louvre," while another, gilded and

---

[1] *Vermeil-doré* or *vermeil* are old forms of *argent-doré*, *i.e.* silver gilt.

[2] 1 *marc* = 8 ounces (old measure) = 64 *gros* = 192 *deniers* = 4608 grains = one-half " *une livre de Paris telle qu'elle existait avant le système décimal.*" This livre was worth about 6 francs in modern currency.

larger, and also " after the Chinese," was from the hand of Etienne Sager, "master-worker in the imitation of Chinese art." In one of these cabinets were bestowed the Queen's most valuable possessions, golden caskets, vases, and jewels ; the key was held by the faithful valet de chambre, Nicolas Roger, who was also a goldsmith by trade. A precious casket, the gift of a German princess, artistic cups, rare porcelains, silver baskets, a reliquary ornamented with nineteen diamonds and a pearl, a font of crystal for holy water " mounted in silver and having for sprinkler a crystal cup in the form of a shell," and a thousand other objects of value completed the furnishings of this room. As the Queen's cabinet was in charge of a special usher, Jean Mauderon, the bedchamber likewise found its guardian in Antoine Drouin, who, aided by the boy Nicolas Guilloret, was wont to require the profound obeisance prescribed by etiquette from all who passed, even though the bed were unoccupied.

The last room, the *petit cabinet*, was the narrowest of all, being but sixteen feet wide by twenty-nine long. It was built with an entresol, the upper half of which was known as *l'entre-ciel*. This cosy, private, warm, and bright apartment enjoyed the Queen's preference to such degree that she even furnished it with a little bed, and occasionally occupied it for the night. One door opened into the King's bedchamber, another communicated with the " King's little stair," *la petite montée*, built in the angle of the palace and well known to its intimates. A staircase still exists in the same place. Here also were costly trinkets, beautiful specimens of Venetian glass, a shagreen chest with silver lock and key, mirrors framed in ebony, candlesticks of chased gold, and finally a large iron-bound box containing Marie's " Title-deeds and Papers concerning Our Affairs." At the table, covered by a handsome piece of oriental tapestry, she wrote or signed her voluminous correspondence, using the beautiful inkpot presented to her by her brother-in-law, the Duke of Mantua. The dwarf Merlin acted as " usher to the Cabinet." Besides these works of art, "gold, silver, antique jewels, medals," and tapestries were scattered in profusion through the apartments. The Groom of the Chamber, Pierre Courtois, shared with Nicolas Roger the responsibility of guarding these things. The Queen's dresses "and other wearing-apparel" filled numberless chests in carved wood, scattered here no less than through the entresol and above [1] in numberless small rooms set apart for the service—the wardrobe, the rooms of the Queen's women, of the maids and of the Grooms of the Chamber. The wardrobe itself was "fitted somewhat in the manner of a mercer's shop, for there were hats in one place and girdles in another, garters here and ruffs there, some in large, and some in lesser plaits."

Did all stand well between the royal couple—a case by no means invariable—and were the King not absent, as he so often was, the King and his consort awoke side by side. Then, thrice in the week at least—on Mondays, Thursdays, and Fridays—the King held council with his ministers. On these mornings Henry IV. would hastily leave the great bed at some time short of seven, and disappear, for the Council was called to sit between six and nine, and—since he was wont to retire late—the King was frequently late for it. On ordinary occasions, however, he did not rise thus early, and the favoured might then enter the bedchamber. Thus, on the first day of the year, Monsieur de Sully was ever an early visitor, bringing to the King and Queen their New Year's gifts of gold tokens, and on one such occasion, the curtain being yet undrawn, the minister spent some time in profound bows and complete silence. At last the King became aware of something unusual, and drawing the curtains to learn what might be toward, exclaimed : " Ah, my dear, Rosny here has brought us our presents ! " But Sully was not always to find so kind a welcome, for,

---

[1] After the marriage of Louis XIII. with Anne of Austria, Marie de Médicis was compelled to leave the first floor to the reigning Queen and to restrict herself to the ground-floor and the entresol.

having once presented the King's gift, and turned to the Queen with: "Madame, here also are the tokens for your Majesty's acceptance!" Marie averted her face and would make no reply to his salutation. "Give them to me!" the King exclaimed at last. "She is not asleep but in a temper, and has done nothing but worry me all night."

The favoured visitors on ordinary mornings were young men such as the brilliant gallant Bassompierre, whom Henry addressed as "thou," as also would the Queen in moments of excitement, or old friends of the war-time, de Roquelaure, Frontenac, Loménie, and la Varenne[1] in particular, always ready to amuse with his somewhat advanced jests. The King's conversation was always gay, lively, and humorous, with a genial lack of constraint and a witty freedom. Any person outside this little group must, however, bow towards the bed on his entry, and would he address the King, kneel upon a cushion or stool. During this audience a morning cup of broth was brought to the King and Queen, who partook of it while yet in bed. Finally, when the King rose, the highest personage present must hand him his shirt.

Henry's departure was a signal for the entry of the Queen's four tire-women—Madame Salvagia, the favourite, a Florentine who had accompanied Marie from Italy; Madame Catharine, also in the Queen's confidence; Madame Canche and Madame Sauvat, all four in high favour. Their first step was to clothe their mistress in a chemise of linen damasked with gold and red silk, "worked with gold thread," or white or black silk. The next garments were silk stockings, carnation, yellow, or blue in colour, for Marie would never wear black unless when in mourning. A petticoat, selected from numerous "heaps" in the chests, followed—of "slashed violet satin," white satin lined with green taffetas, Chinese "tabit"[2] lined with yellow taffetas, yellow satin lined

---

[1] This la Varenne was Comptroller-General of Posts.
[2] A kind of waved silk.

with red satin, carnation satin lined with yellow, thin brocatelle with blue ground, or black satin embroidered with gold flowers. Having made her choice, and still wearing the "high canvas nightcap" in which she slept, the Queen put on a dressing-jacket, and thus apparelled "in petticoat and nightcap," gave audience to the people of her household—her intendant, treasurer, comptroller, major-domo, and first equerry, who attended to receive orders.

On proceeding with the toilet, a valet de chambre, bearing a ewer from the great chest in the sleeping room, went out for water preceded by two Body-Guards of the Antechamber, and her women having placed "the conch, basins, and towel," upon a table, the Queen washed herself with a sponge and combed her hair with an ivory comb. In order to keep Léonora Galigaï beside her at the time of her first arrival in France, Marie alleged that she was the only woman capable of dressing her hair; in point of fact, she dressed it herself, "high, in the Italian manner, in symmetrical puffs." Her audience continued and she talked freely while disentangling her long hair, which she oiled with "oil of orange blossoms from Spain to fix the powder."

The choice of the day's dress was an important question, and of dresses, skirts, mantles, vests, *cimarres*, *pourpoints*, demi-mantles, and capes, and all garments affected by the most fashionable ladies of the time, she naturally possessed a profusion, and these in the richest materials. That in February 1613, at two o'clock on a Saturday morning, a great number of clothes were stolen from the Queen, gives a strange idea of the manner in which the interior of the Louvre was guarded. As Mistress of the Robes, Léonora Galigaï had charge of the Queen's wardrobe, and received from the Treasurer of the Queen's household twelve thousand francs a year "for the purchase and expenses of the stuffs, dresses, linen, and other apparel necessary for our person." Léonora, having caused to be brought before her silks and velvets—as on one occasion, " nine and a quarter ells of black satin of Milan, embroidered in gold and silver," " forty ells of gold-flowered green satin," or " a hundred and two ells of silk brocatelle figured in yellow, white, and blue on a black ground," the cheapest of these materials costing from twenty-four to twenty-six francs an ell, and the whole piece amounting to from one thousand to two thousand five hundred francs—Marie de Médicis herself viewed the stuffs and signified her choice.

Prices such as these were not slow to exhaust the Queen's annual allowance of twelve thousand francs, but fortunately for her finances, her uncle, the Grand Duke of Tuscany, and her sister, the Duchess of Mantua, often presented her with beautiful stuffs which they shipped from Leghorn to Havre. Such gifts were much appreciated by Marie, especially such as had a white ground " figured in many colours." [1]

Did Marie de Médicis wear mourning, as she often must, less extravagant materials contented her taste, as *Montcayar*, "serge, or other woven or twilled stuffs, fashioned in long robes," " a little robe of black bolting-cloth or a dress of black crêpe ; a great cloak very comfortable and full, and on her head a peaked cap with a ruffle, and a scarf falling along the dress, the whole without fastening."

The stuff being selected, and the " mercer and lace-maker Baron " having furnished " trimming and embroidery of gold and silver, silk and spun gold," the costume was fashioned by the Queen's tailor, a confidential person brought from Florence, Jacopo Zoccoli, " our tailor and groom of the chamber," nephew of an old tailor of the Medici, Domenico di Elbeno. Marie de Médicis was, however, remarked as wearing the French mode *con molto gusto universale !*

Setting aside the splendid dresses of ceremony for the

---

[1] Queen as she was, Marie de Médicis did not always secure these presents without difficulty, the officers of the Customs at Lyon frequently detaining the shipments of the Princes of Mantua and Tuscany.

moment—as a dress of cloth of gold on a ground of columbine and with a long train, a dress of gold and silver embroidery, a dress of blue velvet sewn with gold fleur-de-lis—the Queen's choice has fallen upon a more simple costume of carnation satin. This arranged to her satisfaction, her jewels, of which she has quantities scattered in different cabinets, must not be forgotten, nor yet her ring. Her gold bracelets, studded with seventy-two small diamonds, were purchased from François le Prestre, jeweller of Paris, for one thousand and fifty livres ; her earrings, two great diamonds surrounded by lesser brilliants, were made by the jeweller, Jean Subtil. Her gold watch, valued at two thousand one hundred livres, is " oval in shape and ornamented with several diamonds," and she must not forget to place in her pocket for use at Mass the " rosary of enamelled gold, embellished with diamonds," a trifle worth nine thousand six hundred livres. And, thus adorned, the Queen must yet perfume herself.

Marie adored perfumes, but for her scents were as much a necessity as a luxury. Despite his exquisite qualities the King possessed certain infirmities, as even his too good friend, Henriette d'Entraigues, Marquise de Verneuil—a terrible woman at bottom, common and given to vulgar language—coarsely declared in the phrase, " You smell like carrion ! " If, then, it were true, as Agrippa d'Aubigné asserted in *Le Baron de Faeneste*, that " in these days the nose is a very ready guide whereby to recognise a gentleman," the King was surely the first gentleman in the kingdom. Marie " provided herself with the essences of the country," and scattered through all her chests of clothes, in all her pieces of furniture, among all her belongings, " sachets of carnation taffetas, filled with perfume of roses, rose-scented sachets of parti-coloured satin edged with gold or silk, satin sachets embroidered in gold and silver and filled with musk-rose." Of these, one in light blue cost sixty francs, the remainder fifty francs each. In the language of the day, the Queen's many perfumers "perfumed Her Majesty," and Marie did not fail to try all their products in turn—to wit, the perfumes of Simon Devaux, Emmanuel Mandez,[1] a Portuguese from Braganza, subsequently " apothecary dwelling in Rue de l'Arbre Sec, at the house of Madame Jaquette," and a certain Arnauld Maren, also a foreigner. To this clever distiller Léonora Galigaï allotted a lodging in her house in Rue Tournon, and here the Queen often watched him at work, and amused herself, as was her habit at Fontainebleau also, by applying her own hand to his alembics in the presence of Madame de Guise and her old friend and banker, Monsieur Zamet. But not all the perfumes of Paris could satisfy her taste, and she was for ever applying for " oils and powders " from Florence, for " oil of jasmine, amber, and musk," in especial, so rumour said, for " gloves of jasmine and gloves of amber." As " to clasp and secure " these gloves, " six gold enamelled buttons, each set with a large diamond," were sometimes necessary, the cost of a single pair was known to reach eighteen hundred francs.

The adjustment of the Queen's lace collar always required care. Of this it was worthy, being one of those magnificent Venetian [2] point collars, worth the eyes out of a man's head, her fine store of which was under the especial care of her Keeper of the Wardrobe, Marguerite Chartier. When at last the Queen put on her shoes, specially made for her at Loudun, and brought thence by their maker, Judith Leblanc, her toilet was complete, and she passed into the Cabinet to give audience to the nobles, courtiers, strangers of note come to pay their respects,

---

[1] Mandez and Maren were involved in the imprisonment of Léonora Galigaï.

[2] Venetian point became fashionable in France at the close of the sixteenth century, when its costliness rapidly became a by-word :—

> " But the curs't collar cost me more than all.
> 'Twas of Venetian point I'd have the thing—
> The plaguey, sinful, costly luxury !
> To put on such a thing's to be a fool !
> Thirty good vineyard-acres on one neck !"

those newly promoted to office come to tender their thanks, newsmongers and friends, like Malherbe, in quest of gossip. Then arose a rustling and a murmuring, sometimes a very lively murmur if, as often chanced, a reckless-tongued Gascon were present, or an important event had taken place.

Formerly " the Queens of France were held to kiss the princes, dukes, and officers of the Crown," who saluted them, but Marie refused to conform to this custom, " begging to be allowed to kiss the King only." To this Henry IV. acquiesced, according, instead, to the princes, dukes, and other privileged persons the right " to enter the Queen's Cabinet, which had not before been customary." The entrant was expected to salute Her Majesty by a deep reverence at the distance of three or four steps, and on further approach, kneel upon the ground and raise the hem of her robe to his lips. The Queen, raising him, then offered her hand to kiss : her usual greeting was : " You are welcome." Her own manner was full of dignity, and she required strict observance of the forms in her visitors. Woe, therefore, betide the impetuous gentleman who, disputing with another in the Queen's Cabinet, boxed his neighbour's ears, for it was seldom that such "profanation" of the royal apartment earned anything less than the Bastille. Yet, if Richelieu is to be trusted, such scenes were of constant occurrence, while another writer, from whom we must apparently understand that impertinence was a courtier's chief qualification, records that the Gascons were generally held " especially violent and tempestuous."

Audience over, Marie attended Mass, a daily duty incumbent upon the King and Queen of France, and one which they used as an excuse to take the air. For this they never attended the chapel of the Louvre, although the chaplain and the almoner daily celebrated it here, while the Augustinian canons came every morning, from their convent across the Seine, to perform the same office. The Queen had further a little chapel of her own in the tower almost adjoining her antechamber and overlooking the Pont-Neuf, but this also she ignored. Instead, the King crossed the garden on foot to the Church of the Feuillants, while the Queen went either here or to the Petit Bourbon—" went to Mass *en Bourbon*," she said. But this chapel was too obscure for her regular taste, so —unless moved to attend the Church of the Cordeliers, where the singing of the *Salve Regina* upon her arrival was a scandal to pious souls—her most frequent goal was Saint Germain l'Auxerrois, of which she was a parishioner, and where she offered the holy bread on Quasimodo Monday.

Of the Mass-books of Marie de Médicis, two are still preserved. One, a beautiful fifteenth - century Book of Hours, now in the Bibliothèque de l'Arsénal, is bound in gold and colours, has initials and forty miniatures executed in like style, and closes with little clasps of iron adorned with the Queen's arms. Even finer is the second, now in the Louvre, the magnificent Book of Prayers—the successive property of Francis I., Catharine de Médicis, and Louise de Lorraine—which contains the marvellous series of fifty-eight portraits of members of the House of Valois, reputed to be in part the handiwork of Jean Clouet. Wherever the Queen went to attend Mass, one of her gentlemen bore her missal before her, while her valets went in advance with her foot-carpet and the thick cushions upon which she sat. During Mass a clerk announced in a loud voice when the congregation should rise or kneel. On Saturday, Marie de Médicis attended vespers at Saint Victor, and said her prayers " in the lower chapel of Notre Dame de Bonne Nouvelle." From Mass the Queen proceeded to dinner, a meal usually shared by Henry IV. in the Queen's antechamber. Often, however, on account of domestic friction or for other reasons, each dined apart, the Queen in her small Cabinet in the entresol, or wherever the table might be set for her. On such occasions, the King's gallantry always compelled him to send part of any especially delicious morsel to his consort, although, did this occur at one of their times of disagreement, Marie invariably returned it—" for fear of poison," said the Court gossips.

The hours of the royal repasts were very irregular, the Queen's frequent tardiness in leaving her room often compelling the King to send her word to " hurry her dressing." His habit of early hunting, also, continually brought him home with the finest appetite. It was on one such occasion that, crossing the long upper hall of the Louvre, Henry beheld one of his gentlemen, La Clielle, carrying a gilded dish covered with a beautiful napkin, in company with a companion named Parfait, who at once cried out : " Ah, Sire, embrace my thighs, for I have a many and excellent quality ! " alluding to his dishful of melons, a fruit of which Henry IV. was extravagantly fond. " Parfait is overjoyed," retorted the King to his following ; " this is to lard his ribs ! He brings me good melons which pleases me, and to-day I will eat my fill of them, since never did good melons harm me so be I was hungered at their eating. This day I die of hunger, and whiles there come not better meats, with my melons and a thimbleful of muscatel will I set to ! " Should Marie de Médicis at last be ready, the cooks were usually late, and not till the King's second or third summons would the first butler appear to pronounce the sacramental phrase : " Sire, your Majesty is served."

" When the King eats in his palace, not prince nor cardinal shall eat with him, nay not one save only the Queen's Majesty." First, however, Henry must wash his hands in a bowl of silver-gilt, and the Queen hand him the napkin on which to dry them. Swiss guards, posted all round the table, maintain order, as the whole court is admitted during the repast. These rest upon their halberds, clothed in their ample costume of striped velvet, " tan, blue, and carnation," the colours of the house of Bourbon, with caps of the same colour, long-bearded old Switzers all, speaking the German of the Four Cantons, and ancient servitors of the Crown. To serve the meal the gentlemen-in-waiting attend, three for the King and three for the Queen ; they receive the dishes from the hands of the officers of the King's kitchen, by whom they are brought into the room. This service from the kitchen was an innovation, but since " Monsieur le Prince de Condé was poisoned by a tart " brought at the hand of one, his own page, the officers of the kitchen declared that they would no more be responsible for the King's viands if served by any hand other than their own.

The beautiful damask cloth for the royal table bore the arms of the King and Queen, " woven in Flanders in the style of Damascus." The cover consisted of two silver plates for each, and in front the royal ship [1] of silver gilt containing the King's finely folded napkin, knife, and fork, and destined to receive the Queen's fan and gloves. Henry's economical spirit had brought his knife, fork, and spoon from Pau, and as King of France he thus used the ancient silver of the King of Navarre. This was none the less of the finest quality.

The midday repast in the Louvre—Henry IV. loved heavy and rich meals—always included four entrées, four soups, a course of boiled meat—" a ten pound joint of beef, a side of mutton, a capon, veal, and three chickens " —roasts, " to wit a shoulder of mutton, two capons, a brace of game-birds, a loin of veal, three chickens and three pigeons, a joint of mutton and another of veal." On Sundays, Tuesdays, and Thursdays, these were reinforced by a capon pasty. A pike and carp helped out the lighter fare on days of fast. The evening menu was little if at all lighter. At neither meal were vegetables served ; partridges and quail graced the table only when the King's shooting had prospered. The Court of Mantua sometimes added variety by its gifts—from the Duchess of Mantua " Bologna sausages and cheese," from the Duke presents of fruit and " carp."

A dessert was always provided, though it did not

[1] Such a ship upon the table denoted a great noble. It was usually of crystal mounted in bronze.

D

appear in the menu which was drawn up by the chief steward of the Queen, the Vicomte de Charmel, and countersigned by Marie de Médicis herself. The dessert usually consisted of preserves—those sent from Rheims by the Abbess of Saint Pierre were delicious—"apples, oranges, grapes, muscadines, lemons, pomegranates, and citrons," sent from Provence by Claude Roquette and Barthélemy Saiche, "fruiterers to the King." The Queen's own fruit-garden at Saint Germain was her especial delight, and her children, who lived in the château, were expressly forbidden to set foot in this "little garden." "You will answer to us for all the fruit," she wrote to Madame de Monglat, their governess, "and especially for the apricots, which have been counted. If a single apricot is picked, though it be for our own children, the blame shall fall upon yourself." Of wine, served in a wicker-covered bottle—"claret," white or red—was daily set apart for the Queen's dinner and supper two gallons or seven and a half French quarts; and before a drop was poured into the crystal goblet for Henry IV. or Marie, the gentleman-in-waiting must taste it in their presence, and in his especial glass. This gentleman having once taken the King's glass by mistake: "Eh, friend," cried Henry IV., "at least drink my health and I shall not find you in fault!"

Henry IV. ate and drank inordinately, and none too nicely, and despite his loud assertions to the contrary, the royal indigestion was frequently due to over-indulgence in melons. He might have adopted the saying of Malherbe which so amused Marie de Médicis: "There are but two beautiful things in the world, roses and women ; but two good morsels, melons and women ! " The Queen's appetite was more moderate. While at meals, the royal couple would talk, did humour so dictate, with the gentlemen in attendance or such curious persons as gathered to view the ceremony from behind the line of Swiss Guards. A strict rule forbade the mention of any business to the sovereigns at this time, " stories or other matters of learning or virtue " being alone lawful subjects for conversation. On Sunday, the King's orchestra of fifteen instruments performed during the repast, whereas Henry III. had been wont to eat to an accompaniment of psalms. From the customary bodily removal of the table at the conclusion of the royal meal comes the expression, "*les tables sont levées*." Their Majesties then retiring to their several apartments, the curious went their way convinced that they had beheld something extraordinary, for does not the journal *L'Estoile* record a general belief that one dish of the royal table cost the treasury eighteen thousand crowns a year ?

"When Kings hold council," writes Malherbe, " the people believe that they discuss a changing of the arctic and antarctic poles ; in reality, they are probably catching flies." However this be, Marie de Médicis usually spent her afternoons in very simple and varied occupations. The first was a visit to her animals, of which she maintained a regular menagerie—monkeys, parrots, and dogs—amidst which she loved to " pleasure herself." Dogs were the special object of her adoration, and a number of fluffy little lap-dogs always occupied a place in her carriage. "I must tell you," she writes to a friend, " that my little Bichette has three beautiful puppies, and the prettiest of them, which has two noses, I have dedicated to you." This Bichette was undisputed favourite, but Mignonette, for whose benefit the Duchesse d'Angoulême was required to provide a dog of pedigree as a suitable husband, was not far behind. The theft of " white and grey " Turquette on one occasion caused the greatest distress to the Queen, who despatched footservants and gentlemen in pursuit—her chief anxiety being lest the poor beast should have been waylaid by some too gallant playfellow of contrary sex and quite unworthy of her favours. Roquette, which from time to time enriched the earth " with puglets," and a host of others, formed quite a world of gambols and barks about their indulgent mistress during her daily visit to their realm. In consideration of his care for her pets, Pierre

Guilloret, the Queen's " chair-man," received each four-teenth day of July a gratuity of seventy-five francs, while the royal household must daily provide two pounds of bread for their nourishment. But while lap-dogs were her first care, Marie possessed several breeds besides—water-spaniels for retrieving birds, of which she often made a present ; " greyhounds in leash," the subject of many exchanges, and highly appreciated by such fortunate persons as might receive a present of one at her hand. As she had a preference for white greyhounds, the country must be scoured for them ; when found, a dozen at a time often went to Italy, Concini having charge of their due presentation there. For their maintenance the house-boy, Henri Dubois, received a salary of eight sous per day.

Having visited her animals, Marie at once retired to her small Cabinet. Here, her eyes being weak—she was short-sighted and obliged to wear glasses—the Queen did not spend much time in reading, nor was so serious an occupation exactly to her taste. She wrote, however, to those who presented her with books or dedicated them to her, both frequent occurrences. These volumes were occasionally presented in a most original manner, as one left for her on the altar of the Church of the Feuillants " in a box of cloth of silver and yellow satin, embroidered in silver and covered with lace." But her stock phrases in such cases, " I shall be glad to see it," or " It will give me pleasure to see its treatment of the subject," were but empty words and no more. Books of devotion, " A History of the East Indies," by Père Dujarric, " The Panegyric of the Virgin Mary," " Eulogies of Henry IV. in Latin Verse "—truly the weight of these books might excuse the coolness of the acknowledgments, even had the Queen not known that they came in the hope of that gratuity which she never failed to give in some kind—were she in generous mood to the amount of perhaps six hundred francs, on occasion as no more than a quire of " very fair Florentine paper," a solatium which enraged

the recipient.   Patronage of men of letters was always a
point of honour with her.   Thus a certain poet of Verona
being banished from Venetian territory for participation
in some murderous encounter—when twenty men fighting against seven by night succeeded in sending these
last " from life to death "—her active intervention secured
a repeal of his sentence.   She used her influence with her
aunt, the Grand Duchess of Tuscany, to obtain for
another disciple of the Muses permission to print his
" beautiful poems," and a certain literary interest also
warrants mention of her benevolent intervention, in 1610,
on behalf of a certain Captain Scudéri, imprisoned at
Havre for a theft committed in 1606 in company with one
Barthélemy la Motte, upon " a Flemish vessel which was
off the coasts of Brazil, in the island of Saint Dominique."

The Queen's chief occupation when in her small
Cabinet was, however, to indulge in lotteries in which
each player contributed his share of the cost of the prize.
For this amusement, and other " small pleasures " of the
same kind, the Queen received a regular annual allowance
of thirty-six thousand francs, a sum which will provoke
the less surprise if considered in connection with the cross
of gold and enamels won by the Marquise de Guercheville
—" the face whereof was studded with ten emeralds and
the back fashioned of crystal, in weight a matter of two
ounces, and valued at four hundred and eighty francs."
Another winner obtained a " German cabinet " valued at
one thousand six hundred and fifty-six francs.   Marie's
companions in this expensive relaxation included the
Princesse de Conti, the Duc de Guise, and the Prince de
Joinville.   That on one occasion the Queen staked and
lost two.hundred and seventy-six francs need not astonish
us.   She usually lost, and that the conduct of the lotteries
of the Cabinet was scarcely irreproachable cannot be
doubted.   The Concini took part in the costly game and
were not financially embarrassed in consequence, but
others, like Bassompierre, frequently left the Cabinet
both penniless and deeply in debt.   Stakes ran high on

occasion : we hear of a diamond chain costing one thousand three hundred and fifty francs, eighteen diamond buttons of the same value, and a portrait embellished with a frame of diamonds valued at six thousand francs. Whatever her other qualities, thoughtfulness for those about her was scarcely a virtue of this Queen. She loved excitement, and the lotteries in her Cabinet were certainly calculated to provide it.

The Queen's liking for music, at once more agreeable and less dangerous for her circle, amounted to a passionless but intelligent and instructed taste. She had been well taught—Henry IV. was proud of her *schola ;* and she herself was more than once at great pains to reorganise her company. For " Masters of the Music " the Queen successively employed Gabriel Bataille, Antoine Boisset, Michel Fabry, and Pierre Guédron—the most famous composer of the moment, author of the Court ballets, and " director of the music of the King's Chamber," who succeeded to the post in 1613. For sopranos the Queen employed children ; but her choir was extremely composite, including even dignitaries of the Church, as Monseigneur Guy le Page, canon of Saint Julien du Mans. Her favourite musician, the lute-player René Fancan, the Queen installed as " master of grammar to children of the King's choir." To another, Robert Ballard, she paid, as " salary in respect of his services," twelve hundred livres tournois, besides perquisites amounting to an additional six hundred francs.

The afternoon concerts, given at the Tuileries, were attended by the Queen, always wearing a mask and accompanied by the princesses and ladies of the Court. Here famous singers were occasionally to be heard— Villars, sent to her successor by Henry IV.'s first queen, Marguerite, or Isabella della Camera, a Spaniard, on her way through Paris to Flanders : but Marie did not fail to summon famous companies from Italy. Among others, she begged the Grand Duke of Tuscany to " lend her, for a few months, Julio Romano with his orchestra and singing-girls," a plea in which the King actively seconded her. These concerts afforded exquisite pleasure to Marie, but it must be confessed that her taste sank to a lower plane on occasion, as when her " pastime " was to spend hours together watching Jean Baptiste Capra, called Montalboto, doing his card-tricks, and exhibiting " the greatest cleverness and quickness in sleight-of-hand, and other feats of remarkable dexterity." The Queen's appreciation of this went so far that she presented him with a gold chain valued at two hundred and twenty livres. She begged the Duke of Lorraine to send her for a little while a jester, Nicolas Dalleret, surnamed Caporal, of whom she heard wonders, and whose drollery caused her to " shriek with laughter." Quips and merriment were certainly to her taste.

Marie de Médicis always went out in the afternoon, though sometimes no farther than into the garden of the Louvre, kept so strictly private for their Majesties' peace and enjoyment that Monsieur de Brèves, Governor of the Duc d'Anjou, could scarcely obtain leave to traverse it on his way to the palace. Within this, she made for herself a small enclosure just below that part of the building in which her apartments lay—between the fosse of the Louvre and the road skirting the Seine, upon the present site of the Jardin de l'Infante. To clear this corner of waste land, she removed many " pieces of marble and other stones," and " several little shops and sheds " occupied by workmen. Later, during her regency, when in consequence of the marriage of Louis XIII. with Anne of Austria she gave up the first story to the reigning Queen, and moved down to the ground-floor, she threw over the moat dividing her new apartments and the ' small ' garden the drawbridge which a scandalous public called the " bridge of love," alleging—a pure libel—that it formed the road by which Marie de Médicis obtained secret access to Concini's little house at the corner between the garden and the quay. The river side of her new garden—" the small garden of the Louvre "—Marie closed by a wall supporting an arcaded gallery, on the terrace above which she kept her orange-trees and aviaries.

The garden of the Tuileries was another favourite afternoon haunt of the Queen—so much so that this palace came to be known as " the Queen's house." Here she amused herself with flying hawks, but their quarry, it must be owned, was never more noble than a crow.

The Queen never entered the city either afoot or in her chair, but always in her carriage, the ordering of which was quite a ceremony, since word must first be passed to the first equerry, and so through him to the Queen's stable in the old Hôtel Combault near Saint Germain l'Auxerrois. Even when ordered and brought up at the appointed hour, the heavy carriage could only enter the too low and too narrow gate of the Louvre by dint of the utmost care and skill. The Queen's coach was magnificent, gilded without and within all crimson— the linings of velvet and the hangings of the doors and windows of damask. The splendid team of six white horses was always in charge of one of the two " coachmen of the household " in their superb livery of the Queen's colours—white and blue. This consisted of a doublet and breeches of cloth slashed with velvet and edged with lace, a cloak of cloth also slashed with velvet, white stockings, and belt and epaulettes of gold. An immense hat completed this attire. The riding postilions wore the same livery, and the footmen, mounted at the back, were clad in " velvet mantles and hosen, doublets of chamois leather, and a sword-belt."

Preceded by two equerries, the equipage described the curve necessary to bring it to " the curb below the Queen's stair," and was duly met by a crowd of gentlemen, pages, and lackeys, while the usual crowd of nobles in the courtyard of the palace came forward to assist at the departure. But when, masked according to the custom always affected by ladies of quality while driving, the Queen at last set out, she drove without an escort, a mounted troop being calculated to cause altogether too great an obstruction in the narrow, winding, and busy streets of the capital.

The Queen never drove without an object, the pleasure of a mere passage through shady roads being unknown to her. La Muette was a frequent goal, her house at Chaillot, or the Hôtel de Gondi, a walk in the gardens of which always caused her much pleasure. Given an excuse, however, Marie de Médicis was always ready to drive to humbler haunts. Having heard that one Guitard, dwelling on the Quai des Augustins, was possessed of a cabinet of curios collected from the Orient, she at once honoured him with a visit. Overjoyed at her condescension, Guitard produced a vase, "which hath the virtue that it can by no means contain poison and remain whole. Whosoever useth it to drink cannot, therefore, be poisoned." Marie's reply doubtless recalled a quarrel between the King and herself: "Alas, but of how much more worth were a vase that should dispel the melancholy of whosoever should drink therefrom." For such a one she would pay its weight in gold, aye and promise constantly to use it! A "strange and wonderful accident" claimed her attention on another occasion, and while her less curious consort hawked magpies in the Pré aux Clercs, the Queen, "for the novelty and the rarity of the thing," visited a woman who had given birth to a deformity — two children joined together! On other occasions the royal couple drove out together, as when Monsieur de Sully provided the pleasant entertainment of the casting of certain culverins at the Arsenal. The Arsenal was also the scene of frequent brilliant festivals —by night as well as by day—"tilting at the ring in masks" of an afternoon, jousts organised by Queen Marguerite for the benefit of the reigning couple, "tilting at dummies or in the lists, and every kind of feat of arms, masquerades, and gallantries." These exercises had formerly taken place within the Louvre itself, the cavaliers jousting around a maypole planted in the centre of the great paved courtyard, under the eyes and applause of princes, princesses, nobles, courtiers, and the household. In 1605, however, young Bassompierre, jousting with five other gentlemen in the courtyard, which had been sanded for the occasion, was accidentally pierced through the body and borne gasping into one of the lower rooms of the Queen's suite—an accident which caused the King henceforth to forbid all such sports within the palace.

Shrovetide was, of course, the season for open air carnivals. Marie de Médicis accompanied the King to the bridge of Notre Dame, where "was tilting at the quintain" and the spectacle of twenty-two princes and noblemen, Messieurs de Nevers, d'Aiguillon, de Rohan, de Soubise, de Termes, and others, splendidly caparisoned and mounted, masked, and armed at all points, tilting at each other with the lance and cutting and slashing with their swords before an enormous concourse of people. Another no less exciting occasion was the picturesque fair of Saint Germain, which occurred annually at the beginning of Lent and lasted for a period of two or three weeks. In booths, erected upon the usual site of the market of Saint Germain, were offered to the public wares of every conceivable description—stuffs, books, jewellery, linen, trinkets, earthenware, spices, faience, and laces. Hither flocked merchants from all quarters of France, from the various provinces of Germany, from Flanders and from Italy. This fair served as a general exchange for information of all kinds, so that Pierre de l'Estoile could here learn what were the latest foreign books, while the rabble and populace thronged round the tents pitched on its outskirts, where seemed to be gathered together all the mountebanks of the world. Pages, lackeys, students, and soldiers of the Guard also, crowded round these until this part of the field was a very hotbed of insolence, intrigue, and drunkenness.

King and Queen alike took particular pleasure in this fair. Henry IV., indeed, conducted Marie thither on the very first day of her arrival in Paris in 1601, leading her by the hand through crowds so closely packed that the Guards accompanying them opened a passage with difficulty, while they were jostled and crushed on all sides. The King never missed attendance for a single day, and he would even postpone his journeys if there was a risk of losing a day of the fair. In the year of his death, 1610, when the abominable weather, " snow, sleet, and a driving rain," which froze as it fell, with every now and then a sharp shower of hailstones, had filled Paris with a " universal chill and whooping cough," so that the receipts of the merchants were as " beggarly, lean, and cold as the weather," the King's attendance was probably the sole factor which prevented its utter failure. Indeed it amused him vastly : he bought " figurines from Arezzo," and improper prints, doubtless by Marc Antonio, which he laughingly showed to Monsieur de Montpensier and the other lords in attendance. Once, seeing a couple of Franciscans selling pearls at eight crowns the ounce, he and his friends gathered round and jeered them so unmercifully that the honest friars incontinently fled. His chief amusement, however, was to gamble at the " banks and gaming tables of the fair." Here also he had a " box—a stall in which was set out a table covered with a cloth whereupon to play at dice." In this manner he one day lost seven hundred crowns to Monsieur de Villars. The King's passionate addiction to play was undoubtedly his reason for extending the duration of the fair by a whole week, although he alleged that he did this " for the pleasure the Queen hath to walk therein."

The Queen was not behind her consort in patronising the games of chance at the fair—her choice among them being the game of " *blanco*," a lottery in which the white ticket—whence the name of the game—lost, and the ticket " with profits " [1] won. She also indulged in raffles similar to those held in her own Cabinet, first buying an article in common with a number of her

---

[1] The ticket known by this style.

friends, and the entire company then drawing lots for it. The stakes were by no means small : a gold watch studded with diamonds, in value nine hundred francs, was raffled for by six persons : the Queen's share for a chain of gold set with diamonds—in which raffle she was a loser—was eighteen hundred francs. A gold watch set with diamonds cost the winner, the Duc de Guise, four hundred and twenty francs—rather more than a tenth of its price, for ten people took part in this raffle. The prizes on these occasions were always articles of jewellery or choice works of art, such as " a veronica of enamelled gold, full open like a sun, garnished with many little diamonds ; a figure of St. Jerome in enamel, fashioned as a reliquary," similarly ornamented ; "six fruit-baskets in pierced silver work, and another in silver gilt, pierced." The goldsmiths Jean Chancel and Nicolas Chrestien presented the Queen with a bill for seven hundred and sixty-eight livres on account of a single day at the fair, while that of François le Prestre, " merchant goldsmith dwelling within the Gallery of the palace in Paris," amounted to twelve hundred livres—sums which represented merely the Queen's share of the day's losses. Some idea of the extensive gambling in which the royal couple indulged at the fair may be gathered from a letter written by Henry IV. to Sully, dated February 28, 1607 : " My friend, during the fair of St. Germain I have gambled away goods to the value of three thousand crowns. The merchants from whom I had the said goods have pressed me for payment, wherefore I send you this line to bid you pay all such my debts."

Besides these expensive indulgences the Queen always made presents at fair time to all her children and relations, and to her friends, accompanying the gifts with some such letter as : " While walking here about the fair of Saint Germain des Prés, I bethought me of your fairing, which I send with this." At other times, Mademoiselle de Montpensier, it might be, received a sum of money to expend in whatever manner best pleased her. Each of these " fairings " cost the Queen from fifty to three hundred francs, so that it is small wonder that Shrove-tide and the booths of Saint Germain invariably caused a sad depletion of her exchequer.

The Queen's airing occasionally assumed the proportions of quite a little tour, as when on Sunday, seated in her coach between her Lady of the Chamber and the Mistress of the Robes, she drove to " hear vespers at Poissy," and on the return journey paid a visit to her children at Saint Germain. Marie de Médicis was never slow to accept Queen Marguerite's invitation to take a meal with her at her estate of Issy, for she loved a ride as dearly as do all good horsewomen, and on a return from Issy she always galloped her Spanish jennet as far as the beginning of the Faubourg Saint Germain. To Saint Germain itself, naturally the usual goal of her outings, she rode in summer, and in winter was carried in her litter. This litter, which was closed on all sides, had glass windows, and was warmed by the combustion of perfumed balls ; it was upholstered throughout in red velvet embroidered in gold. Italian bearers had carried it on her first arrival in France, but Henry IV. soon replaced these by two good Poitevin mules, the muleteers being escorted by Pages of the Stable. Did the Queen desire to hunt by the way, she left her litter " and coursed a hare, mounted upon her palfrey." With one good mule in front and another behind, such a litter was by no means a bad method of locomotion in an age when the surface of even the chief main-roads was seldom above reproach. The use of one would probably have spared the royal pair that accident which overtook them when, crossing the Seine by the ferry of Neuilly on the afternoon of June 9, 1606, the cumbrous coach missed the gangway and was overturned in the water. The Queen disappeared from sight, and there was a general commotion, but the bath was, fortunately, the worst that any one suffered. Henry IV., indeed, averred that the fates had clearly intended to present them with a good draught of water, seeing that they had partaken of too many salt meats at dinner. The shock had also cured him of a toothache ; he was delighted with the new specific.

Once a year the Queen and King were compelled to leave Paris while the Louvre was cleaned : the rooms were then aired and disinfected "by perfume of juniper wood," and the moats were scoured. During this period of three weeks, they usually wandered from place to place. The months of September and October, sometimes November also, they spent at Fontainebleau, thus originating a custom observed by the Kings of France until the end of the *ancien régime*. The Queen's marked preference for this palace ran directly counter to the opinion of the Parisians of her day, who " considered the air nowhere so clear as at the Louvre, and Paris comparable with no other place." Hither, then, she came often, at Easter, in May and June—the spring here was her special delight—and usually with but few companions ; for whatever the accommodation of the Château in point of space, its furnishing was meagre in the extreme. Strangers desiring to visit there—as Vinta, the Florentine envoy, or the Venetian ambassadors—were asked to bring with them their beds, hangings, china, often to send some one in advance that a lodging might be ready against their arrival.[1] Did the Queen invite her friends to visit here, they must come one by one : the royal orchestra was quartered at Avon.

At Fontainebleau Marie de Médicis was particularly fond of the beautiful apartment which overlooks " the Queen's garden "—now the garden of Diana—and of the spacious bedroom in which she was to be succeeded by all the Queens of France until Marie Antoinette. In the

[1] The following anecdote does not seem inapposite here. Monsieur de Cavoie, Grand Marshal of the Royal Palaces, laid a complaint before Louis XIV. on this same score—the miserable inadequacy of the furniture at Fontainebleau—in 1701. "But," objected the King, "they served for Francis I., my grandfather Henry IV., and my father as well !" "Sire," replied the marshal, "you tell me of kings who had their humour !"

adjoining oval room, she desired that her children might
be born. To what Henry IV. called "our delicious
desert of Fontainebleau" she took only such parts of her
wardrobe as were essential, modestly wearing the Grand
Duchess of Tuscany's gifts of "hats of fine Florentine straw,
trimmed with taffetas or carnation satin." She walked
freely and unattended in the Park ; her parasol was
fashioned of "two whole metres of violet taffetas."
"Feeding the birds in the aviaries was her great pastime,
but she was no less fond of watching the carp-fishers,
and of guessing the traditionally venerable ages of these
creatures." "They caught two great carp," she writes
Madame de Guise, "one of which was eight hundred
years old, although some said it was of the time of Noah
and the Deluge ; the other was only three or four hundred
years old. I ate the head of the first one, and enjoyed
exploring it as if it were a beautiful cabinet ! "

The great pleasure of Fontainebleau, during the
regular royal residence there, were the forest hunts. The
enormous crowds of gentlemen which attended them—
four or five hundred according to Bassompierre — and
ladies mounted on richly caparisoned palfreys, made a
gay and many coloured crowd.

Having returned to the Louvre towards the close of
the day, Marie de Médicis enjoyed a light repast of fruits,
preserves, and a little wine, served in the antechamber to
her and the ladies of her train. Having changed her
costume and made a slight toilet, she then entered the
Cabinet, where waited a numerous assemblage—a busy
crowd on the watch for intrigues and news, and bound to
be there that they may say next day: "I was at the
Cabinet, or at the circle. . . . I heard yesterday at the
Cabinet. . . ." Here she remained until seven o'clock.

The Queen and King hardly ever entertained at
"supper"—that is to say, great dinners. Only under
very exceptional circumstances, such as the marriage of
the Duc de Vendôme, natural son of Henry IV., with

Mademoiselle de Mercœur, the greatest heiress of France, or the baptism of the Dauphin at Fontainebleau, did their Majesties organise a banquet; for besides the fact that etiquette forbade any man to sit at the King's table in the Louvre, Henry IV. had no taste for wasting his money in this way. The few men invited to such banquets—great nobles and officers of the Crown—served the King and Queen ; the ladies dined. The three tables in the great hall were arranged in " the form of a gallows " —in modern phrase, " in the form of a horseshoe." At the upper or central table—occasionally raised two or three steps above the rest—the King sat, under a canopy, the Queen upon his right, upon the left the cardinals and ambassadors. Near the Queen sat the great ladies, such as Madame and Mademoiselle de Guise, the Comtesse d'Auvergne, the Princesse de Conti. The further side of this table was never occupied, but the other two tables had on the contrary, seats down both sides. Prince de Conti, the Comte de Saint Pol, and Monsieur de Guise served the King, while Messieurs de Nevers, d'Elbeuf, and de Joinville enjoyed the office of Gentlemen Servers to the Queen. Halberdiers of the Swiss guards surrounded the tables, and stewards, " officers of the kitchen," pages and waiters, squeezed between them as they came and went.

Every now and then the King and Queen bestowed the honour of their company at dinner upon some private individual in the city. The King, then, invited himself and issued all the invitations, none but himself having the right to do so. The host, who naturally paid the bill, seldom sat at the royal table, standing instead behind the chair of the King who was graciously pleased to talk and laugh with him. Although he did not dine, the host must test all the dishes before they were handed to his august guests, thus guaranteeing them against poison. The happy person most frequently honoured with the King's company was Zamet, the banker, known to all on account of his dark and serious face and his habit of perpetually bowing. His vast and luxurious mansion in Rue Beautreillis, on the Marais, was hung with superlative tapestries valued at four hundred thousand florins. An Italian by birth, whose immense fortune accumulated in the course of his profession allowed him to render the greatest financial services to the King, Monsieur Zamet was a confidential friend of the royal family long before he became Superintendent General of the Queen's household in 1603. The King and Queen constantly invited themselves to his house, and should Henry IV. be passing through Paris alone he never failed to visit the Rue Beautreillis for his meals; frequently he quartered himself there as well, an apartment in the house being commonly known as "the King's room." When Henry IV. desired to give a dinner in honour of his own birthday, it was always at this house that he received the princes, princesses, nobles, ladies of the Court and ambassadors, and the owner never failed to appear altogether delighted as he stood behind the King's chair.

Monsieur de Sully, at the Arsenal, was the second favourite host of their Majesties. The Concini's mansion in Rue Tournon was not, however, far behind in popularity with them, notwithstanding that Henry's appreciation of his magnificent reception there, of the extraordinarily rich furniture and abundant silver, and of the quality of the concert which followed the dinner, was always tinged with surprise. Others who were occasionally permitted to receive the Sovereigns were the Maréchal Balagny and the First President of the Parliament. The Queen on her part affected the houses of Madame de Guise and the Princesse de Conti, to which latter mansion she once invited a supper party of no less than twenty-six persons, one only of whom was a man, Cardinal de Joyeuse.

Failing anything better to do the King and Queen supped quietly in the antechamber—together as they had dined, or separately. In the latter case Marie de Médicis often took her repast in the little Cabinet, served only by the women of her chamber. The royal evening was spent in diverse ways, occasionally at the theatre of the Hôtel de Bourgogne, where the comedians " were in the habit of seldom playing anything worth listening to," so that Henry frequently went to sleep. At this theatre was once played before their Majesties the " amusing farce " of a drunkard who tells his wife that he would far rather spend his money in drink than waste it in paying the King's taxes. The better to put this into practice, he would henceforth drink wine at six sols instead of at three sols as heretofore. " The King's a sharp fellow," he cried, " but he'll scarcely lay hands on that ; out and fetch me some as fast as your pins can carry you ! " At this point the tax-gatherers arrive, but on the good man's evoking three devils from a chest, they are carried away after suffering a tirade on their pretensions to be " officers of justice." Henry IV. laughed at this foolery till the tears came, but the ministers, greatly annoyed, took steps to arrest the company. The King, however, called them fools and compelled them to withdraw the order.

Marie de Médicis' extreme preference for Italian actors led her yearly to arrange for a visit from some such company, who performed their comedy at least once a week before the Court and the remainder of the time in the town. Among her favourites were the *comédiante* Isabella Andreni, " never yet equalled for elegance, promptitude, and facility in all manner of patter suitable to the scene " ; Julio Romano and his company were also in favour, but no one approached Arlequin, the arch-favourite and most fashionable actor —spoilt, fêted, petted, and overwhelmed with presents. The Duke and Duchess of Mantua received her special prayer to use their powerful influence to the full in order to induce the " finest company that ever could be had " to accompany Arlequin across the Alps. To him she wrote letter after letter, assuring him that three thousand six hundred francs to defray the expenses of his journey were held to his order by the Receiver General at Lyon.

Such negotiations were complicated enough even without the vanity and quarrelsome pretensions of the actors. Arlequin cannot come, now because so-and-so refuses to accompany him, then because so-and-so asks too much ; two of the company are at daggers drawn ; lastly, the season is too late and he fears the snow on Mont Cenis. Marie de Médicis cannot imagine what will happen to her without " this good company, promised for her recreation and that of the Court during the sad winter days." He must, absolutely, come for the carnival.

At last the company arrive, among them old Petrolini and Giovanni Battista Andrini, called Lelio, with his wife Florinda. They are to play before the Court, first at the Louvre in the Salle des Gardes—now the Salle des Cariatides—later in the Salle de Bourbon, on the opposite side of Rue d'Autriche, at the Hôtel du Petit Bourbon. For their appearance in the city, the Queen kindly hired the hall of the Hôtel de Bourgogne, though not without some difficulty. The proposal having been made to " the caretaker and the governor of the Hôtel de Bourgogne," and by them transmitted to the company, the latter, aware on whose behalf the application was made, and snatching at an opportunity for gain, variously demanded sixty crowns a month, and one hundred, with " the addition that several boxes be reserved." The Queen, much incensed with " such factious, inconsiderate, and stupid people," offered two hundred livres a month and not a penny more. She finally demanded the intervention of the King's Procurator at the Châtelet, also that of the Civil Lieutenant of Paris, in order to put sense into "these creatures " ; matters were then arranged.

Marie de Médicis' enthusiasm for Arlequin, whose real name was Tristan Martinelli, was not universally shared. In 1613 he was fifty-six years old, and his colleague Petrolini eighty-seven — "no longer fit ages for the theatre," as some one wrote, where a "gay humour and quick mind are needed, qualities not found in such old bodies as theirs. They are now playing a comedy which

they call *Dui Simili*, but which is the *Menechmi* of Plautus.
It gave me no pleasure." But Marie, under the charm
of "all this harlequinery," as she says, treats Arlequin
familiarly, writes to him not only the friendliest letters,
but stands godmother to his children, consoles him for
his troubles with the treasurer in a wrangle over certain
promised payments, helps him to recover pledges from
the pawnbrokers of Florence, and compels the Duke of
Mantua to intervene in his disputes with a debtor.   In
proof of Arlequin's high favour with the royal household,
indeed, no more than this anecdote need be adduced :
" Ho there," says the actor to the King, " you have
impersonated yourself long enough, give me my turn
now ! "   Thereupon, and sitting in the King's chair, he
cries, " Well, Arlequin, you have come with your troupe
to amuse me !   I am well content !   I promise to protect
you and give you a pension ! "   The repertoire of this
troupe was limited to comedies, but its members included clowns, female rope-dancers, and acrobats who
turned fearsome somersaults and did "other feats so
appalling that many ladies and even men must turn
away lest they see them break their necks."

    Failing a performance at the theatre, the royal couple
often enjoyed a musical evening—royal regulations prescribed fixed days on which the King's orchestra should
play before their Majesties—or the Queen might give a
dance.   A curious letter written by the old Queen
Catharine de Médicis to her son, Charles IX., explains to
that Prince that he must give two balls a week at the
Court, " for I have heard your grandfather (Francis I.)
say that to live in peace with the French, and to insure
their love for their King, need is to make them joyous
upon two days, lest otherwise they find them occupations
more dangerous."   Before the King and Queen had concluded their Thursday and Sunday dinner, the custom
was that candles should be lighted in the great hall, and
the musicians assembled.   " Chairs and stools " being
brought in, the Captain of the Guard erected the separat-

ing barriers, and the dances began. In these—round dances—all present shared : they were double flings, single flings, dances of Burgundy, of Hainault, and of Avignon —of which last the rhythm and cadence are preserved in the popular song :—

> " Sur le pont d'Avignon
> On y danse . . . . ."

More formal dances followed, canaries [1] and galliards ; in which the men danced with hat on, and sword at side. A nobleman, having the honour to dance with the Queen, must show his respect by touching no more than " the hem of her hanging sleeve." Supper was subsequently served in another apartment. Henry IV. and Marie de Médicis were far from giving as many dances as usage prescribed.

Another amusement of the Queen's evenings was the ballet, in which she took extreme pleasure, personally organising them, and even, on occasion, herself taking part in their representations. These elaborate, costly, and magnificent performances were given in different places —in the upper hall of the Louvre, in the Queen's Ante-chamber, or in an apartment on the ground-floor, where the ladies sat upon platforms raised against the walls. Another favourite room, the " grande salle de Bourbon," in the Hôtel opposite, was a beautiful hall measuring a hundred and eight feet long by forty-eight wide, with vaulted ceiling strewn with golden fleur-de-lis, and upheld by columns with Doric capitals. Here, on gala days, twelve hundred white wax candles in silver sconces lighted up a profusion of tapestries, sculptures, and paintings. More frequently than in any other place, however, these ballets were staged in the Arsenal, where Henry IV. expressly caused to be built the magnificent hall, with a double row of galleries, opened on December

---

[1] So called, it is variously said, because copied from natives of the Canaries, and because first danced in a ballet, the performers in which were disguised as natives. In no case was the dance formal—in a modern sense.

6, 1609. The Queen, as director of the performances, selected the princes, princesses, ladies and nobles who took part in them. Duret, Durand, Palluau, and la Clavelle were among those who wrote the scenarios—*The Joys of the Golden Age, The Amusements and Pastimes of the Four Seasons*, with dances, figures, couplets, transformation scenes and grand tableau. The performances, which lasted for hours, were prepared with the greatest care. The Queen occasionally consented to "take" her piece on tour to various houses—the Bishop's Palace, the Hôtel de Condé, the Hôtels of Queen Marguerite and of Madame de Retz. Did she herself appear upon the boards, it was always in a mask.

When, as sometimes happened, a piece was acted exclusively by men, ridiculous disguises concealed the performers, who came on in pairs as twin towers, colossal women, pots of flowers, screech-owls, bass-viols, or windmills. Marching on in file, these would dance, divest themselves of their trappings and dance again in fours; all together then resumed "their machines" and disappeared. The women were elegantly costumed for their performances—Marie often in Italian dress. The Queen's most magnificent ballet was given in 1609—the ballet of *Dian's Nymphs*, rehearsed in the great hall of the Louvre, and presented at the Hôtel of Queen Marguerite. Marie de Médicis had long "planned and designed" this piece, which lasted until six in the morning.

Ballets, at this time, were danced everywhere and by all the world—"the carnival swarms with them"—yet even in the presence of the Queen, they often became mere tomfoolery. "I believe I never saw one laugh as I saw the Queen laugh," wrote a dancer in one such which ended in "agreeable buffoonery." Another spectator of similar scenes did not agree in his view of the matter, for to him these entertainments at Court were spoiled by their "great, shameful, and unworthy disorderliness." Small rooms and a too numerous company, suffocation and uproar, and the impossibility of movement on the part of the audience, or of obtaining proper space for their evolutions by the performers, are charges which lead us to incline to his view. At the grand ballet of 1614, staged at the Arsenal at a cost of ten thousand crowns, the Captain of the Guard who was charged with keeping order, yielded free entry to all comers. The Queen, flying into a furious rage on her arrival, departed, declaring that the performance would not take place, and was followed to the Louvre by a message that the guard had evicted the populace. Louis XIII. was thereupon snatched once more out of bed, and dressed in haste; the Queen returned, and the ballet was performed "as well as might be." Yet, on her departure, the crowds at the doors clamoured and jostled for "souvenirs."

Being unable to do without her amusements, Marie, when in mourning, enjoyed light comedies upon the stage of the little theatre which she had erected, on the ground-floor of the Louvre, to seat eighty persons. Or, alternatively, she would dine with the Princesse de Conti at Saint Germain des Prés, with Madame de Guise in the Rue de Grenelle, or with Madame de Guercheville, her lady of honour. On such occasions the younger guests, as Bassompierre, Messieurs de Chevreuse, de Vendôme, and others, would dance a miniature ballet for her diversion.

Not every day being, unfortunately, a day of festival, the royal couple often remained at home, but it was impossible that they should remain alone. When the Queen "gave her good-night" to the company in her Cabinet, there remained with her certain intimate friends, among whom the entertainment at once took a new lease of life: the Princesse de Conti, Madame de Guise and her mother, the Maréchale de la Châtre, Madame de Ragny, Messieurs de Guise, de Joinville, Bellegarde, Créquy, Bassompierre, Saint-Luc, de Termes, de Rambouillet—a brilliant circle of the nobility full of spirits and a cynical wit. But the pleasure of talking has its limits, and the cards were soon brought out. The King had a great

taste for chess, dicing, and card-playing; virtuous bur-
ghers, indeed, considered that he set a very bad example. "There is neither beggar nor rascal who does
not set up his gaming table at the corner of the street,
such weight hath the bad example of princes." The
King, however, caring nothing for such criticism, continued his play, varying it with a game at Reversi, very
fashionable at this time, or with watching pretty game-
sters matching each other "with the three dice, thrown
from out of little boxes so devised that there can be no
cheating."

Marie de Médicis' particular game was *prime*.[1] This
she played with a wonderful set of cards painted and
illuminated to represent diverse animals by Louis de la
Haye, goldsmith, whose work cost her one hundred and
twenty livres. Bassompierre was her favourite adversary; she played with vigour and punted heavily, so
that in one evening she was known to lose seven hundred
pistoles,[2] "which did not make me happy," as she afterwards lugubriously wrote. According to Bassompierre,
a single day's play at Fontainebleau saw twenty thousand pistoles change hands. The lowest stake was fifty
pistoles, the highest five hundred. Fifty thousand pistoles
might hang upon a single chance. Bassompierre, again,
relates that one evening in 1607 his sole goods in life
consisted of seven hundred crowns, whereas he had just
ordered a suit for the Dauphin's baptism at the cost of
fourteen thousand crowns; by the favour of fortune
he rose from the table with the said fourteen thousand
crowns in his pocket, a sword mounted in diamonds
valued at five thousand two hundred crowns, and five or
six thousand besides. If we are to believe his statement,
his winnings at cards in 1608 amounted to half a million.
The Queen was a good player, but the King, if luck were
bad, would pass his hand to a companion.

[1] An early card-game, in which but four cards were dealt to each player.
' Avoir la prime " in this game was to receive one card of each suit in the deal
[2] A pistole = a gold crown of Spain or Italy, so called because smaller
than the French coin of the same denomination.

Never late, and in no case later than eleven o'clock, the last intimates took their leave or were dismissed, and Marie retired within her little Cabinet to deal with her correspondence, often abbreviated on the plea of weariness : " Gli e ora di dormire, e voi sapete che io non scrivo se non a quest' ora." Léonora Galigaï now descended from the next floor to talk with her, and to help her to bed.

The Queen often sat late talking or writing with her Mistress of the Robes, but nevertheless, as the Court clock of the Louvre struck eleven, the sentries of the bodyguard having given " three consecutive calls in the courtyard with intent to warn all to withdraw into their own place," closed the gates of the palace and handed the keys to the Captain of the Guard, who gave them the night's password.

CHAPTER III

THE QUEEN'S HOUSEHOLD

NEGOTIATIONS between the Court of Florence and the government of Henry IV. were manipulated with a view to sending with the princess a numerous suite of Italians, all to be provided with lucrative positions in France, a question that occasioned quite a shower of diplomatic notes. Monsieur de Sully angrily signified that he would recommend " neither a doctor nor a cook," while those holding offices, protesting that " the bread would be taken from their mouths," declared that " in France there are vested interests." Marie de Médicis was with difficulty able to find place for some few Florentines— her childhood's friend, Léonora Galigaï, a few gentlemen in waiting, women of the chamber, and little pages. One by one she subsequently sent back her disappointed compatriots, and gently discouraged all those who for years solicited her good-will and a position at Court.

The Queen's household was, on principle, a close corporation. " Long experience and habit being necessary for those in command," old servitors were greatly valued, and must all be " good men and healthy in their persons." Honest ushers and faithful grooms of the chamber thus grew old in the Louvre, under the reigns of three or four Queens—

> " Who will his house well rule, must him surround
> With men all worth, virtue and honour found ;
> Who, fearing God, shall, under Him, be free
> Their profit by their master's to agree."

To maintain a tradition of good service, each servant was allowed to place his family, his sons and nephews, in the household. Beginning very young, as scullions in the kitchens for example, these mount the ladder of the hierarchy step by step, and under the very eye of their fathers and uncles—a veritable system of domestic dynasties. Wages were possibly inadequate, having stood unchanged for a hundred years, but any such deficiency was made good by gratuities. The servants of the King enjoyed, besides, the royal favour, an ample table, exemption from taxes—their pensioned widows were also exempt—and the privilege of *Committimus*, providing that any suit to which they are parties must be brought before certain special tribunals. Finally, though a simple groom of the chamber, every one of their number was duly enrolled in " the general Protocol of the State immediately after Councillors of Bailliwicks, Seneschalships, and the Courts of Justice, and before the Officers of Elections, of the Salt Wharves and all inferior judges "—an appreciable dignity ! All the world being, for these reasons, desirous of entering the Royal House-hold, while there were here more functionaries than places, a system of quarterly rotation was devised, under which four titulary occupants of the same post served, turn about, for three months in the year, their salaries justly varying as they were or were not *en quartier*.

Henry IV., imbued with a spirit of economy, rigorously reduced the Queen's household, abolished the Superintendency, dismissed the Gentlemen of Honour, and retired the Ladies of Honour.[1] Thus disappeared the countless personages who followed Catharine de Médicis, most pompous of queens—twenty-five Maids of Honour, forty-four Ladies of the Chamber, and eighty waiting-women. Nevertheless, in 1606, an average year, Marie's household comprised four hundred and sixty individuals, of whom eight alone were unpaid. Of these four hundred and sixty persons, two hundred and one owed regular daily service.

Her Majesty's immediate attendants, whether of the Household of Honour or servants proper, were under the direction of the Queen's sole lady of honour, the sweet and gentle Madame de Guercheville. Twenty years earlier Henry of Navarre had paid his court to her as the beautiful Madame de Guercheville, attached to the court of Catharine de Médicis ; full of esteem and respect for one who had been able to resist him, he now chose this lady to guide his foreign Queen upon her arrival in France, and to instruct and advise her in her new life. A woman of forty in 1600, the good sense writ clear on her tranquil countenance enabled her to conduct the household with great tact, and to ensure respect for all traditional forms. She had control of all that regarded the Queen's " person and chamber" and all expenses connected herewith, countersigning orders and furnishing certificates. The extent of Marie's love for her was open to a doubt, but she certainly loaded her with favours—sixteen hundred francs at the New Year—the salary of a lady of honour was twelve hundred francs a year—an annual pension of six thousand francs, a beautiful gold cross studded with diamonds, and supported her in her lawsuits. Madame de Guercheville

[1] Louise de Lorraine, Queen of Henry III., had sixty of these.

was privileged to " carry the train of the Queen's mantle in processions " ; Marie secured to her precedence over the wives of the Marshals of France. She assigned her the handsome suite of rooms on the second floor — directly above her own and those of the King—afterwards occupied by Constable de Luynes. She once persuaded the King to make her a grant of one hundred thousand crowns.

The Mistress of the Robes—though without any further authority—as superintendent of the Queen's apparel, designed, ordered, and approved her toilets. This office—important in that it carried with it the right of free access to her Majesty at any hour—was held by Léonora Galigaï, whose beautiful suite of three rooms on the second floor was encumbered by twenty carved chests filled with the Sovereign's clothes and " effects."

The Maids of Honour to Marie de Médicis usually numbered from six to eight *filles et demoiselles*, or *filles d'honneur*, all of the highest birth — Genevieve d'Urfé, Victoire de Cadaillac, Sabine de Coligny, Anne de Saint Mars, Marie de Pontcourlay, Madeleine de la Meilleraye. Their rooms were on the ground-floor of the Louvre, in the " old part of the hotel " beneath the Queen's apartments. Besides maintaining them, the Queen dressed them and watched over them. On occasions of great ceremony, these young girls wore magnificent gowns of " cloth of gold and silver." Their salary was two hundred francs, but the Queen's gift to them on marriage " for a wedding-gown " was always twelve thousand livres, to which the King added two thousand crowns. Their special attendants were a governess, Madame de Malissi, an under-governess, Mademoiselle de Courtenay, an usher, honest Girard Passetemps, to keep the door of their apartment, three grooms of the chamber and three footmen. Marie de Médicis, whose cold temperament was proof against all motions of the heart, would by no means tolerate them in her Maids of Honour, so that it was an evil day which found young

Baron de Termes in the room of Mademoiselle de Sagonne at an hour which admitted of no excuse. The Queen asked Henry IV. to "have his head off"; "the Sagonne was ignominiously dismissed and maltreated," the governess suffered a like dismissal, and not the urgent prayers of Père Cotton himself could obtain their pardon.

Marie de Médicis was, none the less, prone to conceive an affection for her young companions, whose cause, if need were, she would vigorously espouse. Thus she desired to marry one of them—an Italian named Catarina de' Medici, daughter of one Cosimo de' Medici, a distant relative of her own and of Diana, Countess de Bardi—with Baron de la Musse. The Baron, having heard certain gossip, hung back, and the Queen learned that a shameful scandal had been invented and circulated by his mother, Madame de la Musse. The project of marriage she declared "a thing about which I care nothing at all;" but no one, for all that, was free to steal "her little Catharine's reputation." Madame de la Musse must either designate the authors of these stories that they may be punished, or "I will teach her, to her cost, how much I am offended!" Interrogated by the Civil Lieutenant, Miron, by order of the Queen, who desired an action to be brought against her and to have her imprisoned, Madame de la Musse could only offer her excuses. "Little Catharine" subsequently married Maréchal de Marillac.

A marriage being duly arranged—and the pretty heads of her girls were full of nothing but dreams of fine marriages —Marie de Médicis was pleased to permit the young man to pay his court by instructing the governess that he may have "such honest access to the young lady as a servitor may desire to his mistress." This elegant and dainty little band of *filles et demoiselles* lived retired in the apartments, appearing only upon occasions.

The domestic service was performed by ten or twelve women of the chamber, under the direction of an old and respectable dame, "good La Renouillière," a toothless grandmother, well fitted to uphold traditional customs, whom the little dauphin called "that old beast." Some of these women were Italians, who had served the Sovereign from her infancy, knew little of French customs, and were sometimes difficult to manage. The most influential of these Italians was Madame Salvagia Vincenze, or, as the French called her, "Madame Selvage," who, as well as La Renouillière, slept in the royal chamber. She was employed by the Queen upon confidential errands, and as the wages of a woman of the chamber were very moderate—one hundred and twenty francs a year—received gratuities amounting to nine thousand francs. She, or her daughter, was still with the Queen at the time of the latter's death in 1642.

Three other women, Catarina Forzoni, a particular favourite, daughter of Marie de Médicis' nurse; Madame Sauvat, daughter of a groom of the chamber to Queen Louise of Lorraine; and Madame Canche, wife of a Comptroller General of Finance at Poitou, remained in the apartments, where they relieved each other, in watches, throughout the night. This they called *être de chevauchée*. The other women were occupied in the wardrobe—one in charge of the table-linen, another of the *linceaux* or bed-linen, a third in starching the Queen's linen. The furniture or other property of any deceased stranger or natural child were their perquisites.

Besides these women the household included a certain number of subsidiary personages, first among whom were the dwarfs, a couple of Italians, Margarita Zavizanca and her brother Alberto. Merlin and Marin Noué, *porte-manteaux* in ordinary; a negress, Madeleine, "the Queen's Moor," whom, by the aid of a dowry of six hundred crowns, Marie succeeded in marrying, and for whose wedding she made "a festival worthy so superb a beauty;" a crazy girl, Mathurine, very famous at the time, and a jester, Pierre Navarre, were also of the number. Among those whose service was of a more practical kind were one Nicholas Guillois, "chair-man," whose duty was to bring the chair whenever called for, and to any room, from the wardrobe where it was kept ; the washerwoman, Madeleine Maupart, who has washed "Her Majesty's body linen since her departure from Florence " ; and finally, young Gaspard, in charge of the birds belonging to the women of the bedchamber.

The first place in the household of a queen of France was held by the almoners, the number of whom Marie de Médicis greatly increased. Her predecessor, Louise de Lorraine, had been content with a single Grand Almoner, twenty or so honorary almoners, and four chaplains. Now, a Grand Almoner, first almoner, almoner in ordinary, four almoners serving quarterly, thirty unsalaried almoners, a confessor to the household, a confessor in ordinary, a preacher in ordinary, and ten chaplains—more than fifty ecclesiastics in all—bore witness to the solicitude of Henry IV.'s wife to appear a good Catholic.

According to the custom initiated by Anne of Brittany, under which the Queen's Grand Almoner was always a bishop, Marie de Médicis appointed to this post the Bishop of Béziers, Giovanni Baptista Bonsi, a Florentine Senator, who left his bishopric to be administered for him by his uncle, Tomaso Bonsi. Ill-paid, like every one else, with three hundred francs a year as salary, but four thousand five hundred as gratuity, Giovanni Baptista Bonsi was charged with the by no means arduous duty of distributing the Queen's regular alms, and of acting as Her Majesty's secretary in religious affairs. This office carried with it many honours and profits, such as exemption from ecclesiastical taxes and the possession of various benefices and dignities. Bonsi did not even wait for the death of the Archbishop of Rouen, Cardinal Joyeuse, to ask for a share of the abbeys held by the dying man, while he also took good care of his nephews and nieces, marrying the latter richly, and procuring for one of the former, Dominico Bonsi, the office of First Almoner and the Priory of Solesmes. Moreover, as the first cardinal created by Louis XIII., he obtained the purple in 1611. Four years later, in 1615, he was dismissed. But one of his successors —the Bishop of Luçon, Jean Armand du Plessis-Richelieu —more fortunate or more clever than he, also honoured with the red hat, left the office in 1624 only to become prime minister.

None of the ecclesiastics, of whatever grade, attached to Marie de Médicis' household — first almoner, almoner, almoner in ordinary, quarterly almoners, or chaplains— really had more than two definite duties—to perform Mass in the morning and Vespers in the evening, and to say grace at meals. They must be ready to say the Queen's Mass at nine in the morning ; on Sundays, Fridays, and Saturdays all the Bishops and Archbishops at Court must attend High Mass in full canonicals. On these days, Vespers were sung at four o'clock, but failing a message from Her Majesty, the services were delayed for her until noon in the morning, and until six o'clock in the evening. Should Marie attend Mass elsewhere than in the Louvre, " Her Majesty's footstool, with her cushions and canopy," preceded her upon a sumpter-horse to the church which it was her intention to visit.

In consideration of the modest sum of ten francs a year, a preacher attached to the royal household, Frère Jacques Buchon from the abbey of Saint Victor, preached every Sunday and holiday, in the mornings after High Mass, and almost daily during Lent and Advent. The daily Mass for the members of the household was probably but seldom attended by the lackeys, grooms, coachmen, or cooks, but a *Benedicite* and grace was always said at their tables, as at the Sovereign's own, by the almoner upon duty for the quarter-year.

The most important man in the Queen's household after the " members of the chapel " was the Chevalier d'Honneur, a grave and worthy personage who always accompanied the Queen, and was her *chaperon*. To fill this position, as Marie de Médicis herself said, " a blue ribbon and a grey beard " were essential. This official, however, had very little to do, and his position carried with it no

F

authority whatever. At the Louvre and elsewhere he took Her Majesty's hand whenever she had need of assistance, and stood at her right hand on all occasions of ceremony. When she rode it was the first Equerry's duty to mount and dismount her, but the moment her foot touched the ground the Chevalier resumed his charge. He was quartered in the palace—a signal privilege accorded to few men. In cases of emergency, and when the office was held by some one in whom Marie de Médicis placed full confidence, the Chevalier d'Honneur drafted important letters requiring thought and " consideration."

Authority over the Queen's attendants belonged entirely to the First Steward, who was as much the mainspring of this household as is the corresponding official in the households of private persons of means. A supreme arbiter over " the Seven Offices," this official enforced the rules of the household, kept the accounts, and imposed punishments. Having under him gentlemen equerries, the steward was necessarily of gentle birth; he needed to be active, intelligent, enterprising, and possessed of a perfect memory in order that he might know the least of the lesser scullions. Rising at dawn, so soon as " the great canvas lanterns " on the staircase of the royal dwelling were extinguished, he must see to it that the menials "swept and carried away the dirt from the courtyard, staircases, and upper and lower halls, that no stench or filth remain "; also, that all those servants who lodged in the city were punctually at their posts. So soon as the Queen was awake, he attended in the royal chamber to take her orders, which he transmitted to the kitchens, and it was his duty to see that everything was done according to the Sovereign's taste, that the provisions were good, and that the wine was not sour.

Every three months he drew up a list of those who were to serve during the quarter, and presented it to the Queen for her signature—a very important matter, since no salary could be paid to any person whose name was not enrolled in this schedule. On the fourth of the first month of the quarter he assembled the new staff, read the regulations aloud, and reminded each one that it was his duty to conduct himself " with all fidelity, integrity, care, and diligence " ; he strictly charged them to be present every day, and forbade them to send a substitute unless under a special authorisation which must be entered in a particular register, or without " good and regular certificate " from a doctor ; then, dismissing all to their duties, he passed from office to office to learn the new faces, and to renew acquaintance with the old. It was he who advised as to promotion, regulated the prerogatives of each office, suspended and dismissed. From top to bottom he must know everything, and every person, in the household. In the evening and at night, the lighting also came within his province. He " has candles lighted in all the halls and passages of Her Majesty's dwelling, and lanterns placed at the four corners of the courtyard and on the stairs, so that those who enter may be seen and recognised." The First Steward was assisted by the steward upon quarterly duty and the steward in ordinary—the latter occupying an obscure position. On the third day of the first month of each quarter, the first steward, the steward retiring from residence, and he who was entering upon it, assembled " in the steward's office " to consult with the other officials—the Clerk of the Counting-house, the Comptroller General, and the Clerks of the Store-room. They discussed the business of the preceding quarter, and arranged procedure in that next ensuing. The books were inspected ; purchases of provisions and supplies, bills of fare, the condition of the kitchen coppers and utensils and the linen, were gone over, signed, and certified, for the newly installed steward was held responsible for all that was entrusted to his care. The steward-entrant then assumed his staff of office, and made a tour of the kitchens, so as to acquaint himself with the faces of his subordinates. In the absence of his chief, he awaited the Queen when she left her apartments in the morning, and received her instructions for dinner ; he then returned to the kitchen to superintend preparations.   Having informed Her Majesty that a repast was served, and the Queen having taken her place at the table, he handed her the damp napkin upon which she wiped her hands.   As director of the service of the palace he must be ever at hand, was forbidden to take any meal outside the Louvre, or to undertake any other salaried occupation.   At the end of each month he reported to the Queen any shortcomings on the part of her attendants, suggesting suitable punishments ; and he frequently took counsel with the officials already mentioned, conferring with them in order that the traditions of the royal service might be observed.

The Queen being seated, however, the steward's service concluded when she had received her napkin at his hands.   No domestic, indeed, might serve at her table—such service requiring to be performed by persons " of birth."   The office accordingly devolved upon her gentlemen servants — three gentlemen who bore the ancient titles of pantler, cupbearer, and trencherer.   The first of these served the bread, the second filled the glasses, and the third cut the meat.   When it was time to prepare the table, these three personages—preceded by an usher and followed by numerous underlings — repaired in procession " to the buttery "—the first of the " Seven Offices " —where was kept the table furniture for Her Majesty's personal use.   Here each took the article for which he was responsible — the pantler, the royal *nef* — a crystal vase in the form of a ship, mounted on a chased metal stand, and containing the napkin ; the cupbearer the cup ; the trencherer the knives.   Returning to the hall in the same order, they superintended the laying of the table. Alone permitted to serve the Queen, who received nothing unless direct from their own hands, they now handed her the bread, offered her her glass on a tray—first tasting the wine and water in her presence to prove that it was not poisoned—and handed her the meat which the trencherer received from the officers of the kitchen.   Theoretically their duties ended here, but as Marie de Médicis maintained no Gentlemen of Honour, the responsibilities of that office also devolved on them. They were thus obliged to attend at the Louvre by seven or eight o'clock in the morning, there to wait in the antechamber until Her Majesty might go abroad. Each was obliged to keep two horses. Failing need of their escort, the Queen would use them for every sort of errand, sending them often on long journeys, as into Berry or Touraine. Although allowed no lodging in the Louvre, they were forbidden—like the stewards—to dine or sup elsewhere. On a salary of scarcely four hundred francs a year a good appearance at Court must be maintained, with all its obligations—to wear handsome and costly clothes, often renewed, to spend two thousand five hundred crowns in preparation for the Shrovetide carnival, on occasion to take part in dangerous gambling, to participate in costly ballets, and much else of the like kind. This, rather than the large number of aspirants to the position, originated the system of quarterly service. Three months of the latter, with its ruinous expenses, sufficed ; and for the rest of the year, as a contemporary says, "the simple and retired life of the châteaux demands neither great expense in rich apparel, or horses of price, banquets, or yet the other magnificences required of those at Court. Thus, and by wise economies, may a man make good the costly necessities of the service."

Members of the domestic service, properly speaking, came from the commonalty — first among them being the ushers, addressed as " Mr. Usher," of whom one was allotted to each room. Posted at the entrance of the room of which he was in charge, Mr. Usher held in his hands " a rod "—a reminder of times not yet so remote when his progenitors reproved with blows, and maintained order with the cry, " Out ! Clear the way or suffer the rod ! " The ushers arrived at the palace at five o'clock in the morning, helped with the cleaning, and permitted none to enter before his appointed hour.

The most onerous duties fell to the Usher of the Antechamber, for here the courtiers and members of the household gathered in the greatest number. Etiquette forbade any one to sit upon the chests against the walls of the room, or to approach the buffet—the first prohibition for decorum's sake, the second by way of precaution. The usher, indeed, was at times obliged to "mount guard" over the buffet. When Her Majesty took her repast in the antechamber, the usher was charged with clearing the room before her table was laid. A thorough knowledge of all with whom he was brought into contact was required of an Usher of the Cabinet, since while no unknown or suspected persons must slip into Her Majesty's "salon," he must be no less careful not to irritate some touchy nobleman, or offend a little-known gentleman, by questioning his entry. This duty was naturally not without its difficulties, as on the occasion when the usher was compelled to eject a couple of garrulous Gascons, friends of Henry IV., who quarrelled and boxed each other's ears—a criminal offence against the dignity of the royal House.

Next in order of rank came the Grooms of the Chamber —four in number, serving in quarter by rotation, under the direction of old Pierre Sopitre, first Groom of the Chamber and head of a dynasty which held this office for many generations, a Sopitre being first Groom of the Chamber to Henry III., while his descendant served Louis XIII. in the like capacity in 1633.[1] These servants arrived at the Louvre at five o'clock in the morning, lighted the fires in the antechamber—in winter in the Cabinet also—and set the rooms in order. As soon as the Queen awoke they repaired to the kitchen for her "broth," and she had no sooner gone to Mass than they took possession of her sleeping-apartment, made the bed, and arranged and dusted the furniture. Having attended in the antechamber during the remainder of the day, they at evening lighted the candles and lanterns. The fruit-room[2] furnished them with the necessary lights, for which they gave a receipt in due form "by weight and by tale,"

---

[1] Henry IV. endowed a member of the family with an abbacy.
[2] The royal fruit-room purveyed lights as well as fruit to the household.

as also they did for the firewood and the towels. Snuffing the candles and trimming the lanterns was their especial duty. Of a somewhat lower rank than these were three grooms of the wardrobe, who helped Her Majesty's women in the handling of the Sovereign's effects, and their arrangement in the chests.

The doctors, of whom there were five, ranked next below the grooms in the domestic service—the first doctor, the doctor in ordinary, and three doctors for the quarter —among them the doctor to the household—assisted by two apothecaries, two surgeons, and a barber to the household. The regulations required their presence in the antechamber every morning in case their services should be needed, and their scrutiny of the wines at every meal. Measured by their position in, and the wages of the remainder of, the household, their salaries were disproportionately large, for while the first steward received a stipend of eight hundred francs yearly, Monsieur Delorme—successor to Monsieur André du Laurens, a very learned man, and a doctor and professor of Montpellier—drew a salary of seven thousand four hundred francs, in addition to three thousand seven hundred francs of perquisites—in all, eleven thousand francs. Monsieur Petit, the doctor in ordinary, received nine thousand francs. Marie de Médicis' weakness for foreign doctors explains her patronage of Italians, Spaniards, and Portuguese Jews. These latter she favoured greatly, Philotée Montalto—whose real name was Pompilio Evangelisti—a pretended " doctor of Palestine," in especial. These doctors attended the household also, a careful list being kept of some five score of persons who enjoyed the right to their services. Elaborate regulations providing for possible cases, and defining the limits of these claims on medical attention, medicines included, forbade summoning the doctor for any malady not contracted in the royal service or in case of certain unmentionable diseases. The doctors were specially recommended to draw up their prescriptions with sincerity and severity, not to include in them " any superfluity, delicacy, or refinement, these tending rather to please the invalids than to cure them." " Sugar, preserves, sweet odours or other blandishments which might cater to the palate of the patient without conducing to his recovery," were forbidden ingredients, with intent—as Robert Etienne says—that " the using of apothecaries' ware by the gourmand in perfect health " be prevented. The apothecary who furnished hippocras for the King's Day, as well as a beverage of sugar and cinnamon on ordinary days, was also bound to deliver quarterly statements of these, carefully dated and endorsed with the names and rank of the beneficiaries, which were then checked.

The kitchens and offices of the Louvre—extending beyond the palace buildings to what are now the sites of the Daru and Denon pavilions, and to the garden in front of the Pavilion de l'Horloge—consisted of a mass of low buildings backed by the houses bordering the Rue Froidmantel, " Her Majesty not desiring that cooking be done within her château, in that such were a thing unseemly and unworthy the respect which is her due." The fear of poisoners caused admission to these offices to be strictly forbidden to the public, a rule so rigorously enforced that the discovery of an intruder probably resulted in dismissal of the stewards. Of the Queen's two kitchens the one supplying the food for her own table was known as *la cuisine bouche, la cuisine de corps*, or simply *la bouche ;* the other, where was prepared the food for the remainder of the household, being known as *la cuisine commun.* The staff of *la cuisine bouche* numbered fourteen persons—a regular hierarchy as usual. The squire in ordinary held supreme command here, and remained in office throughout the whole year, his assistant being the squire in quarter. These squires were not "noble," but were ordinary members of the kitchen staff, who rose by long service ; they received the meat and were responsible for the various dishes. The head-cook who prepared the entrées, the soup-maker who made the soups, the roaster who roasted the meat, the pastry-cook who made the pastry, the kitchen-boy who had charge of the strings and skewers, two scullions who swept and cleaned for a wage of forty-five sous monthly, kitchen-knaves who turned the spits, two carriers whose duty it was to bring water and charcoal, and finally the usher who guarded the door, completed the establishment. With the exception of the scullions, the service of all these was limited to three months in the year. The Queen of France had therefore no famous cook skilled in preparing rare dishes. The head-cooks, having begun life as scullions at a wage of forty francs per annum, and so become masters of the roast at one hundred and twenty francs, attained this position with its salary of one hundred and forty francs by seniority. As vacancies occurred, they then became squires at one hundred and sixty francs. The heavy and simple food served at the Queen's table called for no great art in its preparation, and sufficient skill was easily acquired. To those who pleased her, the Queen would grant gratuities, which added materially to their very slender emoluments, and in order to secure her favour some of them were not backward in offering her surprises connected with their profession. Thus, the soup-maker presented Marie de Médicis with "a design of butter in the shape of a rock," receiving for his trouble sixty francs—exactly half his salary for the year. The bills of fare for the royal table were drawn out at the beginning of each quarter by the first steward and the steward in quarter, who submitted them to the Queen for her approval and signature. The regulations required that "the officers—all persons holding any kind of office—shall use such care to dress the Queen's meat well that nothing be served her which is not very good and tender." The "broth" must be "well cooked and boiled down, and not thin and greasy as it sometimes is"—above all, particular attention must be paid to the wine, to ensure the quality of which the first doctor "shall taste it to make certain that it be of the requisite standard." The kitchens must have Her Majesty's meals ready at half-past nine in the morning and at five o'clock in the evening. The conveyance of the meat called for a most dignified ceremony. At the head of a procession marched two archers of the guard in embroidered coats, halberd upon shoulder; an usher followed, rod in hand, then the steward in quarter with his staff, after him a serving-gentleman—the pantler—and finally, Her Majesty's meat borne by pages. The squire of the Queen's kitchen, a keeper of the plate, and two bodyguards with their halberds and sometimes their arquebuses, took care that no one approached the joint destined for the royal table. On reaching the Queen's antechamber the entire procession uncovered, the usher, stationed at the door, removing and pocketing the cap of each page as he passed in. The kitchen for the household employed the same number of servants as the *cuisine bouche*—fourteen—but as they bore the same titles and enjoyed the same salaries and the same distinctions of rank, it need not be described.

Around the kitchens were grouped certain accessory offices, such as the fruit-room with its two superintendents, two assistants and a registrar, in charge of the fruits and salads; the storeroom—its staff one superintendent and two assistants—where were kept wood, charcoal, faggots, straw, lanterns, and other matters of the like description; and a room in which were kept the leavings from the tables, those from the royal table being conveyed thither by one of the gentlemen-servants.

Of the two hundred persons in daily attendance upon Marie de Médicis, one hundred and seventy-five, supplied with board at her expense, were known as " companions of the King's household "—folk having *bouche à cour*, or being *à pain et à pot* in the Queen's house. These sat at fifteen tables, from five to twenty-two persons at each table, each of which bore a distinctive title—the table of the gentlemen-servant, at which sat also the almoner and chaplains; the table of the Maids of Honour, with their governess and assistant governess; the table of the First Steward, most important of all on account of those who sat at it; the tables of the women of the chamber and of the grooms of the chamber, of the storeroom, the King's kitchen, &c. All these were surrounded by noisy diners " talking together, and making a great uproar all through dinner with their shouting and laughter." An abundance of silver plate sufficed for the use of all; candlesticks of silver-gilt lighted the table of the fruit-room; and countless " saucepans, basins, baking-dishes, and plates and dishes " of silver lined the ranges in the kitchen. Twice a week a comptroller checked the attendance to see that no unauthorised persons were present, and strict surveillance was, indeed, the rule. Unpunctual diners might not, for instance, recall a course, nor might any sit elsewhere than at his proper table. It was forbidden to carry off anything, bread in particular, in the pockets; the cooks were on no pretext whatever to change the bills of fare arranged by the Queen, or the number and names of the diners. The dishes—of the same description as those served at the Sovereign's table—were heavy, abundant, and unattractive, but the choice varied at each table, the midday dinner of the Maids of Honour, for example, consisting of three entrées, three soups, boiled meats—as a joint of beef, a fowl, some mutton, or for roasts, a shoulder of mutton, a capon or chickens; in the evening various roasts, and on Sundays and Thursdays game. The grooms of the chamber would, however, have choice of only two entrées, three dishes of boiled meat, and two roasts; no boiled meats were allowed them in the evening. Of wine, the daily allowance to each person was a *pinte-chopine* [1]— except to the higher officers, who received about half as much again; a half-pound loaf was the allowance of bread.

The daily memorandum of supplies to Her Majesty's household shows that its average requirements were forty-six pounds of beef, five sheep, two and a half calves, twelve capons, eight fowls, thirty chickens, four head of game, twenty-five dozen of eggs, of fat four pounds, and thirty-two of lard. The quantity of wine was about forty-five gallons and three quarters, or three hundred and twenty-three litres; of loaves, five hundred and five. " Extras "

[1] *i.e.* about $1\frac{1}{2}$ litres : 1 litre = 1.76 pints.

occasionally occur despite the regulations—hen, turkey, pork, kid, "cow's udder," a dozen black-puddings ; but such entries are very rare. A small quantity of sugar and spices were also furnished by the apothecary. During the month of January 1610 the total expenditure on food for the Queen and her household amounted to fourteen thousand one hundred and eighty-two francs, four sous, and six deniers.

Some hundred and seventy-five persons alone of the two hundred in the household were privileged to sit at Her Majesty's tables, but she supported yet a further number under a different arrangement. Madame de Guercheville, Léonora Galigaï, the Chevalier d'Honneur, the First Steward, the Treasurer General, and all the high dignitaries of the Court received, in the first place, large gratuities—an ingenious device to supplement meagre stipends. Three hundred francs monthly were thus allotted to the Mistress of the Robes, three hundred to the Dame d'Honneur, five hundred to the Chevalier d'Honneur, two hundred to the First Steward, one hundred and fifty-five to the Secretary—sums sufficient for the ordinary expenses of living. To them, also, the Queen's household further supplied—under the name of "liveries"—a daily allowance of bread, wine, and meat—an allowance sufficient even without the gratuities. With a gallon, or seven and a half litres of wine, twelve loaves of bread, two capons, two joints of veal, two of mutton, a pound and a half of lard, three quarters of a pound of candles, six logs of wood and six faggots—to which he was entitled by his "warrant of livery"—the First Steward might well put by the two hundred francs allowed him for his living.

The Queen's kitchens were provisioned by contract. To the sound of a trumpet announcements were made in the squares and thoroughfares that public tenders should be made on such and such a day, when the contract would be awarded by extinction of the candle." [1] These proclamations were made not only in Paris but also in the

---

[1] The equivalent of the modern "fall of the hammer."

towns "round about, and on the banks of the Loire." Crowds attended on the day in question, for the position of purveyor to the Court was an honour much appreciated as affording double profit—such tradesmen being "privileged, free, and exempt from all bridges, ports, thoroughfares, tolls of entry and of egress, salt-taxes, and all other duties and taxes whatsoever." For the supply of bread to the Louvre, four bakers—Martin Gallet of the Rue St. Honoré, Crespin Grillet of Chatillon sur Loing, Andre Moreau of Poissy, and Jean Bardin of Rue Coquillère— entered into a joint agreement with the Sovereign, represented for the occasion by the Chevalier d'Honneur, the First Steward, the steward on quarter by duty, and the Treasurer General of the household. By this the bakers undertook to furnish during a period of two years the bread for Her Majesty and her household—" well-baked and stale," in loaves weighing from nine to ten ounces at the fixed price of twelve sous the dozen loaves, " all averaging the same weight," to be paid for at the end of each month. The bread was delivered to the pantry in leather bags and wrappings marked with the arms and colours of Marie de Médicis, and any failure on their part to supply correct weight or quantity was punished by the purchase of the shortage elsewhere, and the deduction of the cost of it from their accounts. When the Queen travelled they were bound to supply her wherever she might be, and were indemnified for the expenses of carriage. For the Fête des Rois they made the cakes prescribed by tradition for the whole household at a cost of forty-four francs ten sous.

The King of France maintained no cellar, but was daily supplied by the wine-merchant. The purveyor to the Queen was Monsieur Vincent Voiture, " citizen of Paris, dwelling in the Rue St. Denis, in the parish of Saint Eustache," who engaged by agreement to furnish white or " pale " wine for the Queen's table at the price of eighty francs the hogshead—" the Paris hogshead containing thirty-six gallons," that is to say, about two hundred and seventy litres—and *vin ordinaire* for the household at forty francs. The Sovereign's wine must be "all old wine from the commencement of the New Year till Easter Sunday, and all new wine—the best obtainable—from Easter to the last day of December"; for the household wine it sufficed that it be "good, honest, and of fair measure." In Monsieur Vincent Voiture's wine vaults and cellars were long rows of casks destined to supply the royal household, and the clerks of the wine-cellars came hither daily to obtain the requirements from the wood. The merchant particularly stipulated that "casks already broached shall be emptied before others be drawn upon." The comptrollers verified the quantities drawn, and paid the reckoning at the end of each month.

Meat—beef from the Poissy market and from Florence, mutton from Madrid, and veal from Rome ; fish, received every Friday morning, fat, wood, charcoal, candles, and other provisions were supplied by the merchants, Robert Allard, Augias, Begny, Gilles Fournier, and Claude Pommier—all of whom were under similar agreements. For heating in winter, the household received a daily allowance of one hundred and eighty-six logs of wood, and one hundred and ninety-three faggots. Lights were also provided in fixed quantities—each day twenty-one pounds of candles in winter, in summer twelve. The Lady in Waiting, the Mistress of the Robes, the Chevalier d'Honneur, and the First Steward, severally enjoyed the right to two pounds of white candles a day; yellow candles were supplied to the remainder of the household.

The Queen's stables were situated in the little Rue des Poulies, leading from the quay to Rue Saint Honoré, near Saint Germain l'Auxerrois. Here, in 1605, the Queen rented the Hôtel Gombault, causing it to be furnished by "Master Saloman Brosse, architect of our buildings," who arranged "certain sheds for the keeping of our coaches under cover." This work was so satisfactory that the Queen wrote : "The aforesaid building is so convenient that I have a mind to buy it, but

funds must first be found for the payment thereof."
These were never found. For each of the thirty coach-
horses, thirty saddle-horses, and twenty mules in Marie
de Médicis' stables, five measures of oats, two trusses of
hay—weighing twenty pounds and a half—and one truss
of straw were daily furnished by contractors. A farrier
was also under contract to shoe the horses for a consideration of six hundred francs a year, and for a further three
hundred francs to " tend the horses when wounded or
sick." The horses came either from Henry IV.'s stables
at Mehun, or were purchased of dealers who, in virtue of
royal letters patent, could not offer any horse for sale in
Paris until the royal equerries had waived their right of
pre-emption. The Queen's coach was drawn by the old
and quiet horses, the younger animals being allotted to
the carriages of the suite. The Queen's litter was always
drawn by mules, a hackney of medium size—" which comes
up to the block well, and usually goes at an amble "—
following with panniers containing bread, preserves, fruits,
and Her Majesty's table furniture, so that, whether travelling or taking her pleasure in the country, a light repast
should be obtainable without delay, " did the sumpter-
horses, provided for this purpose, not arrive in time."
Four ostlers, with six assistants, were appointed to shake
down the straw, groom and harness the horses. On gala
days, these ostlers wore a beautiful costume in the Queen's
colours—blue and white—a jerkin of fustian, breeches of
cloth with velvet bands, cloth capes, white stockings, and
gold garters and shoulder-knots. The mules were in the
care of a " captain of muleteers " and his assistants.

First in the sheds and coach-houses, full of heavy,
lumbering coaches, stood the regular coach, slung " on
main-braces with double straps and a simple cross-tie,"
upholstered in red velvet and often harnessed to as many
as eight horses. The " rich " coach, built in 1604, upholstered in red velvet and gold, stood next to this, with
close at hand the gala coach presented by Henry IV. to
Marie upon her arrival in France, in 1600—" all tan-

coloured velvet and silver tinsel, and lined with carnation
velvet embroidered in gold and silver, with curtains of
carnation damask "—to be drawn by four dapple greys.
The four coaches for Her Majesty's suite—" the coach for
the women, the coach for the girls," &c.—were each drawn
by six horses. The oldest coach was yearly replaced at the
stipulated price of one thousand francs, while the wheel-
wright as often renewed the weak parts of each vehicle for
one hundred and ten francs, and greased the wheels at
the fixed rate of one franc and ten sous per month.

Of the eight coachmen, the two " coachmen to the
body "—alone allowed to drive Her Majesty—wore a
superb livery, as usual of blue and white velvet covered
with gold embroidery, with gold belt and shoulder-knots,
white stockings, and a large hat. Five postillions led
the horses. Finally two footmen, *grands laquais du corps*
and *grands valets de pied*—in mantles and breeches of
blue velvet, with " doublets of chamois leather " and gold
shoulder-knots and belts, stood behind each coach.

To lend anything from the Queen's stables—whether
horses, mules, or wagons—was strictly prohibited, but
Marie de Médicis maintained the animals of her immediate attendants in the royal stables and at her own expense,
as those of Madame de Guercheville, and the saddle-horses
of the equerries, the first of whom, being head of the stable,
must make a daily inspection and receive a general report.
The equerry on duty for the quarter repaired every morning to the Queen's antechamber to take her orders, and
always accompanied the Queen's coach on horseback. On
the occasion of the festival of their patron, Saint Eloi,
Marie de Médicis granted to her coachmen, ostlers, muleteers, lackeys, and stable-boys, a gratuity of one hundred
and twenty francs with which to make good cheer.

The pages—a little band of twelve boys of good family
entrusted to the Queen's service, with a chaplain as tutor
to instruct and direct them, a squire " cavalcadour " to
teach them to ride, and a " baladin " to teach them
dancing—should be mentioned in this place. On days of

great ceremonial, the pages, wearing a beautiful uniform "of cloth of gold, with borders two fingers wide of silver," were mounted on richly caparisoned horses; their ordinary wear was a skirt, breeches, and cap of velvet, a satin doublet, white silk stockings, shoulder-knots and sword. Eight shirts and the same number of caps, handkerchiefs, neck-bands, pairs of cuffs, and stockings; twenty-four pairs of morocco-leather shoes and four pairs of boots, was the outfit of these young gentlemen. Three servants were at their orders, a barber "to arrange their hair and dress their wounds," and a laundry-man. The evil reputation of the Court pages and lackeys is attested by the saying: "While God made his angels, the devil was devising pages and lackeys." They would spend their time in company with the King's pages, the pages of the stable and of the chambers, playing in the courtyards, staircases, and halls, gambling at cup and ball, fighting, creating disturbances with the cry of "Kill! kill!" swearing, mocking at everybody, stealing caps for a joke, and talking nonsense to the women. Among the numerous regulations made to keep them in order was that issued to the captains to post their Swiss Guards everywhere—"on the staircases, in all passages and avenues, to restrain their disorderly riots, oaths, thieving of caps, affronts to women, and other violence and iniquity—an execrable thing!" The scapegraces, when caught redhanded, must be carried to the kitchen by the seats of their breeches, and there whipped. The number of these rascals maintained in a large house was, at this time, held proof of its greatness. The Queen's pages subsequently passed into the care of experienced captains, whose duty it was to train them in the carriage of arms. Marie de Médicis maintained a number of Italian pages during her first years as Queen. Like the pages, the Marshal of the Lodgings and his three quartermasters should be named with the stable establishment. Travelling in advance when Her Majesty went upon a journey, they marked the apartments reserved for her use with a white cross : quartermasters of the Court or Army used yellow chalk for the like purpose.

No account of the Queen's establishment can be held complete without mention of her " galley," the costly and useless whim of a young woman and a Florentine. To beg Henry IV. that a little ship should be built for her at Marseilles was one of the young Princess's first acts : its progress proving slow for her taste, she subsequently purchased another already in course of completion. At first refused the money by Monsieur de Sully, Marie borrowed the sum necessary for its purchase and completion from the banker, Zamet, who also furnished the salary of four hundred francs for its captain, Monsieur Jean Baptiste Vassal. To obtain the needful half-hundred or sixty rowers, recourse was had to the Grand Duke of Tuscany, whose intermittent expeditions to Barbary [1] placed him in possession of Mussulman slaves. The Grand Duke, none too willingly, consented to send the " fifty Turkish galley-slaves " required ; having arrived one by one, they were found to include two Jews, whom the Queen's conscientious scruples forbade her to accept. The " gang " was finally completed by application to the General of the Galleys of France. Thus was the *Regina*, a large and graceful galley, ultimately anchored in the harbour of Marseilles, its fifty-two unfortunate rowers—dressed in shirt, linen breeches, and jacket of red cloth—lined-up on the twenty-six leather-bound benches, there henceforth to spend their days and nights. For artillery, she carried five cannon, a cannon-royal, two demi-cannon, and two which fired small-shot. In the hold were stacked arms for a troop which might be carried : 43 muskets, 86 arquebuses, 13 partisans, 12 halberds, 69 pikes, 24 round shields, 16 " bourguignotes " of white metal, 6 tabards, and 2 drums ; and provisions—189 barrels of drinking-

---

[1] These expeditions of the Grand Duke of Tuscany were reprisals. Between 1570 and 1619 he was said to have freed 6000 Christian captives, and to have enslaved 10,000 Turks. That French galleys were frequently manned by Turkish slaves at this time is proved by documents—among them one of 1685 : *Un Marché de Turcs pour les galères royales.*

water, 4 barrels of wine, 10 barrels of victuals, 2 tubs of
salted meat, and the "candle-box." At the stern was the
little apartment to be occupied by the Queen—had she
ever found occasion to go on board—a salon furnished
" with a little hanging of red damask," arm-chair of red
velvet, twelve small chairs to match, also small tables,
velvet cushions, and " small lamps to light at night."
This apartment was used by the captain and the " scriv-
ener of the galley," otherwise the accountant, Monsieur
Mathurin Daniau. But alas for the embarrassments of
queens ! By constantly lying at anchor in the harbour,
the vessel suffered such deterioration that endless repairs
became necessary before each of her rare voyages ; but
funds for these had to be advanced by the captain. Perpetual complaints, requisitions, and protests to Paris
proved vain, and in 1611 he finally retired in despair,
left his ship to one Monsieur Dori, and presented a claim
for twenty-two thousand five hundred francs, for which
he finally took a mortgage on the hulk. The conveying
of the Duc de Nevers and a Capuchin father to Civita
Vecchia in 1608, was, indeed, the *Regina's* sole real commission. The whole affair taught Marie a lesson, for when
the inhabitants of Nantes presented her with a galley and
its crew on the occasion of her solemn entry in 1614, the
Queen then and there handed it over to the Ensign of her
Guard, Monsieur de Launay.

Monetary affairs were in the charge of the Treasury,
or Pay-Office to the Queen's Household, the members of
which were known by the general style of " Gentlemen of
the Council." The most influential man here was the
Private Secretary—Monsieur Phélippeaux, Seigneur de
Villesavin,[1] a very intelligent, active, and authoritative
person, who had the Sovereign's ear, and wrote the greater

[1] Paul Phélippeaux certainly rendered good service to his mistress. He
practically controlled appointments by controlling all access to the Queen's
person. The extent of his secretarial labours may be gauged from the bundles
of forty-one letters to relatives and friends in Italy, despatched by the hand
of M. de Brèves when he left Paris on first taking up his post of ambassador
at Rome.

part of her letters, and whose recommendation was of the highest value to any one seeking advancement or a "gratification." Seldom seen in the antechambers or at Court assemblies, he attained his ends more surely in audiences in the "Cabinet," and spent the rest of his time discreetly working at his table with his two clerks, Messieurs Samuel Lechalas and Laurent Deshaye. Nominally subordinate to the "Superintendent or Intendant General of the Finances of the Queen," so long as this functionary was honest Monsieur Sebastien Zamet, who was quite otherwise occupied, or easy-going Monsieur d'Attichy, Monsieur Phélippeaux remained unquestioned master. In 1614, however, the succession of Monsieur Claude Barbin began that weakening of the Private Secretary's power which ended with his dismissal when Richelieu assumed the office of Superintendent in 1619.

The duties for the most part honorary and never arduous of the "Chancellor to the Queen," old Monsieur Potier de Blancmesnil, *Président à mortier* to the Parlement de Paris, chiefly consisted in presiding about once a month over a council of four or five jurists—Messieurs Florent d'Argouges, Bullion, d'Ocquerre, Marescot—which advised the different agents of the Queen's domains upon the bringing or defending of lawsuits. Marie de Médicis never parted with this worthy Chancellor of the venerable beard. The Treasurer General, Monsieur Florent d'Argouges had, on the other hand, many responsibilities and duties, as manager of accounts and signatory of all orders for payments.[1] To him, the Treasurer of the Savings—the Cashier General of the State Treasury, as it were—made over at each quarter-day the total amount of the "credits" allowed to the Queen's household for the distribution of which he was responsible. As the Treasurer of the Savings was frequently late with his payments, the unfortunate household often besieged the Treasurer General's door, of which Monsieur Florent d'Argouges com-

---

[1] His son succeeded him in this post in 1615, while his grandson was Superintendent of the Household to Anne of Austria.

plained, humiliated by the torrent of their recriminations. The study of the budget and finances of Marie de Médicis, to follow later in this work, will make clear something of the desperate straits in which the Queen's caprice and extravagance continually involved her Treasurer.

The multitude of lawsuits brought about by difficulties of this kind, added to countless disputes over the property accruing to Marie de Médicis under her marriage-settlement, necessitated the retaining of quite a number of lawyers. As members of the household, these gentlemen enjoyed fine titles similar to those of the dignitaries of the Parlement. The Attorney General to the Queen, Monsieur Louis Dolé, was a vigorous, eloquent, and somewhat intriguing lawyer, at times so high in favour at Court as to be quite a factor in politics; his good offices were sought by great nobles, his name was put forward for the Comptrollership General of Finance, and even for the Chancellorship of France. Other like dignitaries were the Queen's Solicitor General of Affairs, Monsieur Pierre Basouin; her Advocate General, Monsieur Guillaume Marescot; the Advocate in Ordinary, Monsieur Adam Thévenot; and, lastly, in the Audit Room, a "solicitor" and a Judge Advocate, whose duty it was to deal with the endless criticisms presented by the captious Sovereign Court when auditing the Queen's domestic expenses.

Next to the Queen's Treasurer General stood the Chief of the Department of Accounts, her Comptroller General, Monsieur du Buisson. Towards the end of each year Monsieur du Buisson drew up "a detailed estimate" of the expenses of the household for the following year. The statement required the King's personal approval, and the expenditure for the year must subsequently be kept rigorously within the limits of this budget. The Comptroller General was also responsible for the proper appropriation of its several parts, for as to the Treasurer General were entrusted the salaries of the household, so to the Comptroller fell the purchase of supplies. The steward having,

therefore, given him nightly a signed memorandum of the
day's expenditure, the Comptroller must add them up,
record them, enter the several items whether of price or
of quantity upon the account of each tradesman, and
compare them with the particulars of the past year's
account. Application being made at the end of the
month by the aforesaid tradesmen, he took out " the
signed certificates of the parties employed," and made out
orders for presentation at the cashier's office—*La Chambre
aux Deniers*—where all payments were made. The Comptroller had clerks who copied the registers, drew up
the duplicates, transcribed the memoranda, oversaw the
kitchens, assisted at the " receipt of fish and meat," and
scrutinised the memoranda to see if they tallied, the
cashier's duty being limited simply to the payment of
orders at sight. This officer—" the Master of the Cash-
room "—having early shown a tendency to raise objections
and to criticise, was rather sharply reminded that his duty
ended with the receiving or paying out of the moneys of
the Treasury. He was, at the utmost, authorised to represent the Queen in company with his fellow officials when
entering into agreement with the purveyors, examining the
papers of the officers of the household in the Steward's
quarters, or reading over their certificates of office with
such as were newly installed. This last was by no means
a nominal duty, since the meanest scullion might not be
engaged by the kitchens without a certificate, or " letter of
engagement," signed by the Queen's own hand. Armed
with this, and then only after it had been read in the
Chambre aux Deniers, the newcomer swore his oath of
fidelity before the First Steward, and witnessed the
enrolment of his appointment upon the household roll.
These formalities over, the Master sent the formal papers
to the Chamber of Accounts, which accepted them after
scrutiny, or referred them back in case of irregularities.[1]

[1] The *Chambre aux Deniers* is the *Camera Denariorum* of the time of
Saint Louis. Marie de Médicis supervised her household to the extent of
summoning officials to the *petit Cabinet* for her personal reprimand.

Marie de Médicis retained a large staff of occasional advisers—magistrates, Judge Advocates, advocates, and lawyers—in Paris and in the provinces, especially in the vicinity of her domains. Under such titles as Master of the Queen's Requests, or Secretaries in Ordinary to the Queen, these men drew petty emoluments varying between ten and fifty livres, or, when occasionally summoned to her side for a month or two's regular work, a reasonable " gratification," thus ensuring their services in case of future need.

Such Masters of Requests and Secretaries in Ordinary numbered seventeen, and twenty-six in 1601 ; in 1630 these numbers had respectively increased to sixty-six and sixty-eight. Many of their names naturally fail to arouse interest, but some few—as Edouard Colbert de Villacerf,[1] or Monsieur Bénigne Bossuet,[2] Avocat au Parlement and Conseiller aux Etats de Bourgogne—carry us forward to the by no means distant but, in style and magnificence, very different age when the seven thousand personages at the Court of Louis Quatorze, at Versailles, shall stand contrasted indeed with the little and decent household of Marie de Médicis.

[1] This Colbert was otherwise interested in the establishment at Paris of a manufactory of cloth, silk, and cloth of gold and silver.

[2] The great Bossuet always exhibited a portrait of Marie de Médicis in his rooms—doubtless an heirloom from his ancestor.

CHAPTER IV

PALACE LIFE

DURING the few hours immediately subsequent to the arrival of Marie de Médicis in Paris in 1601, Henry IV. presented all the personages of the Court to her at the Hôtel de Gondi. "All the ladies of the principal houses of France, and of the most honourable of the city, came to kiss her hand and to bow before her," when suddenly, beside the old Duchesse de Nemours, appeared a tall young beauty, Mademoiselle Henriette d'Entraigues, whom the King playfully introduced with the remark: "This lady has been my mistress; she desires to be your personal servant." The company was a little surprised; Marie de Médicis remained very cold. Etiquette required that the person presented should "bow right low before the Queen, and kiss the hem of her robe." Mademoiselle d'Entraigues, scarcely bending, was about to raise the royal dress at the height of the knee, when Henry IV., with a sudden gesture, seized her hand and carried it to the ground. The presentation concluded amid general constraint, and the Court was next day unanimous in their censure of the incident. " This lady who has been my mistress " was so to remain for many a year : indeed, Henry's passion for the haughty and spirited Henriette d'Entraigues, Marquise de Verneuil, was to poison the ten years of his Queen's married life.

Henry IV. is one of the few historical characters the defects no less than the qualities of whose personality have been accurately handed down by tradition. So short as to be obliged to mount his horse from a block, he was yet robust, vigorous, a rapid walker, light of tread, and determined in all his motions. His hair and beard early turned grey, but he long kept " his ruddy skin and red lips, the fresh colour betokening perfect health." At his death, aged fifty-seven, the outward signs of age had overtaken him, nevertheless—writes Priuli—he still seemed *di natura prosperosa e forte*. He remained vigorous until the end of his life. He paid no attention to the laws of health, and was very irregular in his hours ; " waking and sleeping," writes Sully, " whenever and as much as he wished." Ignoring the claims of hunger under stress of passion, war, or his amusements, he at other times ate and drank to excess. Horses, hunting, and every form of exercise he loved ; while, habituated from early youth to a roving life and to long marches, he ignored fatigue. His hard usage of himself being rather careless than deliberate, he would remain in the saddle for whole days, without concerning himself particularly as to whether the physical endurance of those about him was equal to his own. It is therefore hardly astonishing to learn from Héroard that when visiting his young son at Saint Germain, the King's exhausted body occasionally succumbed to the inevitable ; with drooping head, he would ask the Dauphin's permission to lie on his bed, and instantly fall into deep and refreshing slumber. This capacity for occasional "naps," learned doubtless as a soldier in the field—the school of the greater part of his life —certainly stood the King in good stead. Indifference in the matter of his personal appearance again betrayed the soldier whose taste was all for simplicity. Henry IV. raised this preference to the dignity of a rule, and loudly proclaimed that what he loved best was to see his gentlemen well-mounted and modestly attired. During an adventurous career he had a hundred times been obliged to want for everything, and to ride for days and nights without wash or change of dress. Certainly inured to it, the King was even accused of not disliking this dusty carelessness and untidy dress: " I have many times seen him very badly dressed," says one of his circle, " and once in a doublet of white linen, worn and sorely stained by his cuirass, and frayed at the sleeve, with breeches worn and torn by his sword-belt. They say he usually wears old clothes." He was often seen by his Court, his " face and arms bathed in sweat, and his beard and hair covered with thick and filthy dust." In respect of his objection to dressing his hair or permitting it to be touched by others, and his despite against those who were careful about such things, Dupeyrat remembers one evening, when " Henry IV., noticing at his table certain gentlemen with curled hair, feigned not to see them, but discoursed upon the vanity of those who spent a whole morning in combing and crimping, loudly declaring that he had no love for folk who amused themselves with such superfluities." Superfluities apart, however, his neglect of certain elementary duties of the toilet drew constant, and by no means private, complaints from Marie de Médicis, Henriette d'Entraigues, and others.

No constitution could remain proof against the irregularity of his meals and his gluttony, and Henry was early troubled by his stomach. The doctors setting this down to indigestion, treated him with a diet of asses' milk injection, and doses of aloes and wormwood. Besides his systematic use of the waters of Pougues, which he caused

to be brought wherever he might be, Henry yearly underwent a " course " of twelve or fifteen days at Montceaux.
Gout apart, the ten years between 1600 and 1610 nevertheless passed with only one serious indisposition—a stricture.

First troubled by the gout in 1602, when, in his fiftieth
year, a slight attack in the toe was cured by fur boots,
each subsequent winter saw a recurrence of the trouble :
" The snow wakes up the chilblains on my toes," he
writes, still gaily, to Henriette d'Entraigues. Spreading
from the foot to the knee, his gout increased in painful-
ness. " Yesterday morning," he wrote to Rosny from
Saint Germain, in 1605, " I wished to go a-hunting, thinking that the pleasure of the chase would cause me to forget
my pain. Having got not half a mile from here, however,
and notwithstanding I had slit my boot, I had to return
immediately on account of the cruel pain I felt—such
pain that were half my estate in jeopardy, I should not be
capable of listening or making any decision." This suffering presently became intolerable : it was remarked " that
he was so racked with pain that his face and disposition
had altered," and that, " contrary to his nature, he was
very fretful, irritable, and inaccessible." He tried to dis-
tract himself by playing at dice.

Henry IV. was pre-eminently intelligent, and may be
considered the most remarkable of the French kings. He
was endowed to an extraordinary degree with the quickness of mind which seizes instantly the most delicate
shades of meaning, and perceives the exact bearing of
things with precision and penetration. Posterity has been
especially struck with his soundness of judgment, while
his contemporaries principally admired the alertness of his
mind. Père Matthieu writes in regard to a scene at which
he was present : " I noticed the quickness and vivacity of
his mind, which always went faster than his eyes, and
penetrated into the things that he desired to find out.
His mind was everywhere, and everywhere was master."
Sully could not sufficiently admire " this brilliant, prompt,
and active mind, of quick intelligence and comprehension."

We know the easy manner in which Henry conducted his affairs. In the morning, walking under the trees in the garden of the Louvre, his hands behind his back ; with no papers to study laboriously, no notes to take, he listened to the minister who explained, asked questions, informed himself of the facts, turned and returned the problems that nothing might be forgotten, then swiftly made a decision. On rainy days, the King's rapid strides up and down his cabinet in the long gallery of the Louvre soon exhausted the minister, who had trouble in keeping up with him. He seized upon the root of the matter under discussion without effort, and obtained a comprehensive idea of the question. He never devoted more than two hours in the morning to business, before Mass, but always made a point of seeing everything, learning all details, and deciding important questions. Only an intelligence sure of itself, confident in its quickness as well as its clearness, could venture thus lightly to treat momentous, and often complicated, affairs.

With as subtle a wit and a rather more powerful understanding, Cardinal de Richelieu appealed far less to the sympathies of his generation than did Henry IV., who joined great charm of manner to his other qualities. Affable, smiling, and gay, he was always, says his Intendant of Finances, "amiable, kind, and friendly"; *di dolce natura*, remarks a foreign ambassador, "gay and gentle," though often quick to anger. Extremely polite, he never ignored the customary obeisances of all who met him, being in this respect very different from his grandson, Louis XIV., to whom, as Saint-Simon says, one might do homage for three years before he deigned to remark it. Henry IV., on the contrary, lifted his hat in response, adding a few gracious words : " Serviteur, So and So ! Serviteur ! " an easy expression which would have been very startling on the lips of one of his descendants. He waved at his friends from his coach, usually calling them by name ; seldom used the title " Monsieur " unless in anger, and often simply addressed them as " My friend."

" This tractable and gallant " king was master of a finely deferential address towards the ladies, whom none treated as did he. In a fit of high spirits, he was known to dance to his own whistling when in the privacy of his Cabinet. *Les Estrennes au roy et à la rayne*, printed at Paris in 1606, asserts that, " There is none but knows you as sweet and affable in your conversation, wise of words and subtle in maxims, easy and gracious in act and speech, in act and temper frank and without haughtiness." The familiarity that would laughingly exhort his gentlemen " to be good comrades," or tapped one upon the shoulder, another upon the knee, succeeded in making his circle very informal. He was surrounded by an atmosphere of spirited, bold, and reciprocal joviality, in which gentlemen of high and low degree joked with their King in perfect freedom and good-humour. Parries and thrusts, even though a trifle barbed, were admissible, for the King's wit sufficed not only to provoke them but to take them well. In this spirit of good fellowship in the Louvre, gaiety, vivacity, and the best French wit alike found free expression. Henry IV.'s reputation for wit has come down to us not least on account of the frequency with which he would invite himself to sup with his friends, when, sitting in their midst like any other guest, his high spirits and good-humour amused the entire company. " He would jest with all, to the very humblest, and a man might dare speak truth before him."

It has been questioned whether this daily familiarity was not excessive, and whether it did not bring trouble in its wake. Scaliger impatiently wrote : " These two things Henry IV. cannot do—keep his gravity and read ! " and he finds that the King lacks seriousness. Scaliger's opinion on this subject notwithstanding, Henry IV. did read. Without being learned, his education was superior to that of the nobles of his time ; he had a good knowledge of history, spoke Spanish and Italian, and took pleasure in the new books of the day. As weak sight compelled him to wear glasses, his doctor, Du Laurens, read these to him—for example, " Amadis of Gaul " immediately on its publication. It is true that Henry was in bed, and that this work put him to sleep. When he had the gout, Messieurs le Grand, de Grammont, and Bassompierre relieved each other in reading *A strée*. The King's natural gifts for speaking and writing, which he neither cultivated nor neglected, are well known : his addresses to the parliaments and those delivered on other state occasions were models of clearness, and his brief and vigorous letters give him a place among the first writers of the language.

This gay exterior of Henry IV. really concealed a deep melancholy, and even sadness; for his unsettled existence as King of Navarre—a period of many reverses, more full of dangers, risks, and failures than of happiness—brought him to a precocious maturity and disillusionment. Thus, walking one day with his intimates at the Tuileries, he gave expression to ideas which surprise us a little, saying to Messieurs de Montigny and de Cicogne that he wished he were dead : when they expressed their surprise, and remarked that he certainly had no reason for such sentiments, he shook his head and answered: " You are happier than I ! " He declared that he would gladly change his condition, praising solitude, and affirming that in it alone could true peace of mind be found : " But this life is denied unto princes, which are not born for themselves but for the kingdoms and peoples upon whom they bear rule. In this sea have they no other port than the tomb, and they must die in action ! "

Neither more nor less religious than his contemporaries, his religion was sincere. " He once confessed to Marie de Médicis that when he first made profession of Catholicism, he had only pretended to embrace the truth of the religion, to ensure his crown, but that since Cardinal du Perron's conference with du Plessis Mornay at Fontainebleau, he had come to detest a Huguenot on conscientious grounds as much as he detested their party for reasons of state." Without doubt " he was no bigot, and made no

account of outward appearances." He had ways peculiar
to himself of reconciling his Evangelical precepts with his
love-affairs, feeling, as he did, less sure that he was vio-
lating the laws of the Decalogue than that he conciliated
them by his broad interpretation of divine mercy. He,
none the less, attended Mass daily, according to custom,
read his hours and prayed.

He could be serious as well as genial, and the courtiers,
knowing exactly to what point they might jest without
danger, observed the necessary limits. "There was no
speech or caress so familiar," writes an experienced contemporary, "but he might, within the same hour, remind
those whom he had favoured that he was the master."
Despite his kind and easy ways, indeed, Henry IV.
was very much a King, and B. Legrain insists that his
subjects felt obliged to keep their distance. Too intelligent not to understand his world, and to perceive all
overstepping of the bounds ; too witty not always to have
the appropriate rebuke ready ; the Prince might jest but
always inspired deep respect and awe. His method of
showing his anger when displeased—full of sound sense,
but impetuous and unanswerable—was known to all.
The Parlement learned this to their cost, and the vigorous brevity of the famous speeches to which he occasionally treated them remind one of the characteristic style
of Napoleon I. There were even moments when Henry
IV. was pleased to affect manners reminding one un-
mistakably of his haughty grandson, Louis XIV. Of
this one Chamier, a Protestant minister, against whom
he had some grievance, had an opportunity to judge,
when, having asked audience of the King at Fontainebleau, he was made to wait twelve days, constantly put
off upon mortifying pretexts, only to be at last received
under such humiliating terms—His Majesty being about to
mount his horse at the door—that he suffered a crushing
reprimand with scarcely the semblance of an opportunity for self-defence. Though he had not the disconcerting impassiveness of his grandson, there were times

when Henry IV. certainly anticipated his descendant's pride and haughtiness of manner, and when Tallemant asserts that there was no majesty of appearance in the King, this statement must be taken relatively. That, when he so desired, the King was without a peer for dignity, grandeur, and magnificence, is proved by the case of the Constable of Castile. This person, having permitted himself to pass certain unbecoming remarks upon the French, the King resolved to take a high tone with him, left him to cool his heels in the antechamber for a great while, and when at last he did give him audience, treated him in so cold and lordly a manner as to astound him, Spaniard though he was. The reception of the ambassadors from the Swiss Cantons in 1602 was, however, the occasion upon which he most fully displayed his talent for pomp and magnificence. The forty ambassadors, solemnly conducted by the Duc d'Aiguillon, the Lord High Chamberlain, and sixty noblemen, entered the Louvre between two lines of the French guard extending from their own lodging—the Hôtel de Longueville—to the palace, at the gate of which waited the Duc de Montpensier—a Prince of the Blood, with an escort of Knights of the Saint Esprit. At the foot of the grand staircase, the Comte de Soissons, also a Prince of the Blood and Grand Master of France, attended by governors of provinces and aged knights, received them anew before they mounted the staircase, now known as that of Henry II., between two lines of the Swiss Guards. Crossing the long gallery of the first floor, where the Bodyguard held a whispering crowd in check, they at length arrived at the royal chamber to find—in the midst of a brilliant circle of Princes of the Blood, Officers of the Crown, Governors of Provinces and Knights —Henry IV. seated upon a gilded throne, richly dressed, covered with precious stones, and wearing an aigrette of diamonds in his hat, and a beautiful white and black scarf. The King who devised so effective a scene, certainly understood something of pomp and ceremonial. To contemplate him again as, composedly dignified and naturally simple, he listens to the *landamman's* German discourse—summarily translated for him as it is delivered—and replies " in truly royal manner," is to understand that, did he so desire, Henry IV. very well knew how to don the garment of imposing majesty. When, also, at the conclusion of the reception, the King smilingly invited the forty ambassadors to defile before him while he shook each one by the hand, we may well see in this no lapse from the grand manner, but a nicely calculated conclusion to a brilliant scene, the more impressive to these modest mountaineers by its contrast to all that had gone before. Certainly no slave to the outward shows of convention, Henry IV. was as wholly aware of their occasional value as he was, in due season, able to clothe himself in their most striking forms. These characteristics, with his varied and many-sided nature, explain the King's great popularity, and how, according to l'Etoile, " the poor were drunk with love of their prince." Even his weaknesses and his love-affairs may also have contributed to this popularity.

Sully explains that Henry IV. was " a slave to women and was led away by them, and that he was given to philandering, either for amusement, through gallantry, or for simple diversion, or any such light cause." It was not precisely for recreation and simple diversion that, as long as he lived, the King pursued his various passions, and Fontenay Mareuil is nearer the truth when he speaks of " Henry's furious passion for women, which besetting him from his early youth, possessed him always to such degree that neither his second marriage nor anything else could in anywise abate it." Such in fact was the prince's inflammability during his whole life, that it really seems as if the unfortunate monarch suffered rather from the fatal effects of a morbid predisposition than that he lightly followed the fancies of caprice. Each new love was accompanied by great disturbance—failing health, loss of sleep, appetite and spirits, a taste for solitude not easily explained in a man so addicted to the society of his fellows. Until the day of his death, he was subject to such pronounced physical disorders, that Marie de Médicis, distressed and conscious of human impotence to conjure away such ills, had recourse to religion, and caused prayers to be said for him. Richelieu observes that even the King's mind, ordinarily so clear and luminous, was at such times dulled : " excess of passion so enfeebled him that, although he had always shown himself to be a prince of great mind and heart, he in this state appeared devoid of judgment and strength." Henry IV. grew to be unable any longer to distinguish what was fitting and what was not. Theologians, consulted on the subject, stated that "passing faults of levity" might, on occasion, "be deserving of mercy," but that " sacrilege, breaking of the marriage vows, and violation of the sacrament were inexcusable " ; he concerned himself no more about the one than the other. " My dear heart," he wrote to Madame de Verneuil, " it is not my devotions which have prevented my writing you, for I do not think I am doing wrong in loving you more than anything in the world " ; and at another time, " To-morrow I receive the Sacrament for Easter, but that will not prevent my sending you news of myself immediately afterwards ! " Being absolutely without conscience, he was, at one and the same time, Madame de Verneuil's lover, in relations with his wife, constantly philandering with others—Mademoiselle de la Bourdaisière, Mademoiselle de Fonlebon—hovered about the Queen's maids of honour, and at the age of fifty-seven became violently enamoured of the sixteen-year-old Charlotte de Montmorency, wife of the Prince de Condé. Yet, when called upon to reconcile the irreconcilable, to submit to reproaches, jealousies, and justified rage, he was silent, uncertain of his course, weak and vacillating.

The woman who figured most prominently in the King's life was Mademoiselle Henriette d'Entraigues, Marquise de Verneuil. A fascinating and distinguished creature, tall and slim, yet well-proportioned and with a beautiful figure, elegant and harmonious in its lines, she yet lacked the sweetness and grace which made Gabrielle d'Estrées so charming. Her features were regular but rather sharp, her mouth, thin and tightly closed, bearing witness rather to malice than to goodness. A somewhat harsh physiognomy, and coldly commanding eyes, gave to her face an air of decision, of pride rather than sensuality, of ambition and a positive, rather than a romantic, character. Her manners could, however, be quite charming were she so disposed. Her marked intelligence and wit were qualities in which Henriette greatly surpassed Gabrielle, while her conversation was lively, gracious, gay, teeming with brilliant repartee and unexpected malice. Henry IV., who delighted in a merry jest, revelled in her fine wit, her delicate and veiled satire directed against the young blades and beaux of the Court, and in her clever and discriminating flattery. Past mistress in the arts of coquetry and bold audacity, she managed Henry IV. with unexampled temerity, successfully instilling a blind passion, at once his joy and pain, by methods which might have sent her to the Bastile on a score and more occasions. That Henry's passion, as being of the senses far more than the heart, was constantly almost painful in its violence, is clearly to be seen in his letters to this mistress. Lacking the sentimental note of others in the same kind, these are almost brutally direct, while that Henriette was, on her part, under no delusions as to the nature of her power, is patent from the disdain with which she calls herself " *la beste du Roy.*"

The child of a respectable but humble family, her essentially common and vulgar nature was inherited from a father who, having married the cast-off mistress of Charles IX.—Marie Touchet — scarcely waited until Gabrielle d'Estrées was three weeks dead before throwing his daughter at Henry's head. The whole affair was one of sordid haggling. Her mother, father, and brother, having cunningly intrigued to bring the girl's name to the King's ears, and arranged a chance meeting at a hunting-party near Malesherbes, made use of a base agent—one

Naus—to discuss their terms. The family were to receive a large sum of money ; Henriette made it known that she would consent only upon a written promise of marriage from Henry IV. After weeks of parleying, the King consented and signed. Beside himself with rage, Sully snatched the promise of marriage, and tore it to bits before the King's face, declaring to him that he was deceived, that he would not find " the magpie in the nest." Henry IV., confused, made no reply, but re-wrote the promise.

"Far from you," the King wrote to Henriette, " life would be sad and dreary." He repeated to her what he had already said to many others and what he was to say to so many more, those impassioned expressions into which he put, for the moment, so much sincerity and conviction : " My dear love, heart of mine, I kiss you a million times ! Love me well ! . . . Be assured that you alone will always possess my love ! . . . I swear to thee that all the rest of the world is as nothing to me beside you, whom I kiss and kiss again ! . . ." He loaded her with presents, gave her the Château of Verneuil—by which title he also made her Marquise—and showered gifts upon her, in particular, money, for which she begged, for herself and her family, with singular insistence. Not content with lodging her near the Louvre, at the Hôtel de la Force, he granted her an apartment in the palace, and composed mediocre but ardent verses in her honour.

As to whether or no Henriette returned the King's affection, there is but one answer. Flattered by the royal favour, she was too cold and ambitious for deep feeling, especially towards one no longer young, and considered the affair rather as a matter of business than of love. Over and over again, wearied by the prince's affection to the point of regarding him with plain aversion, she was at no pains to hide her antipathy. Storms were of frequent occurrence. Madame de Verneuil affected coldness and reserve, held the King at arm's length, refused to see him otherwise than in public, wrote frigid letters, absented herself and provoked his jealousy. There were constant animated explanations, in which the mistress was haughty and impertinent, the King suppliant. Relying upon the power of her terrible weapon, the written promise of marriage, Henriette dreamed of herself as Queen of France, and her future as assured by her children. When the marriage with Marie de Médicis was proposed to Henry IV., and the political, financial, and other reasons for it—foremost among them the necessity of preventing an actual marriage with the Marquise—were urged, the King, whether from a feeling of duty to the State and of his royal dignity, or from an understanding of her character, did not appear to be deterred by consideration for Henriette. The final disillusionment and anger of the mistress may be imagined, but King and ministers were in accord, general approval was unanimous, and resistance was vain. Henry's infatuation was greater than ever. Making no open protest, Henriette consulted jurists, who explained that the promise of marriage, if drawn in form, made the new union void, and Madame de Verneuil might either choose her time and bring a suit for annulment at the court of Rome, or await the King's death and claim her rights and those of her son. As a third alternative, she might take the place of Marie de Médicis, should the latter presently die. Much concerned by this problem, the Queen subsequently asked advice from the Roman canonists, and received the hesitating reply that, should the King's second marriage indeed be found invalid, it was conceivable that the Dauphin's legitimacy might still be affirmed.

Knowing Henriette's biting wit, caustic humour, and the feelings with which she must necessarily have regarded Marie de Médicis, we may imagine in what tone the lovers conversed upon the subject of the Queen. Henry IV.'s letters to the Marquise, in which we find discreet and mocking allusions to these conversations, are sufficiently explicit. A haughty and passionate but base soul, Henriette pursued Marie de Médicis with implacable hatred—*un odio e una rabbia domestica*, wrote the Florentine envoy, Giovannini. She let slip no chance of expressing herself concerning the young Sovereign, in language outrageous beyond all measure : " Your Florentine is a concubine," she cried ; " I am your real wife." The Dauphin she called a natural child, and her own son the real Dauphin. When Henry IV. proposed to her that her children should be brought up with the future Louis XIII., she angrily replied : " Let the Florentine keep her bastard, and I will keep my Dauphin ; I will not have my son brought up with bastards ! " She asked the King whether the son of the " Florentine " resembled him, or whether he had not rather all the characteristics of " that hateful race of Medici " ; she heaped ignominy upon—" your fat banker's daughter." At first, amused by these insults, Henry, when the Marquise's freedom of language, which was known to all the Court, was repeated to him, tried to palliate it, and to excuse the impetuous young woman. Annoyed at length, he retorted in kind, meeting : " When is your banker's daughter coming ? " with such gentle speeches as : " So soon as I have rid my Court of all the —— " Later, his annoyance became serious, and there were scenes. " She has been speaking of the Queen," he wrote in indignation to Sully, " and called her by such a name that I thought I was like to give it her on the cheek ! " Henriette had scant consideration even for the King : " As you grow old," she said to him, " you become so distrustful and suspicious that there is no living with you ! " She accused him of incredible things, of being father to the Prince de Condé among others. " You scoff," replied the enraged King, " and think to carry things with a high hand. You threaten to leave me : go if you please. Five years have finally convinced me that you do not love me. Your ingratitude has worn out my passion ! " In her rage, Henriette spread the rumour that she extended her favours to others—to Monsieur de Bellegarde, to the Duke of Guise : Henry IV. furiously notified her, through Sully, that it was *aut Cæsar aut nihil*.

A breach being discussed, she claimed an income of one hundred thousand francs "in landed property," which would make her independent, and the right to leave France with her money at will, as she had no wish "to die elsewhere of hunger, and because she knew well that once the Queen was mistress, she would ruin her and those belonging to her." She asked for Metz as a place of safety, and a thousand other things, but the King's passion was, unfortunately, too strong. "I cannot lose a battle," he sighed, "either against men or women!" Sully, commanded to negotiate the reconciliation, having bought it by money, legitimisation of the children and promises, Henry IV. returned to her more amorous and more humble, and life was resumed with the daily "rubs" and "roughnesses," as he called his tyrant's exhibitions of temper. The reserved and cold manners of the young woman he called "grimaces, wry faces, and airs—all pure hypocrisy." Things came finally to such a pass, that, to assure the validity of the rights which she claimed for herself and her son, Henriette entered upon the plot known as the Entraigues conspiracy, the aim of which was nothing less than the murder of Henry IV. and the Dauphin, the subsequent proclamation of Madame de Verneuil's son as king, with the connivance of England and Spain. The King of England apprised the King of France of this plot, and Henriette's family were arrested, together with the Comte d'Auvergne, who was also implicated in the affair. Chancellor de Bellièvre was for "cutting the heads off" all concerned, but Henry was too weak, and Madame de Verneuil, kept under the surveillance of the Captain of the Watch in a Hôtel of Faubourg Saint Germain, boasted that she held Henry "in the hollow of her hand." The King was persuaded to exact a solemn restitution of the promise of marriage, and, after endless hesitation and delay, allowed the trial to proceed. But Parliament had no sooner decreed that the Marquise de Verneuil should remain in confinement until further orders, and the rest be executed, than he pardoned them all, and fell more than ever under the spell of his dangerous mistress. Having held the King for nearly nine years—from 1599 to 1608—this passion gradually weakened under the constantly recurring quarrels and disputes, and was yet more undermined by his violent and sudden love for little Charlotte de Montmorency. Henry continued to see the Marquise, but his new feeling for her may be gathered from the manner in which he now referred to " that thin and yellow lady " ! At another time, still in reference to her, he wrote amiably to Marie de Médicis : " Here be henceforth no wares for my shop ; I deal only in the white and fat ! " The day after Henry IV.'s death, Madame de Verneuil, considerably frightened, flung herself at Marie's feet, and Louis XIII. compassionately conferred upon her an annuity of ten thousand francs. She " grew old gently," becoming " fat and monstrous," and thinking only " of her victuals," but always retaining the trenchant and mischievous wit —once part cause of her success.

Marie de Médicis, in the pride of her new position as Queen, arrived in France fully informed as to Madame de Verneuil, and resolved—among other matters—to make proof of a stoic patience. She loved the King, and would have pleased him. When he was absent, her letters to him were sad : " I do not regret the tears that I have shed, for I am ready at any moment to shed more, when I reflect upon your absence." Was the King hurt by a fall from his horse, she sent post-haste for news of him. Her letters to him were humble and touching : " Sire, I kiss your hand humbly, begging you to keep me in your good graces."

Henriette d'Entraigues she at first treated coldly, but with no especial animosity. The Marquise's insulting re-marks about her, however, and still more Henry's in-difference to them, soon clouded the horizon seriously. Humiliation and pain gradually worked their way into her soul ; she shut herself up in her apartments, weeping and refusing to see any one or to eat—" being decided to die."

Henry IV., greatly vexed, proposed such compromises as that Madame de Verneuil should not enter the Louvre, and forgot them next day. Henriette's feelings in regard to the Queen were less and less concealed, and her coarse way of showing them, and threats against the Dauphin, threw the unhappy Queen into a fever of sorrow and rage. " The Marquise makes my life here nothing but trouble and uneasiness," she wrote to her uncle, the Grand Duke, and later, seeking help from him in her distress : " I have no one to appeal to except Your Highness, and commend myself to you with tears in my eyes ! " An Italian, still less a Medici, could not thus suffer and remain silent, and Marie rebelled at last : " This creature knows no other end than to torture me and to overwhelm me with sorrow ! " " Whoso declares for her, is self-declared my enemy, and when I can, when the opportunity offers, I shall avenge myself ! " To her uncle she repeated : " I shall avenge myself cruelly when my time comes ! " Richelieu says that the King, being informed that Henriette had serious reason to fear for her life, was so much alarmed that he thought it necessary to remove her from Paris under escort sufficient to protect her from the menaced vengeance : " It was, however, a feint," adds the Cardinal, " the Queen having, on this occasion, no other purpose than to intimidate the Marquise." The King's informant on this occasion was Concini, who was, at the same time, advising Marie to excite the King's jealousy by attentions to others. The following extract from one of the King's letters to Henriette has its interest in this connection. " Dear heart, I showed your letter to my wife last night, and watched her face if I might read upon it such signs of emotion as have at other times appeared there, was there question of yourself. She answered me with not a sign of feeling, that I am master, and so may act as I will. It is long since she has named you without a blush ! "

From this moment, the life of the royal pair was an uninterrupted succession of scenes and quarrels. Henry IV., being unable to defend his passion on reasonable grounds, became aggressive, and declared that the fault lay really with Marie, who was too cold, hard, and lacking in gaiety. " He swore to his intimates and confidential attendants that had the Queen sought his company, caressed him, conversing with him and showing her love in a friendly manner, he would have had nothing to do with other women ! " He reproached her, partly in sincerity, partly out of wilful exaggeration, of overmuch favour to the Duc de Bellegarde, Gondi, Concini—baseless insinuations one and all. With more foundation, he accused the Queen of being too much in the hands of a few members of her suite—her Mistress of the Robes, Léonora Galigaï, and Catharine Selvagia, her Woman of the Chamber—in whom she reposed blind confidence, and to whose judgment she deferred. Marie de Médicis, on her side, tried " to touch the King by considerations of his health, his reputation, and finally of his conscience, representing to him that she would willingly suffer whatever pleased him, were it not displeasing to God. But all these reasons, the most powerful in the world, were not strong enough to restrain this prince ! " At last, irritated beyond measure, she said that she would end by publicly insulting the unworthy mistress, and, growing excited, that she " would have her life ! " She wrote wrathful letters to the King. " My friend," Henry IV. wrote to Sully, " I have received a letter of the utmost effrontery from my wife, but I am not so offended with her as with those who have prompted it "—an unconsciously amusing remark on the King's part, since Sully had himself inspired the offending letter.

A public scandal occurred in 1604, when Henry IV. declared that he would bring up his legitimate and illegitimate children together. The Court was then at Fontainebleau, and the Dauphin at Saint Germain. Under pretext of the cold weather, Marie de Médicis gave orders that the little prince and his sister Elizabeth should remain where they were, and notified the King, through Sillery, that she would never endure " this shame ; that her dignity as Princess forbade her submitting to such opprobrium!" Henry IV. drily replied "that he was master and meant to be obeyed." Madame de Verneuil was to join him at Fontainebleau; he requested Sully to prevail upon the Queen to accept his decision, then rode to La Mivoie to meet the Marquise. Having awaited the Queen's reply in vain, Henry brusquely left his Court and family and went off with Madame de Verneuil. Sully wrote respectfully remonstrating with him upon this great scandal, telling him that he was lucky in having a " good and prudent " wife, and that every one took her part. Henry IV. grumbled, addressed some affectionate letters to Marie, and returning as though nothing had happened, caressed his wife, and owned to Sully that he had been in the wrong. The minister was to arrange a definite explanation with his wife, informing Marie as of his own initiative, of the King's grievances against her. " The King could not bear to have his wife growl and sulk whenever, on his return to the palace, he wished to kiss and caress her, to laugh and enjoy himself with her." Also she had a difficult character, and if offended, " took five days over it " and everything went wrong. Henry IV. was also annoyed " that she displayed such extreme animosity towards his natural children, some of whom were born long before he either saw or heard of her." He objected to the high favour in which Concini and his wife were held, to the Queen's bestowing all her money upon them, so that she was always " short of funds," and to the ready ear which she lent to their disparaging remarks about himself. The Concini, he said, spied upon him— " good-for-nothings, hearth-breakers, liars, scapegraces, whom he should have packed back to their own country the moment they set foot in France ! " As for Henriette d'Entraigues, " she was agreeable company, pleasant to meet, and was ever ready with a jest to make him laugh, which could not be said of his spouse, who gave him neither her company, amusement, nor consolation ; who either could not or would not treat him pleasantly and with gentle words, or accommodate herself in any way to his moods or temperament; who, when he came to kiss her, caress her, and joke with her, was always cold and disdainful, so that he was obliged to leave her in chagrin and seek recreation elsewhere!" Sully availed himself of the opportunity afforded by a request for money by the Queen to discharge this far from agreeable errand. "Certainly," he insinuated to the Princess, "your Majesty has causes for vexation, but I do not despair of their diminution if you will only consider the King's character, and the need of accommodating yourself to it." "Why," he asked, "did she always receive him coldly, as if he were an ambassador, instead of meeting him half-way, kissing him, embracing him, praising and entertaining him gaily?" Marie retorted with heat that "the King's love-affairs were cause of all the trouble, and that she felt neither sufficient 'courage' nor 'spirit' any longer to bear with Madame de Verneuil and her insults." She demanded whether there was a woman in the world who could endure "such language as that polecat used of her children." Sully tried to calm and encourage the Princess, and to induce her to accept the inevitable. "It is important," he said, "that the weaker party and the one under the greatest obligation, should not wantonly discover causes of offence." He spoke of the "infirmities" of which "the King, who has been called the wisest of men," could not cure himself; enlarged upon the kindness of Henry, who loved her at heart, and upon the necessity of following the counsels of patience which must have been instilled into her before she came to France. He finally promised to use all his influence to persuade the King to amend his ways; the Queen wept and promised to follow his advice. For a time, things now looked better. Marie de Médicis even went so far as to receive Madame de Verneuil, who, while talking with her one evening, dared to tell her that if Her Majesty had not seemed so ill-disposed towards her, she would have come and told her that she had not seen the King for a long time, and that, with God's help, she would never again see him—by which words she trusted to regain the Queen's favour. Marie, deeply affected, replied : " If you do this, I shall love you as my sister," and, replying no long time afterwards to Henriette's congratulations upon her lucky escape from some accident, wrote : " You wished by your letter to let me know your affection for me, of which, though already well assured of it, I am glad to have this evidence. May God give me the grace to recognise those who, like you, love me and desire my welfare ! " It was not long, however, before Madame de Verneuil's duplicity, her bitter and venomous wit, and Henry IV.'s passion, interrupted this agreeable truce, and led to a new breach between the royal pair.

In her distress, Marie blamed every one. She accused the ministers, particularly Sully, of falseness. " They are deceivers," she cried to Giovannini, the Grand Duke's representative, " sold to the King : in their presence I must be reserved and dumb." But her angry outcry to the Grand Duke that all Frenchmen were " traitors," brought the indignant reply that her language was immoderate, that she was behaving with great impropriety, and that instead of winning over the nation of which she was Sovereign, she " insulted it." In all her differences with Henry IV., her uncle did his best to calm her, and was constantly advising her and remonstrating with her, being of opinion " that the Queen had no judgment." Twenty times did Sully make peace, counselling gentleness and patience, and going back and forth in the Louvre while the Queen renewed her complaints against Madame de Verneuil, and Henry IV. repeated his charges against Concini, adding to the number of the Queen's friends of whom he complained, the Dukes of Florence and of Mantua, her cousin, Virginio Orsini, Trainel, Vinta, and Giovannini ! " " Stuff and nonsense," answered the minister : " at least be generous, and see that these affairs go no further than the threshold of your room ! " Henry replied that that depended not upon him, but upon the Queen's pigheadedness." To Sully's advice " that four or five people be sent beyond the sea, and four or five others over the mountains "—*i.e.* the Entraigues and the Concini—the King replied that he desired nothing better, but knew not how this might be done. Solidly rooted in the Queen's affections as were these Italians, not Henry IV. himself felt bold enough to exact or obtain their dismissal, while without Madame de Verneuil what should he do ?

So far from abating, therefore, the disputes between the King and Queen became the more embittered and violent. " The Duc de Sully has often told me," wrote Richelieu later, " that a week never passed without a quarrel." After these scenes, the unfortunate Marie would shut herself up in her cabinet to weep, refusing her door even to the King's self. Finally, exasperation so far destroyed her sense of proportion that utterly losing her self-control after one of their frequent and violent scenes, she one day, in Sully's presence, rushed at the King with raised hands. Sully, just able to intervene, dashed her arm aside with such roughness that she at first thought she had been struck : " Are you mad, Madame ? " he cried. " He could have your head off in half-an-hour ! Have you lost your senses not to remember what the King can do ? " Trembling with rage, Henry IV. left the room, while Marie de Médicis, her face convulsed with tears, held her arm, repeating that the minister had struck her.

This scene exhausted the King's temper, and he declared that the Queen must go : his first idea was to confine her in some distant provincial château. Then, his irritation getting the upper hand, he determined to have her conducted back to Italy, " with everything as she brought it from Florence," and informed Sully that " He would bear with this woman no longer ; but be rid of her to her own country ! " The alarmed minister tried to reason with him. " Whatever were the case," he explained, " had she borne the King no children, God had given her issue, and any such action would be a great blunder ! The King must be wise, prefer the State to his private interest, and dissimulate his feelings. Thus he, whose valour had overcome so many enemies, might yet master a stubborn and shrewish wife." Long reiteration of these and the like arguments gradually calmed Henry. The mention of his children clearly carried weight and, as he afterwards confessed, was the argument that finally prevailed with him. Peace, " such as it was," was once more re-established.

These constant scenes and brooding on her wrongs embittered the Queen's temper : she became bad-tempered and cantankerous. Her circle observed that her obstinacy became more marked every day : trifles infuriated her. *La natura sua e non poco ombrosa e collerica*, wrote Guidi to the Grand Duke. She no longer evinced " either obedience or fear " toward the King, the result " of her new knowledge of the Prince's weakness in private life, and of her familiarity with annoyances and vexations." Henriette d'Entraigues, not without some apprehension, spoke to Henry IV. of Marie's " vindictive Florentine blood." The Queen set spies upon the mistress. When Madame de Verneuil received permission to visit her children at Saint Germain, Marie de Médicis expressly forbade her seeing the Dauphin or the other legitimate children. Under pain of certain public insult, Henriette was obliged to avoid a meeting with the Sovereign at Court, and the Queen's attitude became aggressive even towards Henry IV. Seeming to expect the King's possible and not far distant end, she spoke openly with the ladies of her Court, notably the old Comtesse de Sault, of queen-mothers and their regencies. She even sent to Monsieur du Tillet, Master of the Court of Requests, for the registers of his grandfather, sometime Registrar of the Parlement, " that she might learn the conduct of affairs under Catharine de Médicis, and those other queens which had beforetime been in that position."

Happily, little was known abroad of the disputes of the royal pair, and although Marie de Médicis occasionally made imprudent remarks to her intimates, or clearly showed her indignation at some unexpected annoyance,

her temper was no sooner calmed than she spared no effort
to convince even the members of the royal family that
there had been no misunderstanding.   To a princess who
alluded to these quarrels in a letter, she vigorously protested against " this absolute falsehood," averring that
such tales come only from those "who, jealous of our
great friendship and the good understanding between us,
seek to make trouble. " There has," she stoutly added,
" been no quarrel, as hath been said, between the King
my lord, and myself." [1]   " Florentine and vindictive,"
Marie de Médicis may have been, but the fact remains
that she could never bring herself to hate Henry IV.   As
with all sanguine and nervous people, the inveterate and
implacable hatred proper to bilious temperaments was
wholly alien to her nature.   Also, taken all in all, lasting
anger was impossible against a royal husband who, so
soon as the tempest was over, forgot both his own anger
and whatever cause for irritation he still had, and became
charming as ever to his wife.   " Our little disagreements,"
the King wrote to Sully, "should never outlast the
twenty-four hours ! " and he insistently multiplied his
advances.   " A storm was scarcely over," writes Richelieu, " before the King, delighting in the fine weather,
treated the Queen with such sweetness, that since that
great prince's death, I have often heard her rejoice over
the memory of her life with him, and extol his kindness
to her."   Master in the art of pleasing as he could be at

----

[1] The extent of the nation's real knowledge of these difficulties may be
gauged by this passage from a publication dated 1610.   "This alliance has
so pleased God as to be free from all the thorns, crosses, and troubles of other
marriages."   The King's own entourage were little less in the dark, for he
confided nothing on this subject unless under strict oath of secrecy.   "For
your ear and none other, I may say that one of the great embarrassments to us
of the King's service, and one greatly traversing all affairs, is the matter of a
certain trouble that is arisen between the King and Queen on account of
Madame de Verneuil.   This vexeth sorely the King's mind, putting him in ill
temper, and causing great trouble to us his servants.   I mean not that they
company no more together, but that their agreement runs not smoothly.   These
be things not well set upon paper, and truly this much were more than enough
had I any doubt but that the hand which beareth this were sure " (*Mémoires
du Duc de la Force*, i. 444).

wish, and not the less effectually that he was a self-willed king, Henry IV. on no occasion found it difficult to dominate the impressionable nature of Marie de Médicis.

At heart, Henry IV. sincerely loved his wife with an affection compounded of real attachment, a sense of duty, and habit: she was his Queen, his legitimate wife, and the mother of the Dauphin. Did he enter the Queen's cabinet, Marie's mere presence " had power to alleviate his melancholy, and dissipate the clouds from his heart. . . . His sadness vanished, as it were, and he felt supreme contentment of mind in her company." On the testimony of Priuli, the King was really attached to the Queen *con istraordinario affetto*, so much so that she ought to think herself *la più felice donna del mondo*. Marie de Médicis was certainly beautiful, and her personal charms doubtless contributed to her ultimate attraction for her husband, his confidants—witness Richelieu—even surprising upon his lips the singular avowal, that " Marie de Médicis was so much to his mind that, were she not his wife, he would have given all he had to make her his mistress ! "

Apprehension for the future, a vague confidence in her, resulting from the fact that, correctly or the reverse, he considered her capable of keeping her own counsel ; his conviction that, being much younger than he, she would undoubtedly survive him, and hold the reins of government during the Dauphin's minority ; the prospect, in fact, of her being practically his successor—more than anything else, inclined him to her. Had he anxieties or sorrows, he confided them to her, " although he found not in her such consolations as he might have had from a person more sympathetic and experienced ! " She took no apparent interest in affairs of State, with which Henry vainly endeavoured to keep her in touch.

Sully relates how when Henry IV. was—as previously related—ill of the disease that so frightened the Court, he sent for his faithful minister, who found him in his bed, but already somewhat better and smilingly uncon-

I

cerned. Marie de Médicis, alone with him, was sitting with his hand between her own. " Embrace me, friend," said Henry IV., extending his free hand to Sully ; " I am marvellously glad to see you. My dear," he added, affectionately glancing at the Queen, " this is the man who has the greatest responsibility, and the greatest knowledge of the affairs of my kingdom." This little picture may serve, better than anything else, to show the real feelings of the King and Queen for one another, but proofs of the King's affection for Marie abound in his correspondence. " I could not sleep without writing to you. If I held you in my arms, I would cherish you with a will ; " and, lapsing into familiarities which he permitted himself only in strictest intimacy, as being contrary to the royal dignity, he impetuously adds : " I give you good-night, and a thousand kisses ! " These are no isolated expressions but constantly recur in the letters. " Good-day, my heart, I kiss thee a hundred thousand times."

As Henry IV.'s passion for Madame de Verneuil diminished, his affection for the Queen increased, so that, towards the end of his reign, quarrels became very rare, and even ceased altogether. The King became tender and attentive, more frequently sought the Queen's apartments, stayed long hours with her, and always went to embrace her before leaving the palace. " Maréchale de la Châtre, observing these attentions, told him that he became more in love every day, the which gave great satisfaction to his faithful servants who hoped for still more ; he must beware, however, of deceiving them ! " Whether or no the Queen's beauty did become more brilliant towards the end, Henry IV. declared that never had she looked fairer than on the day of her coronation at Saint Denis, a few days before Ravaillac's crime. More probably, however, the presentiments which assailed him during the last part of his life, reminding him that every day might be his last, tended to attach him more and more to the woman for whom he had felt the truest and surest affection.

These presentiments, despite his assumed indifference, became more and more disquieting to the King, who indeed, as one whose life had already been five times attempted, was generally held predestined to a violent death. His uneasiness was at times quite painful, as once when having sat for some time in a low chair, pensively tapping his spectacle-case with his finger, he suddenly struck both knees with his hands, and rose with the cry : " Par Dieu ! I shall never leave this city, but shall die here ! They will kill me ! . . ." Occasionally disheartened, he as often recovered his self-control : " He resigned himself to the will of God, believing the ordinances of God inevitable, and that man must follow his destiny gaily, and with no hanging back." His apprehension soon affected those about him, and even the Queen, who had not enough feeling to be deeply touched, was yet vaguely uneasy.

On the day of his assassination, the King spent the afternoon with the Queen, and when, at four o'clock, he was due to consult with Monsieur Sully at the Arsenal, seemed as if he could not make up his mind to go thither. Having thrice made his good-byes and embraced the Queen, he as often returned seeming in great distress. The Queen, being alarmed, protested that he must not depart in this manner. " Stay, I beg ; you can speak with Monsieur de Sully to-morrow." He replied that this was impossible, " that he could not sleep in peace until he should have seen him [Sully], and have unburthened his mind wholly." Ravaillac struck him at the corner of Rue Saint Honoré.[1]

[1] Attempts to assassinate Henry IV. were made in 1584 by Michau, by Rougement in 1589, Barrière in 1593, Chatel in 1594, and Davennes in 1587. Contemporary records are filled with the presentiments of another and successful attempt, an idea apparently held by everybody. Two or three months before the event, Marie dreamed that Henry was "twice stabbed with a knife," and leaping up with a loud cry was quieted by the King, who warned her against the folly of believing in dreams. "There wanted," says a writer of 1610, "in the character of this great King naught, excepting to trust less in others." Before proceeding to the Arsenal on the fatal afternoon, Henry several times repeated : "I know not what is amiss

It has been insinuated that Marie de Médicis was not entirely innocent of Henry's death—a wholly groundless suggestion, contradicted alike by fact and the probabilities. The Queen herself related the manner in which she learned of the tragedy to the Florentine Cioli, and as Cioli forwarded his account to the Grand Duke on the same evening, we have evidence from her own lips of the shock which overwhelmed her, and for which she was certainly unprepared.

The body of the murdered King was brought from his coach to his small bedroom towards half-past four. Double doors divided his apartment from the little cabinet in which Marie de Médicis, who, on account of a headache, had remained in her room, without dressing or receiving any one, was resting on her *lit d'été*—a sort of lounging-chair—and talking with her friend, Madame de Montpensier. The sound of many hurrying footsteps being heard in the King's room, Madame de Montpensier opened the door to learn the meaning of this unaccustomed noise, and immediately divining the truth, turned deathly pale, and closed it with a bang. The Queen perceived at once that some misfortune had occurred, and suspecting an accident to the Dauphin, flung herself against the door, crying out in a voice of anguish, " My son ! " Madame de Montpensier tried to hold her back, mechanically repeating, " Your son is not dead ! " but the Queen, pushing her aside, had already opened it to find Monsieur de Praslin, Captain of the Guard, who, in the utmost consternation, exclaimed : " Madame, we are lost." She pushed him aside, and in the alcove opposite,

with me, but I cannot leave this place." The Queen used every effort to detain him. The murderer's knife, entering between the fifth and sixth ribs, "entered the left lobe of the lung, severing the aorta and arterial vein which carries the blood from the heart to the lungs." Henry IV. spat a little blood and almost immediately fell dead. His death caused unexampled emotion and grief. "Not one of us," wrote Bossuet sixty-five years later, "but has heard from his father or grandfather of, I cannot call it the astonishment, the consternation, or horror which followed so sudden and damnable a crime, but such sense of bereavement as a child feels on the loss of a worthy father." There is a passage in one of Henry IV.'s letters which is as justifiable as it is touching. "France is well my debtor, since well do I labour for her."

saw the King, stretched out upon his bed which stood directly in the light of the window, so that his features, white as wax and beginning to turn yellow, at once revealed to her the extent of the catastrophe. Madame de Montpensier caught her as, at this sight, she fell half fainting against the wall, and with her woman Catharine, who ran to her assistance, carried Marie back to her couch. The Duc d'Epernon, who had watched the scene, followed them into the room, and kneeling by the Queen's side repeated that the King was possibly not dead, and that she must not despair. Bassompierre, Monsieur de Guise, and Monsieur le Grand, soon followed. " We fell upon our knees," writes Bassompierre in his *Mémoires*, " and kissed her hand in turn." Then came the Chancellor and Monsieur de Villeroy. When Marie de Médicis regained consciousness, she burst into convulsive sobs. " Her heart was broken with sorrow, she burst into tears, and nothing could comfort or console her." As soon as her grief would allow, the Chancellor, Villeroy, and Jeannin, impressed upon her the gravity of the interests at stake, and that she must immediately occupy herself for the public weal, see to urgent matters, and regain her self-command in order to cope with the complications ensuing upon the King's death. She controlled herself sufficiently to advise with them as to the despatches to be sent, and the necessary measures to be taken.

For nine consecutive days, Marie de Médicis was unable to sleep, a prey to unspeakable emotion and grief. When, on the day after the King's death, she was obliged to be present at the sitting of Parliament, her general distress was as universally remarked as was the difficulty with which she uttered the few words that she had to say, and which were interrupted by sobs. Complying with all the observances which tradition imposed upon a Queen of France after the death of her husband, she condemned herself to remain immured within the Louvre for forty days, seeing only those people who were concerned in the administration of the State, she commanded two years of deep mourning, during which time there should be no

festivities, receptions, or amusements of any kind. She
swathed herself in crêpe, and caused her apartments to be
hung with black, a lugubrious custom by which the walls,
ceilings, and floors of all the rooms were covered for
months in black cloth worked with silver tears and skulls
—" funereal ornaments covering everything and hanging on all sides, on the walls and floor as well as on the furniture." For weeks she was occupied in writing in all
directions, to the provinces and to foreign countries, an-
nouncing the King's death, each day renewing her own
sorrow by her daily expression of it : " My sorrow and
desolation are so great," she wrote to the Duchess of
Mantua, " that I am inconsolable ; " and to the Duchesse
de Bouillon : " I am so overwhelmed with grief, that in
this supreme affliction, I have great need of the sympathy
of my good friends.   You will share my sorrow with me ! "
Besides the prayers offered throughout the Kingdom at
the time of the King's obsequies, she every year caused
Masses to be said, and alms distributed on the anniversary
of his death.

Marie de Médicis has been accused of coldness. L'Etoile
has a story quite different from that left us by Cioli, and
Saint-Simon even goes so far as to affirm that " every one
knows with what presence of mind, unconcern, and in-
decency the Queen received the terrible news which
should have startled and overwhelmed her." Michelet,
too, writes that Marie was informed of Henry IV.'s death
by Concini, who joyfully shouted through her door :
" E ammazzato ! " (" He has been assassinated "). These
statements are quite groundless.

It was Henry IV.'s desire that his heart should be
committed to the care of the Jesuits of the College which
he had founded at la Flèche, and that his wife's heart
should afterward be laid next to his own—a wish realised after a space of thirty years. This touching thought
of their hearts being united in death, found preliminary
realisation in Marie's sincere mourning for the King who
loved her, despite the storm and stress in which his
actions plunged their married life.

CHAPTER V

THE ROYAL FAMILY AND ITS ITALIAN CONNECTIONS

Henry IV. remarks on Marie de Medicis' small tenderness for her children—The extent of her care for them—Sickness, discipline, and gifts—She entrusts them to their governess, Madame de Monglat—Headstrong and wilful nature of the Dauphin—His mother's failure to control him—Chastisement and mutual coldness—Her second son, Duc d'Orléans, dies early—Richelieu's version of the cause of Marie's regret at this—The Queen's marked preference for the Duc d'Orléans, her third son—The three Princesses less prominent—Their gentle and sweet natures—The Queen inclines to them—The royal bastards educated with the children of the Blood—Intolerable characters of the Vendôme children—Charming dispositions of Madame de Verneuil's children—Common amusements of the "royal troop"—Ballets and comedies—"Aunt" Queen Marguerite de Valois, old, plain, and ill-famed, but all kindness to the children and full of cares for the Queen: an accomplished entertainer—"Aunt" Duchesse de Bar —Multiplicity of Marie de Médicis' Italian relations—Their place-hunting and importunities — Bourgeois correspondence, commissions and intercourse with these—Jean de Médicis in Paris—Scenes and coldness—The Sforza cousins from Rome— Their exacting demands.

LIVELY maternal solicitude would seem to be expressed in Marie de Médicis' cry of " My son ! " when on May 14, 1610, the first hint of unknown disaster led her to fear lest some accident had befallen the Dauphin. More than one courtier, however, may have thought that she was less anxious about the life of her child, than concerned for the existence of the future King whose inheritance she was most probably destined to govern. Marie de Médicis, indeed, never manifested much affection for her children, and Henry IV.—a tender father—once remarked to Béthune upon the Queen's " strange " indifference, " accusing her of a lack of feeling for her children." That she did at first feel something of their childish grace and prettiness would seem apparent from such a letter as this—written to the Duchess of Mantua in 1603 : " You have here as pretty a nephew and niece (the Dauphin and his sister Elizabeth) as are to be found at their age. I hope that you will some day enjoy with us the pleasure of seeing them." But in all the Queen's correspondence there is scarcely another such sign of affection for them. Thus, she will be absent upon a journey for a month or six weeks—as the Norman tour in 1603—and write not a word to them. Madame de Monglat, the children's governess, sends her news of them, but she either makes no reply—" I do not reply because of the inconveniences of this place "—or sends a brief and purely formal note. During the journey to Metz in 1603, an absence of more than a month brought one short and insignificant letter. She occasionally visited the little princes at the Château of Saint Germain ; Héroard's journal gives us the impression that these visits must have fallen like a passing shadow, cold and forbidding, upon the children whose delight in receiving the caresses of their father—tenderly welcomed as " papa "—was sadly diminished by the appearance of their mother. She commanded and punished, but—as was openly said and believed—made no effort to win their love, and Tallemant even asserts that she never kissed her son, a statement so extraordinary as to appear incredible, notwithstanding the belief that it obtained at the time, were it not supported by Balzac's detailed statement that : " During the four years of her regency, she did not once kiss the King her son. I learned this from an old courtier of that time, who had even ventured so far as to speak with her of it."

She took trouble on their behalf, nevertheless, for the children were in the care of women who naturally referred all matters of health or discipline to her and not to the King. Other questions, such as that of expense, were decided by the proper authorities, but so soon as one of the children was ill the Queen was informed, and gave the necessary instructions. She was consulted as to weaning the children. When, upon the advice of the midwife, Madame de Monglat proposed to delay the weaning of Princess Elizabeth, Marie withheld her consent until she should have consulted Héroard and the great doctors, Messieurs de la Rivière and du Laurens ; while, little Chrétienne's nurse being no longer able for her task, the Queen ordered the child to be weaned, but " after the cold weather, if that could be done without inconvenience." Reported indispositions of the children caused no great anxiety to the Queen, who commonly ascribed them to teething : " My daughter's discomfort proceeds doubtless from the pain attending the cutting of her teeth ; she will presently get over it." She was philosophically assured that little children were subject to ailments, and that proper care was the only remedy needful. " Certain illnesses are unavoidable, especially to children of my daughter's age ; attention must be given to curing them." The most frequent causes for the Queen's intervention were the epidemics, only too prevalent at Saint Germain, owing to the crowded little houses and dirty narrow streets which, at this period, rendered the little borough almost as insanitary as the foulest quarters of Paris. No sooner was one of these scourges notified in Paris, than Marie de Médicis warned the governess of it, begging her " to watch lest this disease get a footing in Saint Germain " ; should it already have appeared there, " let none from elsewhere remain within the borough, and admit no person whatsoever to see my children ; send the children of the nurses and the household into the borough, or elsewhere as they may please, and in all ways curtail the household for so long as the disease shall continue. . . . There are very many cases of small-pox, measles, and other contagious diseases in Paris and in the towns and villages about Saint Germain ; be on your guard against them." [1]   Marie's grand remedy was change of air, and even though the

---

[1] The Queen's preoccupation with affairs of hygiene was in the fashion of the day. Madame de Monglat constantly received orders to take the children away from Saint Germain while the palace underwent a thorough cleaning.

change were slight—from the old Château of Saint Germain to the " new building " on the top of the hill—still she distrusted Paris and the unhealthy fosses of the Louvre.   The children, when in Paris, must reside in some high and healthy faubourg, surrounded by trees and fields : Marie, therefore, hired Monsieur de Luxembourg's hotel at the head of the Rue Tournon.   This she afterwards purchased, and built the famous palace upon its site.

The Queen's disciplinary methods had the merit of simplicity, being bribery and the birch—for a good and obedient child " a little box of toys," and the assurance of " still prettier things to follow " ; for an " obstinate " child, a severe note from his mother, if not—as was more usual—one requesting the governess to be " inexorable." Marie de Médicis, however, paid no serious or regular attention to the education of her children, being at no time concerned with what they did or did not learn.   The manners of the times, and those of Henry IV., permitted a disconcerting freedom of language and of gesture ; but whether from carelessness, the difficulty of contradicting the King, or from simple indifference to what concerned " the little band " at Saint Germain, she never interfered. The governess, Madame de Monglat, who enjoyed the Queen's absolute confidence, was the wife of the King's first steward, Baron de Monglat, a violent and disagreeable man.   Tall, gaunt, and horribly thin, she was considered autocratic and severe, perhaps necessary qualities under the circumstances, and the reason for the confidence placed in her by the King and Queen.   This confidence was boundless, and resisted all the insinuations by which ill-natured courtiers would have discredited her : " I shall pay no at-

The Louvre was to be carefully scoured, " that no dirt or smell be found there,", at 4 A.M. in summer, and at 5 A.M. in winter ; the fosses were drained annually, the royal family carefully absenting itself during the process.   Contemporary architects designed houses to secure a thorough draught between the windows of a room, thus proving themselves in advance of their modern representatives.   The Louvre and Saint Germain are examples of this practice.   De Serres, writing in 1600, categorically asserts : " Free passage of air through a chamber is of great benefit to health."

tention to what they say of you, I trust you entirely," writes Marie de Médicis ; and again, when starting on a journey : "I know that you are so careful of the children that no suggestions are necessary during our absence ; send news of them at every opportunity." Madame de Monglat was known to the whole family ; uncles, aunts, princes of Italy and of Lorraine, all wrote to her, so that the letters received by her from distinguished persons formed a brilliant collection of royal autographs. She almost seemed one of themselves, and the children—who called her " Mamanga," an abbreviation of " maman Monglat "—continued to write to her until her death, using always, even after they had become kings or queens, this familiar and childish name. Henry IV. treated her like a friend and exchanged remedies for the plague and the gout with her. On the occasion of the death of Monsieur de Monglat, he sent her an extremely affectionate letter, which does honour to them both, while Marie de Médicis, more practical, wrote : " You have in your charge that which is the dearest thing in the world to us, our children, and as it is necessary to keep them in a gay humour and to give them no reason for sadness, we find it inadvisable that you should pass through any period of mourning, and we beg you to abstain from grief and tears in their presence. You have enough goodness and constancy to do this for us, and to bear your affliction with moderation and resolution." Madame de Monglat's charges undoubtedly held her in sincere affection, but it was an affection principally due to esteem and habit, and a dim consciousness of the real devotion of her who was indeed a mother to them. That Héroard finds her deficient in tact with the children does not alter this, nor does the fact that, by contradictions which excited him, she frequently and utterly failed to control the Dauphin's obstinacy. This refractory child, rebelling against his governess, often raised his hand against her until the scene concluded with a punishment. Not unnaturally, the little Dauphin felt no tenderness towards her, but he respected her, and continued, like the others, to write to " Mamanga " when, a king and a grown man, he realised that she had fulfilléd her duties conscientiously, and with a devotion which should command his gratitude. The little girls, more gentle and sweet by nature, encountered less severity in their governess, and evinced a correspondingly fuller affection towards her, until self-consciousness presently tempered this with its sense of the dignity obligatory upon a royal princess towards one " in domestic employ."

Madame de Monglat was assisted in her duties by a large staff of attendants : each little girl was allotted an under-governess besides the large number of officials usual in royal establishments [1]—domestics proper, grooms of the chamber, women of the chamber, wet-nurses, dry-nurses, and others. Special mention must also be made of good Jean Héroard, the devoted, simple, and affectionate doctor, beloved by every one, whose diary has recorded for us a minute account of the daily life of this little Court of Saint Germain, so modest, peaceful, and monotonous.

Marie de Médicis displayed less affection for the Dauphin than for any of her children, on account perhaps of his " obstinate," headstrong, and wilful nature. Yet the birth of this heir—the first Dauphin born to France in a half-century, caused unprecedented rejoicing throughout the realm, while, after the Queen's happy delivery, Henry IV. exultantly embraced the whole Court of Fontainebleau. The joy of Paris was unequivocal. At two o'clock on the afternoon following the great event, chimes rang out from the palace ; at half-past two, the bells of Notre Dame announced the chanting of the Te Deum at the Cathedral before the red-gowned Members of the Parlement, while cannon boomed from the Arsenal and Hôtel de Ville, and bonfires blazed upon the Place de Grève. On the next day, St. Michael's day, a general procession of the clergy of all

[1] The Dauphin's household alone numbered 174 persons, and was modelled somewhat upon those of the King and Queen. Many of these functionaries, as five gentlemen, the fourteen children of honour, and the sixteen artisans—among whom were the painters Charles Martin and Dumoustier— obviously had no active duty. Of all the number, indeed, a score only were in personal attendance upon the little prince.

the parishes, accompanied by the Parlement, made the circuit of the city, defiling before the palace in the midst of an enormous concourse of the curious, whose happy faces and enthusiastic acclamations testified to their profound contentment in a birth that was to establish the peace so profoundly desired by a country to which it had of late been too much a stranger. The Grand Duchess of Tuscany sent a magnificent cradle " with a canopy of white damask and silver," the little bed trimmed with the same, all " of rich and exquisite design, made in Florence " ; the Pope, as godfather, presented the layette—" bands, blankets, cap, and other infant necessaries blessed by His Holiness." The baby was from the first a fine and robust child; a letter written by his mother two years later shows him still the same : " We found our children in good health, especially our son the Dauphin, who gains strength daily, and for his age is so tractable that we have every reason to hope that he will never be a source of trouble to us." She took an interest in his development : " My son," she tells the Grand Duchess, " is wonderfully tall, robust, and strong, and I am sure you would admire him if you saw him. He already recognises the King, myself, and others whom he is accustomed to see, understands perfectly what is said to him, and makes himself understood so well that one cannot but find him extraordinarily intelligent for his years." She followed the details of his growth : " I was happy to learn that my son has cut his last tooth ; he will now be yet merrier than is his wont. I send you two pieces of *licorne*[1] that you may use it "—doubtless a talisman. The Italian ambassadors remarked upon the child's excellent condition—" a fine-looking child, well-proportioned and graceful " ; he had an engaging personality, was quick to understand and learn, and displayed great judgment and acuteness for his age. He showed more aptitude for languages and mathematics than for the study of letters, and early evinced great zeal for physical exercise and all things military. The public was pleased to believe that he had

[1] *Licorne*, walrus ivory, doubtless for the Dauphin to suck.—Translator.

inherited his father's mind with his mother's physique, and the Pope was assured of his good health when, as early as 1602, His Holiness broached the idea of marrying the Dauphin to the Infanta of Spain. He was, none the less, imperious and self-willed, unfortunate defects to be manifested only too soon, and, as Héroard's daily notes inform us, with singular insistence. Even Henry IV., though loved and revered by his son, who obeyed him better than any one else, was to experience this obstinacy. Richelieu has a story of a day at Fontainebleau when the King essayed to make his small son jump a stream, and was so enraged by the boy's stubborn refusal that, but for the intervention of others, he would have ducked him on the spot. Gossip occupied itself with stories of this obstinacy, not without reason if it be true that the united efforts of six people were required before he could, on one occasion, be compelled to take medicine. In view of such traits, we can hardly be surprised that Marie de Médicis, neither gifted with keen intelligence nor armed with real love for her child, should fail to have much influence over him. Henry IV., too clear-sighted not to foresee that the mother and son would not long agree together, predicted their future quarrels.

Marie's system of discipline — alternate whippings and presents—tended to a predominance of the former, while the fact that the latter generally arrived on stated occasions, caused them to lack both the charm of the unexpected and the grace of an attention. The child received watches, little knives and silver soldiers at the New Year, and amused himself by sending little presents to his mother in return, as a basket of cherries, in the season, from Saint Germain. To these attentions Marie responded in her cold and chill style, without a trace of sympathy or affection : " I thank you, my son, for the cherries that you send me ; coming from you, they gave me great pleasure. I love you well, for I hear that you are behaving well." The whip, on the other hand, was applied regularly. To every letter from Madame de Monglat mentioning resistance or obstinacy, the invariable reply was : " Use the whip ! " until Jean Héroard interposed on the score of health, since the child received the correction with such outbursts of temper as often brought on a faint. The Queen then modified her orders to : " Apply the whip, but cautiously, so that his anger shall not be followed by any ill effects." Being anxious, for many reasons, to preserve the Dauphin's health, the Queen consulted the doctors, and conceived the idea that chastisement was dangerous in hot weather ; the little prince, in summer, enjoyed the benefit of this doubt. " Have recourse to anything rather than the rod in this warm season, when he might become over-excited ! " Marie's fear of vexing the Monglat led to her corresponding with Héroard by devious means. An idea of the Dauphin's existence may be gleaned from such a fragment as this : " My son has returned to his usual obstinate ways, and no longer fears the Mason [1] nor all her threats." Dauphin or no, a child's heart must have fluttered when every morning's rising and dressing were but preliminaries to a settling of the past day's accounts, and the appearance of a stern governess with her rods and her dreaded formula— " Now, down with those . . ." A child who lived in the knowledge that he would suffer at a fixed hour every morning for the transgressions of the preceding day, not unnaturally felt no affection for his mother, scarcely attempted to conceal his displeasure when she came to Saint Germain, and embraced her only under compulsion.

Time brought no improvement in the direction of increased devotion or affection, whether on the one side or the other. In the year 1609, when the Dauphin was to be removed from " the hands of women," and his education transferred to men, a governor and tutors were selected to give him " an education befitting his high birth and his future position." For governor was chosen an ancient knight, Monsieur Gilles de Souvré, an old friend of both

---

[1] The " Mason " was an ill-featured person, whom it was customary to show the child in order to terrify him.

Henry III. and Henry IV., a veteran who had lived his life at Court, and was thoroughly conversant with its usages and customs. Successively appointed Chamberlain to the Duc d'Alençon, Gentleman of the Chamber, Master of the Chamber, and Master of the Robes to Charles IX. and Henry III., a Marshal of France and Knight of the Saint Esprit—de Souvré enjoyed a pleasant intimacy with Henry IV., who called him " la Gode," and addressed him with the familiar " thou." The correspondence of the royal couple with the little Prince's new mentor was as lively as it had before been with Madame de Monglat. For tutor to his son, the King made the singular selection of the poet des Yveteaux, a peculiar person of suspicious tenets and doubtful morals, and, in spite of the opposition of the Queen, " who wept over it," and general disapproval, blindly held to his choice. Ill-considered speech before his pupil, however, soon led to this tutor's dismissal, and the Dauphin's introduction to studies of a higher order than those which had hitherto occupied him—Latin, fencing and dancing. As the next step, being already almost a man, he " left Latin for wine," but to Marie de Médicis he continued to be a child. As she had advised Madame de Monglat to whip him, so she recommended the whip to Monsieur de Souvré : " I have been well pleased, Monsieur de Souvré, to receive news of my son's health, but I beg you to hold him always to his duty, obliging him to perform his daily tasks. If he would avoid them, you know the remedy which must be used to bring him to reason ; you will let him feel it so often as occasion arises. I command this ! " Never modifying her attitude of icy coldness, " I have been much pleased, my son," she writes in commendation, " to see that you keep well, and to know that you are well-behaved and diligent in your studies and exercises. Continue thus to obey Monsieur de Souvré, that he may ever be able to confirm me in this opinion."

One day when, although after his father's death and his own accession to the throne, the little King had been whipped by the Queen's orders, he entered the apartment where she was sitting. The Queen, as etiquette demanded, rose at the entrance of the reigning king, upon which Louis XIII. brusquely said : " I would be better pleased with less obeisance and less whipping." A laugh ran through the assemblage, while the Queen smiled rather uncomfortably. Daily reminded that the little boy who was corrected was also His Majesty the King, the Queen, to all appearances, seemed incapable of properly appreciating the fact. Yet Marie de Médicis might have suspected that this child was not quite like all others, for had not Lieutenant-General de Fontenay le Comte, an octogenarian, when admitted to see the six-months old Dauphin, knelt in tears before the cradle and, raising his hands to Heaven, said : " God may now call me when He wills ; I have seen the salvation of the world ! " When also, on the occasion of the festival of Saint Louis, on August 25th, the Prince was shown from a balcony at Saint Germain, and the crowd fell upon their knees as in tender and religious adoration, a mother might have conceived that in this child reposed some mysterious and far-reaching virtue. In this the public daily manifested its belief, as when the Dauphin, still "at his nurse's breast," received a deputation from Dauphiny " in his bassinet, on a little bed, under a canopy of cloth of gold " ; the deputies knelt before him, and the Archbishop of Vienne delivered to the unconscious infant a discourse full of encomium and expressions of devotion. Whenever the royal child visited Paris, he was carried in a sumptuous litter, and met before the city-gate, which was " ornamented with armorial bearings and festoons," by the Provost of the Guilds and the aldermen, who addressed a long speech to him ; he always " proceeded " slowly with the curtains of his litter open that he might be seen by every one, and was devoured by the eyes of an enthusiastic crowd who shouted their acclamations, " rendering thanks to God, and glowing with devotion." For this baby was the unconscious and still fragile depositary of royal tradition, and, at a time when the King was the head and keystone of the social edifice—he repre-

K

sented in his person a guarantee of the future of an entire nation.

When the assassination of Henry IV. placed the royal crown upon the child's brow, Marie de Médicis had some fears for his life. Warnings came to her from all sides that the murderers had designs upon the son's life as well as upon the father's. Whether in an unexpected manifestation of feelings which had been hitherto little expansive, or, as her courtiers insinuated, from her anxiety to preserve the precious existence that secured her omnipotence as regent, she took every possible precaution. The Dauphin, become King, was supposed to occupy the royal apartments, of which the bedchamber adjoined the Queen's small cabinet, but his mother arranged that the child should sleep in a little bed, set up every evening in her own room ; she also increased to three the number of women sleeping in her room, and was, herself, constantly with her son. At the proper hour, according to traditional usage, the child was undressed in the royal room of state, with the assistance of the nobles of highest rank—the Prince de Condé having " disrobed him and pulled off his breeches, the little King took his night-robe and boots, and went into the Queen's chamber." For a long time the Queen watched over him apprehensively, and her fears were shared by those about her, for few cared to think what would have become of the realm if some accident happened to a king who had no heir, or what complications were not to be feared if the supreme power were to pass to a younger brother ? Marie de Médicis' care was doubtless due more to policy than to tenderness ; for in 1613, being for the first time obliged to leave her eldest son with the Court at Fontainebleau, to go to the Duc d'Anjou who was ill in Paris, she seemed no more disturbed at leaving the King than she was moved by the really serious illness of the prince. She wrote joyously to Monsieur de Souvré, recounting the incidents of her journey, informing him that she arrived at eleven o'clock in the evening after a day in the coach, of which " the Princesse de Conti found the cushions exceeding hard," owing to the fact that there had been placed " under her five candles without her knowledge," and solicitously giving the news of a little bitch that she had taken with her. When, again, Louis XIII. was stricken with small-pox, a terrible disease in those days, she contented herself with coldly writing to the Duchesse de Lorraine : " The King, my son, is slightly indisposed with small-pox, but he is in such good care that there is reason to hope that with divine assistance, he will shortly be restored to health." He did, in fact, recover quickly, and was but slightly " marked."

The Queen's coldness and indifference to her son grew more and more apparent until the day when, in 1617, the Prince suddenly became King in fact as well as in name, and to her great surprise and indignation took the power from her.

Marie de Médicis' second son, the first Duc d'Orléans, made but a small impression upon the Queen's life. He was a poor, sickly, and delicate child, born after a year of violent disputes and quarrels, and from the first had but a slender chance of existence. He was called Duc d'Orléans, as was customary for the second son, when the eldest son was Dauphin. Born amid deceptive and extraordinary symptoms, he was always suffering. He had an enormous head set upon a little skeleton of a body. " The King did not expect him to live," wrote the Queen a few days after his death, " recognising that he had not the robust health of which, thank God, the King my son is possessed." He dragged out his little life in constant suffering. The doctors did what they could, summoning unofficial physicians, Monsieur Aimedieu and Monsieur Hautin, who went to Saint Germain to put on bandages and apply poultices, and to consult with Monsieur du Laurens and Monsieur Lemaitre as to whether it were well " to administer goat's milk to the sick child, for his first nourishment in the morning, to refresh him before the prescribed baths." When his condition became more serious, the other children were removed from Saint Germain so that he should not be disturbed by seeing them, and also that he might be more quiet. He never left the Château during the four years of his pitiful existence. In November 1611, he was seized with convulsions, which lasted eight or ten days : his brother, Louis XIII., came to see him on the fourteenth, but the sick child lay in his bed " in a sleep so deep " as to resemble unconsciousness." His elder brother looked upon him with tears, and this was the last occasion upon which he saw him. At midnight of the sixteenth the Duc d'Orléans died in convulsions. " As he had lasted so long," Marie de Médicis wrote next day to the Duc d'Epernon, " I began to think that he might recover, as he seemed to gain strength with time. But his illness became suddenly so serious that he was unable to resist it." When, after his death, his head was opened, " the brain was full of catarrh, and was entirely destroyed, being full of black water ; his cerebellum crumbled at the touch." Marie de Médicis was unusually affected. She remained at the bedside of her dying son until the last. " He was well cared for," she wrote, " for besides the care of those near him at Saint Germain, I was myself there, and assisted him as much as my grief would permit." Maréchal d'Estrées observed that " she appeared much troubled," and Richelieu spoke of her " great affliction " ; but he, who knew her so well, and best understood her real feelings, states that she had previously seemed very indifferent to the fate of the child, adding : " He who has some knowledge of the times, will understand the cause of this change, due, in my opinion, to the fact that his life had now become of more importance to her than it was until the death of Henry IV. deprived her of the hope of other sons." After several nights of great sorrow, Marie resigned herself, replying to those who condoled with her : " I will take comfort for my grief in God, and submit to his will in this misfortune."

He who is known to history as the Duc d'Orléans, and who, owing to his quarrelsome disposition, was a constant source of trouble during Louis XIII.'s reign, was born in

1608, a year after the first Duc d'Orléans, and at first bore the title of Duc d'Anjou. He was named Gaston, an unusual name in the royal family, because Henry IV. " desired that he bear the name of one of the most valorous of his ancestors of the house of Navarre," Gaston de Foix. He was always Marie de Médicis' favourite. She is even said to have had the dark design of dethroning Louis XIII., who was not sufficiently manageable, in favour of his more submissive brother ; and in the perpetual struggles which took place after the advent of Richelieu between the disappointed mother and the son who would fain be rid of the troublesome old regent, Marie de Médicis and Gaston were always allies. The Queen's instinctive preference for this child was noticeable from the moment of his birth ; she gave the greatest attention to all details concerning him. Monsieur Florent d'Argouges having suggested a certain nurse, the Queen desired that the woman be conscientiously interrogated—whether " her milk is always good, and whether she has it in abundance ; whether she has a taste for wine ; the character and condition of her parents ; if there be anything against herself. And if she is found to be a proper person, let her be dressed at once, that she be clean and neat and all ready when I send for her." When a governor was to be found for the little prince, there was no personage great enough for this position. The Queen chose the King's ambassador to Rome, Monsieur de Brèves. She gave the child an ostentatious household, with a superintendent, a company of men-at-arms, gentlemen of the Chamber and pages ; as under-governors she selected Monsieur de Mansan, Captain of the French Guards and commander of the troops forming the service of honour of the royal children at Saint Germain, and Monsieur de Puylaurens, chosen upon Concini's recommendation, both of them cousins of Monsieur de Brèves. Two hundred thousand francs were assigned to the annual expenses of this household. Like most mothers, she was early concerned to find a good match for her favourite son, and fixed upon the richest heiress in the kingdom, Mademoiselle de Bourbon,

Duchesse de Montpensier.   In the meanwhile, she solicitously watched over this child.   An attack of the small-
pox agitated her gravely.   She wrote to Madame de
Monglat, from Fontainebleau, "Doubtless this disease
must run its course, and I trust the child will soon be
recovered.   Nevertheless, procure for him, I pray you, all
the care and assistance that may be had."   By her orders,
the sick child was installed in the King's large bedchamber
at Saint Germain: later, on learning that Gaston was better,
that "the pustules were drying up," she ordered that
the room should at once be put to rights and thoroughly
cleansed : "Open the windows to air it, have a good fire
made and burn juniper wood, that not a breath of foul air
remain ! "   When in good health, the young prince walked
out a great deal, and the Queen was not at all averse from his
being taken to Paris and shown to the public.   " I approve
your taking him through any of the great streets of Paris,
that the people may have the pleasure of seeing him so gay
and healthy."   Anxiety would, however, get the upper
hand : "But also I would desire that you do not stop
long, on account of the bad air and the diseases that are
about."   It is fair to say, however, that Gaston was no
more exempt from the whip than was his elder brother.

The three princesses—Elizabeth, Christine, and Henriette—were little noticed at this period, the two latter in
especial.   Before the year 1617 these were, indeed, rather
young to be considered as possessing any real character.
Elizabeth, however, the Dauphin's junior by only a year,
claimed occasional notice.   Madame de la Boissière, her
governess, found no trouble in guiding this docile and affectionate girl ; and if Marie de Médicis evinced little active
affection for her eldest daughter, the Queen did not, at all
events, seem wholly indifferent to the sweet and gentle
nature exhibited in the child's frequent, simple and sweet
letters to her mother.

An idea of these letters may be obtained from Elizabeth's letter thanking her aunt, the Grand Duchess, for a
beautiful doll.   " I have received the doll which you were

so kind as to send to me. I thank you most affectionately for it, and beg you to believe that I shall cherish it greatly, both because it is very beautiful, and because it reminds me of your affection for me." That her daughter did occasionally occupy her real thoughts appears from the plan of bringing from Mantua Marie's niece Eleanor, a child of Elizabeth's own age, a project destined to prove abortive for reasons which included the death of the Duchess of Mantua. Elizabeth was of course petted, and " our very dear daughter "—the Dauphin was always "Monsieur, my son "—-received many presents, " gold bow-knots studded with diamonds, a hexagonal alarm-clock for your table." She was, none the less, no more than fourteen when Marie de Médicis—having arranged a magnificent marriage with the future King of Spain, an alliance of policy supplementing that of Louis XIII., and the subject of momentous crises and interminable negotiations—finally despatched her eldest daughter beyond the Pyrenees.

Less important, and so delicate that the infant was nurtured upon asses' milk, Christine, the second daughter, who later became Duchess of Savoy, grew up quietly under her governesses—Mademoiselle Passart, and from 1610 Madame de Saint-Georges, daughter of Madame de Monglat. The youngest of all, Henrietta, future Queen of England, was still less in evidence. Marie de Médicis, indeed, seldom concerned herself with these children unless they were ill, a frequent mischance, for " these brats," as Henry IV. called them, were constantly the victims of some disease, small-pox not the least often. Marie's first order, then, was to isolate the child affected and remove the rest beyond reach of infection. The doctors most often consulted were Messieurs Delorme, Hautin, and Lemaitre, all attached to the royal household.

Much against the Queen's will, the King's natural children were reared indiscriminately with the children of the Blood. In vain was it explained to Marie de Médicis that this was a recognised custom in France, where the smallest country gentleman had he a varied family brought all up under one roof ; in vain was she told that in Catharine de Médicis' time, there was at Court a bastard daughter of Henry II. holding the rank of Princess, with an established household, and enjoying high favour as " Madame la bâtarde." All her struggles against this order could, however, only end in surrender, since, as Giovannini prettily remarks, the King's bastards are *mercanzia della sua bottega*. Henry IV. drew hardly any distinction between them and his other children, insisted upon their calling him " papa " instead of " Monsieur," as was the custom for natural children in Catharine de Médicis' day, and adored them. Completely forgetful of the declaration which he had signed, prescribing that noblemen's bastards should not enjoy the privileges of that rank, he legitimised all of his own, created them dukes and princes, and insisted upon their recognition.

The three children of Gabrielle d'Estrées were César, Duc de Vendôme, called, before he received a dukedom, " César-Monsieur " ; Alexandre de Vendôme, later Grand Prior of France, and Catharine Henriette, afterwards Duchesse d'Elbeuf. By a not unusual contradiction, the Vendômes, children of a sweet and amiable creature, had unbearable characters, while those of the insolent Madame de Verneuil were most amenable. César, legitimised in 1595, well before Marie de Médicis' marriage, enjoyed the precedence immediately after the Princes of the Blood, and was the most disagreeable of all. Henry IV. blindly believed him to be of " good character," while " from his first years, his lack of education was yet obvious to all the world, and his malice so well known that few escaped its sting." The King loaded him with favours and distinctions, among them the signal favour of an apartment in the entresol of the Louvre, directly beneath his own. An ill-conditioned fellow, violent, brutal, and cynical, he narrowly escaped arrest when one winter's day, on the Pont-Neuf, he amused himself by putting a stone into a snowball, and seriously wounded a gentleman in the face.

This odious child Henry IV. desired that Marie should consider as her own, and—outrageously—obliged her to call him " my son," and to sign her letters to him " your good mother ! " Having complied while she must, on the day after the King's death she changed the formula to " My nephew of Vendôme, my nieces of Verneuil." Outward relations between the Queen and César were cold and formal. The boy wrote dignified and polite letters to Her Majesty, and sometimes even made her small presents, which the Queen acknowledged with assurances of " her friendship and goodwill." In 1609, she was obliged to assent to his marriage, arranged two years earlier by Henry IV., with a great heiress, Françoise de Lorraine, only daughter of the Duc de Mercœur. The entire Court attended on this brilliant occasion : five years later Monsieur de Vendôme was arrested by order of Marie de Médicis. The Dauphin, Louis XIII., detested this half-brother, and subjected him to every humiliation in his power.

Alexander, the second son, was created Knight of Malta in 1604, with much ceremony and ostentation. As he also was treated very roughly and with scant ceremony by the Dauphin, who called him " féfé chevalier " and cordially disliked him, and was himself far from accommodating by nature, frequent quarrels occurred between them. The Queen, even more indifferent to him than to his brother, confided him to a mentor named Monsieur Prudent, and under pretence of sending him to visit the Grand Master of Malta, the head of the order to which he belonged, and of forming his mind by travel, freed herself of his unwelcome presence by despatching him, at her own expense, on a long journey through Italy and to that island.

Mademoiselle de Vendôme, more fortunate, received some consideration and kindness. The princesses were glad to play with her, and Marie de Médicis carried her favours so far as to accord her such occasional small benefits, such as the ordering Monsieur Donon, comptroller of the King's houses, to facilitate intercourse between the children by opening communication between the small apartment of the future Duchesse d'Elbeuf and that of her own daughters.

The children of Henriette d'Entraigues, as has been said, far more amiable and engaging beings, were sad, sweet and timid little creatures—a son called the Marquis de Verneuil, and a daughter happily named by Henry IV. after his former mistress, Gabrielle. These children were generally beloved, even by the Dauphin and his sisters. The Dauphin went so far as to constitute himself godfather to the boy, a surprising favour from a prince usually so inimical towards his natural brothers; he also arranged that his sister Elizabeth should stand sponsor for Gabrielle. Baptism at the age of six or seven being customary, without the assistance of Henry IV., Marie de Médicis, or Madame de Verneuil, they organised a baptismal ceremony of sober elegance at Saint Germain. A procession, headed by trumpets, fifes, and drums, and escorted by gentlemen in ceremonial attire, the domestic staff bringing up the rear, proceeded, for this purpose, through a double line of the French Guards of the Château, to the old chapel, built by Saint Louis. Monsieur de Verneuil and his sister being thus conducted within the chapel, the Bishop of Paris conferred the sacrament upon them. In the evening, a grand dinner under the presidency of the Dauphin terminated the celebration. Marie de Médicis herself had a weakness for " féfé Verneuil " ; she certainly preferred him to her other " nephews," and wrote more often to him. Conscious perhaps of his false position, and seeking to win forgiveness, the poor child was profuse in marks of attachment and respect. When the Queen was on her way home from a journey with the Dauphin, he wrote to tell her of his joy in learning of her return, and begged permission to go to meet her in order that he might the sooner see her. The Queen was touched, and willingly consented to his going as far as Longjumeau. Henry IV. early conceived the idea of making this child a bishop, and he had not long been baptized before he was appointed to the see of Metz. Louis XIII., in his capacity of godfather, interested himself greatly on his behalf, advised him, though they were of the same age, and always followed the career of the little Bishop of Metz with affectionate interest. This intimacy between the two children, one the master and affectionate protector, the other tender and obedient, is very touching. Mademoiselle Gabrielle de Verneuil was later to marry the Marquis de la Valette, Duc d'Épernon, one of the greatest nobles of France.

Madame de Verneuil's children called her " maman mignonne." She was allowed to see them only when she had the King's special permission : one of the gentlemen having, on these occasions, conducted them to her at Paris, Passy, or wherever she were, they remained with her eight or ten days. On occasion she was, herself, permitted to come to them at Saint Germain. In this last case, if no order had been issued forbidding her to see the Dauphin and his sisters, she would hazard a few words to them. " She caresses the Dauphin," observes Héroard, " but, it is said, with reluctance." In the event of the illness of one of her children, she was always summoned, given a room in the Château, and treated with some consideration. When it was a case of the inevitable small-pox, Madame de Verneuil was isolated in the old Château with her little girl or boy, while the rest of the princely band was sent to the new Château. As a rule, whether from real apprehension or simply out of regard for the decencies, Henry IV. was little less loth than was his consort to permit intercourse between Madame de Verneuil and his legitimate children. As the Marquise might visit Saint Germain only with His Majesty's special authorisation, which was granted none too often, it thus happened that she saw the future King but rarely, and then " only by chance, not design."

Five legitimate children, not counting the first Duc d'Orléans who died very young, and five natural children, composed what a courtier irreverently called the little " flock " of Saint Germain. They all lived together, playing the same games, doing the same lessons, eating the

same meals and leading the same life, but the Dauphin
knew how to insist upon his own and his sister's superior
rank. With different attendants, different governors and
tutors, and separate apartments, they were yet as one
family, and as such joined in little fêtes, particularly
ballets, an extravagant diversion then much in fashion.
One of these, organised by the Duc de Vendôme in January 1608, cost fifteen hundred francs, while the bill for
that of the Dauphin, in 1610, amounted to two thousand
crowns. The King and Queen, with some of their intimates, were present at these entertainments. Comedies
were another source of amusement, with the rehearsals,
the devising of costumes and scenery, and the decoration
of the hall of Francis I. The little girls, especially Elizabeth, were very fond of these plays. In 1611, Elizabeth
asked her mother's permission to present Garnier's *Brada-
mante*. " I very willingly accord to my eldest daughter
permission to recite her comedy, but she must learn her
lines well. I intend to visit Saint Germain within a few
days, to observe how she acquits herself, and how well she
knows her part ; apprise her of this, that she be prepared."
This permission was expressly granted on one condition
—" that she do not neglect to serve God and to attend to
her daily tasks, that I may notice improvement therein."
Many actors claimed their part—Elizabeth, Christine—
Henriette was too small—Gaston, Vendôme, the two Ver-
neuils, the Comte de Moret : other little actresses, friends,
were Mesdemoiselles de Renel, de Vitry, and de Frontenac,
and, in an insignificant servant's rôle, Mademoiselle Sauvat, daughter of one of the Queen's women of the Chamber.
Among the boys were Baron de Palluau. The performance was to be given in the ballroom of Saint Germain,
and as candle-light was desired in the afternoon many
pieces of tapestry were requisitioned to cover the great
windows. " As more pieces of tapestry are needed,"
wrote Marie de Médicis to Monsieur Delafont, furnisher to
the King, " to stretch across all the windows of the hall
where the comedy is to be given, it being necessary, in

order to have candle-light though still afternoon, to shut out the light from the windows, I beg you to send twelve or fifteen pieces of average size and the most worn." The invitations were issued by the Queen, in her own name jointly with that of the company: " You are invited in my name and in the name of the whole company of comedians, to be present at their comedy which will be given to-morrow, at one o'clock in the afternoon. Your pleasure in the performance will countervail any trouble or inconvenience which you may suffer from the roads on your way." As the hall was vast, many people were invited and many more hoped to be among the number: princes, princesses, nobles, courtiers, even to the venerable Chancellor, the grave President Jeannin, and the first President of the Parlement. The performance, dated for Sunday, July 31st, was postponed until Tuesday, August 2nd, and, as befitted so grand an assemblage, though announced for one o'clock did not begin until three. The hall was packed. According to Malherbe, who was present, Gaston led off with a little prologue of six lines: " He carried a pike which he waved at the audience with such grace, that by this action and by the little leap which he executed at its conclusion, he drew to himself great applause." Breeches, to which he was not accustomed, unfortunately so hampered the young actor that he had to be put back into skirts. Elizabeth, in a riding-habit, was charming as Brada. Little Christine appeared for a moment, and spoke a word or two, to prevent her from crying. The performance was most successful. On the following day Marie de Médicis wrote to Léonora Galigaï: " I must tell you that my daughter's comedy was well-played in the presence of a goodly assemblage. She, as well as all the others, acquitted herself so well and so prettily that I listened with much satisfaction and contentment." Tallemant, less complaisant, or more accurate, informs us that with the exception of Comte de Moret, the actors were pitiable !

Present at this entertainment, and among the kindest

followers of its progress, was a very plain, fat, and richly dressed person, Queen Marguerite de Valois, first wife of Henry IV. She was devoted to Marie de Médicis' children, who called her " aunt," and really seemed a member of the royal family or their nearest relation. While still his wife, she could not tolerate her husband and lived in constant estrangement from him : no sooner were the couple separated, however, than their relations became most amicable. Henry IV. called his erstwhile wife " my sister," and lavished attentions upon her : they protested mutual affection for one another, and Marguerite's conduct in regard to the King was perfect. Their relations were, indeed, such that in 1605 the former Queen of Navarre asked and obtained permission to take up her residence in that Paris which she had not entered for twenty-five years. The meeting of the two princesses who had occupied the same throne, and married the same King, was not without its interest. Marie de Médicis looked pale and troubled, Marguerite was calm and dignified. But of the brilliant Queen Margot, the pride of the days of the last three Valois, there remained now only an enormously stout and unattractive woman of over fifty, with baggy cheeks, a bushy flaxen wig, and a repellent air. There was a general prejudice against her. Monsieur de Souvré, having one day taken the Dauphin to visit her, accompanied by the Prince's equerry, Monsieur de Pluvinel, she cried out in delight : " Ah ! how beautiful he is ! How well-formed. How happy the Chiron who brings up this Achilles ! " Marguerite affected this literary language, but Monsieur de Pluvinel, who was no great scholar, complained so soon as they had left : " Did I not tell you that this wicked woman would insult us ? "

She had always led a gay life and had many lovers, and it was said that, in spite of her age, her wig, and her flabby cheeks, she continued to do so. Having, upon her arrival in Paris, installed herself in the Hôtel de Sens, near the Ave Maria, upon the death of one of her too good friends she declared herself unable to remain in a house which recalled such painful memories, and Henry IV. amiably presented her with a site opposite the Louvre, on the other side of the river, where she built her superb and costly mansion of the Rue de Seine. When Bajaumont, another of her friends, was taken ill, Henry IV., anxious lest he should be called upon to provide yet a third dwelling, caused general prayers to be said for his recovery. Every manner of scandal attached to this house. Libels of a very Gallic nature were rife concerning the excesses of its mistress, who was dubbed " Queen Venus " or " old whitewashed saint." The outrageous décolletage of her gowns became proverbial, and preachers alluded to them from the pulpit. She was said to beat her lovers.

The truth of these tales may be questioned. Marguerite, who is described in excellent terms by all who knew her well, was brilliant, agreeable, well-read and well-informed, with a taste for literature, *lettere di umanità* and philosophy. She conversed " as well as any woman of her time, and wrote more elegantly than the ordinary condition of her sex at that time would require." She was an accomplished hostess, had no equal in the grace with which she received her guests, was lively, witty, and amiable, all things to all men. Her dinners to literary men were famous, and her frequent receptions, concerts, and balls, were the most successful in Paris. She had by degrees gathered about her a court of authors and artists, among whom she lived " in royal and magnificent " fashion, so that her mansion was named the " Palace of Alcina." Hers was in fact the first " salon " of the seventeenth century, and she the first Princess to become the centre of a distinguished society. Legrain, who frequented her house, wrote : " Her conversation was always so gentle and so serious that at all moments and even at table, she was surrounded by an extraordinary number of men accomplished in all branches of knowledge, from whose discourse, as well as from her own, one might always carry away some instruction " ; and Richelieu added : " She was a refuge for men ; she loved to hear them talk, and her table was always crowded." Upon the shelves of her library, besides a thousand manuscripts, were the Latin and Greek authors, French chroniclers, Fathers of the Church, philosophers and moralists, works of science, medicine, and law, all witnessing to her eclectic tastes. All the writers of the sixteenth century were represented, Montaigne, La Boëtie, and especially the poets. She had herself annotated many of the books of " the humanities," and owned Brantôme's manuscript.

At all times charitable, Marguerite latterly became devout. It was her custom to offer the consecrated bread at Saint Étienne du Mont, and to follow processions through the streets, under a canopy, although, it is true, " upon the backs of men." She attended Mass every day, and partook of the communion three times a week. Her generosity was inexhaustible, but no one could accuse her of giving without discretion. " She dispensed alms so abundantly to the needy, that there was no religious house in Paris which did not benefit thereby, nor did any poor man apply to her without receiving aid. Also did God in his mercy reward with interest her mercy towards his people, giving her the grace to make an end so Christian, that, had she reason to envy others during her life, she was herself by so much the more enviable in her death." Her death was the signal for an unanimous chorus of praise. The writer of the " Lamentations and regret of the poor over the tomb of the Queen Marguerite, Duchesse de Valois " interprets the general feeling, for, after all, as Pontchartrain said : " She had done no harm but to herself."

The ex-Queen's luxurious existence required money: the fortune, indeed, which she inherited from her mother, Catharine de Médicis, was considerable. With her own revenues from the Auvergne, annuities from Henry IV., and the results of profitable speculations and trade, her assured income amounted to the goodly sum of three hundred and sixty-eight thousand, three hundred francs a year. The knowledge that all her possessions were bequeathed to the Dauphin did not, therefore, diminish her popularity with the royal family. Cordial relations between the two Queens, however, did not depend upon this generosity, for their intercourse was throughout most friendly. The Duchesse de Valois, besides being easy and accommodating by nature, was also determined to stand well with the titular Queen. Having no desire to leave Paris, the certain result should they quarrel, she exerted all her powers to maintain this good understanding, which Marie de Médicis, not ungrateful, was equally careful to safeguard. Did some scandal-monger of the Court succeed in raising a shadow between the two women, Marie hastened to write to " her dear sister," to dispel the misunderstanding; she made advances, seemed even to cling to this friendship. Marguerite conducted herself with great prudence and caution : " While lesser women so burn with envy and hatred towards those occupying the place which they believe their own, that the sight of them is unbearable, she, on the contrary, not only frequently visited the Queen, but to the end of her days did render to her all the homage, and duties of friendship, which she might expect from the least important princess." No attentions were neglected by them : Marie invited Marguerite to visit her at Montceaux ; Marguerite responded by gifts ; both mutually protested " their entire affection." The Duchesse de Valois, being asked to stand godmother to Gaston at his baptism in 1614, accepted with effusion. Was Marguerite in any scrape, had Monsieur de Saint Chamans so far forgotten himself as to " say things, in her own dwelling, most insulting to her and of the greatest indiscretion," and had he gone about repeating " insolent words to her discredit," she brought her complaints to Marie de Médicis, who took her friend's grievances much to heart and wrote to the Chancellor, de Sillery, and to the Constable, to have the culprit found and punished. The Duchesse appealed to Marie de Médicis in circumstances of a still more delicate nature, the constant need of money in which her profuse extravagance plunged her. The Queen-regent one day being solicited by her for the amount of twenty-five thousand francs, immediately bestowed them, with cordial goodwill, " though the affairs of the King my son, as well as my own, permit of no unusual expenditure." On another occasion, when Monsieur de Sully refused to provide money for the payment of some such debt, Marie was obliged to insist : " It would give me extreme displeasure, should my sister have reason to complain of me."

Having herself been unable to give the King an heir, and having accepted the annulment of her marriage, expressly that Henry IV. might have issue, Marguerite found in herself depths of tenderness for the young princes, whose mother she would fain have been. She heaped presents upon them, took them to the Fair of Saint Germain to buy whatever they might want, and petted them in every way, often inviting them with their mother to luncheon at Issy, her favourite estate. Marie de Médicis, enchanted with this devotion to her children, desired the Dauphin to call the Duchesse " Maman " instead of " Ma tante." The little boy was nonplussed by this request, and the best he could do, was to call her " maman ma fille." Why " ma fille " no one knew.

On March 10, 1606, Queen Marguerite legally made over all her property, " lands, houses, furniture, and money " to the future Louis XIII. She had just won a great suit, brought for the reclaiming of these same possessions against Charles de Valois, Comte d'Angoulême, natural son of Charles IX. This Charles de Valois had received from Henry III. part of Catharine de Médicis' fortune, but as Catharine de Medicis' will in favour of her daughter was explicit and in form ; as the Count was at the moment disgraced, and in the Bastille, and as Marguerite was supported by the King, the judges discovered more than sufficient reasons for giving a decision favourable to the claims of the ex-Queen of Navarre. Her donation to the Dauphin followed, a deed of gift between the living, on condition that the Princess's property should be incorporated with the royal estate, and should be untransferable, and that she should either retain the use thereof during her life, or that she should give up all claim to it in consideration of a large annual pension. Briefly, by this donation, she bought an annuity, but when she died on April 27, 1615, at her Hôtel of the Rue de Seine, she was found to be deep in debt : " Her room was so full of creditors that one could not turn round in it." She owed more than two hundred and sixty thousand crowns. The inheritance led to an infinite number of lawsuits ; her possessions were all sold ; the beautiful estate of the Rue de Seine was apportioned off by the executors, Brivois and Marsilly, and there remained nothing of this brilliant princess, not even the memory that she had been a bountiful and intellectual woman, an up-to-date hostess, an affectionate "aunt," a faithful friend. There remained only the scandals connected with the name of " Queen Margot."

The King's children had but one real aunt upon their father's side, the Duchesse de Bar, an excellent creature, who having in 1599, at the late age of forty, married the Prince of Lorraine, Duc de Bar, adored her husband. She made a short stay in Paris in 1603, and died in the following year of an internal inflammation, at first, rather pathetically, mistaken for pregnancy. She was therefore almost unknown to the children, and even to Marie de Médicis, whose chief association with her was through the settlement of her debts, which were numerous and heavy.

Marie de Médicis' own connections were very numerous. She had at least a score of near relatives, a sister, a brother-in-law, uncles, aunts, nephews, nieces, and cousins, all of whom overwhelmed the Queen of France with letters. They were content to take the position of modest country-cousins, proud of the success of one of their family, and very indiscreet concerning her.

Among these last, we must not include the Queen's uncle and aunt, the Grand Duke and Grand Duchess of Tuscany. For a long time, the Grand Duke tried to take a father's place with Marie de Médicis, giving her constant lessons, advice, and warning. He kept himself always informed through his envoys of what went on in Paris, and made every effort to promote peace in the royal household, lavishing sympathy upon his niece, always counselling calmness, patience, and resignation, sometimes becoming angry with her and telling her home truths. Though Marie was fond of her uncle, she finally became impatient of his rôle of mentor, and allowed it to be known, through his envoy, Guidi, that she was weary of " being treated thus like a little girl, a child ; that she was Queen of France and mother of five children, and that she refused to submit any longer to this discipline." The Grand Duke was a little surprised, but took her at her word. His relations with Henry IV., too, were far from cordial. Rightly or wrongly the King regarded him as the original cause of those endless and wearisome intrigues, disputes, and annoyances of which the Queen's Italian attendants were the centre, and regarded him with a very natural dislike. He took everything from him amiss. When the Grand Duke, by way of a gracious attention, sent fruit from Italy, Henry IV. bitterly pointed out that the Duke sent to Paris only " oranges and lemons, while to Spain he sent presents of thirty or forty thousand crowns." He wrote to him only when affairs demanded a letter, and then only impersonal official letters drawn up by his secretaries. The appearances were nevertheless preserved. The two families exchanged gifts : the Queen presented her uncle with " six coach-horses " or " a trunk containing many small articles and some clothes," and the Grand Duke sent silks, jewels, articles of food, cauliflower seeds. The news of his death in 1609 really moved Marie de Médicis. Henry IV. broke it to her as gently as possible, and the Court went into deep mourning.

Marie de Médicis' relations with her aunt the Grand Duchess of Tuscany were very friendly. The Grand Duchess, who was almost of her own age, made no attempt to offer good advice, and any friction that had once existed was forgotten on both sides. The Grand Duchess, like a good aunt, was especially interested in the children ; Madame de Monglat must send her news of them. A simple, middle-class person, quiet and affectionate, she was full of small attentions for her nephews and nieces, upon whom she lavished presents : the Queen's feeling for her ripened into a great affection. " No expression of sympathy," she wrote to her, after Henry IV.'s death, " in the great sorrow which I endure, has brought me more comfort than that I have received from you."

The Grand Duchess' letters to the children might be those of a well-to-do shopkeeper's wife, and still more bourgeois in tone is the Queen's correspondence with her sister Eleanor, wife of Duke Vincenzo of Mantua, with its thousand small feminine details. They exchanged recipes, executed commissions for each other, and discussed their children, their health, and matters of dress : " I send you," wrote Marie de Médicis, " these three pieces of linen cloth, which is here called ' quintin,' a material suitable for neck-bands and collars, but not for ruffs. It seems to me almost exactly like the ' fil d'Inde ' of Mantua—it should not be cleansed with lime, but washed with soap. If you think it pretty, and would like more, let me know and I will send it to you." From Mantua the Queen received " cheeses, sausages, and fruits—two mule-loads." When Duchess Eleanor was ill and the Italian doctors did not seem to understand her complaint, Marie de Médicis, after much correspondence, persuaded her to send a detailed description of her trouble, and submitted the case to the King's chief doctor, Monsieur du Laurens, and to her own doctor, Monsieur Martin, " both of them most excellent physicians," that they might consult upon it. Jean André Lumagne, the banker in charge of the Queen's foreign affairs, was commissioned to transmit three hundred francs from the Queen to the Duchess of Mantua, " for matters concerning ourselves, of which we wish no mention or declaration to be made "—doubtless in payment of purchases and commissions. As might be expected, the princesses respectively stand godmother to each other's children. The Queen of France, who was too great a lady to cross the mountains to Mantua, was represented by the Duchess of Ferrara, but the Duchess of Mantua, when asked to act as godmother to the Dauphin in 1606, was obliged to come to Paris. She brought a superb coach with her, but not being rich, her train was but modest : " a rich carriage and a beggar's retinue," said the crowd.

In the course of the year 1608 there arrived in Paris an Italian nobleman, forty or so years of age, the Queen's natural uncle, Jean de Médicis, bastard son of her grandfather. A brave soldier, an eminent engineer, and a man of distinguished intellect, he was also the author of " Political Aphorisms " and " Academic Discourses," and was interested in literature, architecture, and occult science. Jean de Médicis had done brilliant service with the Spanish armies in Flanders, and was newly come from the English Court. Of little stability of character, he was charming, witty, a bachelor, and very extravagant. Being always short of money, he had for some time been in the habit of applying to his niece the Queen of France, who, out of family feeling, had consented to give him the wherewithal to pay his debts. But his demands had become intolerable : " Lend him," she says to d'Argouges, " six thousand crowns, to be paid back in one year. He will pay me interest. I can do no better for him. My affairs are in too bad a state. I am obliged to reduce my expenditure, let him reduce his ! " Henry IV. enjoyed his gay and easy humour, and even thought of keeping him near him, by settling him in France with an annual income of thirty thousand francs. Thus, if Marie should become regent, she would have near her a good soldier devoted to her interests and capable of defending her. Unfortunately, the Grand Duke was not on good terms with his natural brother, and seeing him established in Paris upon a fine income drawn from the hundred thousand francs annually owed to himself in payment of old debts, he was incensed, and laid hands upon Don John's revenues in Italy. Henry IV. also hoped to turn to account the good understanding existing between Jean and Madame de Verneuil—their caustic and sprightly characters had brought them together—by persuading the Italian to give the Queen some good advice on the subject of the mistress. Don John at first replied that he had not come to Paris to " play the ruffian," but did nevertheless try to say a few words to Marie, who received them very ill, and was much displeased. Her uncle found Henriette d'Entraigues most charming, and justly or unjustly attributing the Queen's attitude to the pernicious influence of Concini, flew into a rage with Léonora Galigaï's husband, called him "a valet," and swore that he would run him through, were he not ashamed to soil his hands with the blood of a man of low extraction, who owed his existence to the house of Médici. Concini, to avenge himself, libelled Jean freely, and the quarrel rapidly came to a head. Marie de Médicis was forced to write to Florence requesting her uncle's recall : " I am very ill-content with Don John and his intrigues with the Marquise de Verneuil ; he has harmed me more by humouring the King than have all my enemies ! " Even Henry IV. thought that Jean de Médicis had not been very adroit. Thereupon the gentleman in question declared that he had been disgraced, that neither his own honour nor that of his house would permit him to remain longer in Paris, and that he would immediately depart. This he did so brusquely that the French government complained to Florence. The public deeply regretted his departure, which they attributed to the Queen ; Henry IV. offered the prince a pension, which he refused. Don John was later to distinguish himself by contracting a foolish marriage, at the age of fifty, with a woman of ill-repute named Livia, the divorced wife of a carder of mattresses. By this marriage, he put himself beyond the bounds of society ; his family completely abandoned him, and after his death at Murano, in 1621, they contrived that the marriage should be declared null, the children bastards ; and Livia was left to perish in misery.

Jean de Médicis was but one of the Queen's troublesome Italian relations. Many others tried to exploit her, some of whom were very disconcerting in their demands and unreasonableness. One of her cousins in Rome, married to the Duke Sforza, did not get on with him ; she confided in the Queen, retailed all her trials to her, her husband's brutality and her own despair. One day the husband wrote to Paris asking for a pension in his quality of relation, and, though with some impatience, Henry IV. consented to allow him five thousand francs. On the occasion of the letter granting the pension, Marie de Médicis thought it her duty to address some words of remonstrance to the troublesome husband : " I must tell you that I find it very strange that you should so maltreat your wife. I cannot believe that she gives you any cause for it. For this reason I beg that you abstain in future from such things, as much for your own sake and to prevent the scandal which might come to your house, as out of the regard which you should have for those whom it touches, and myself in particular." The scandal continuing, the Duchess constantly alluded to her cousin the Queen, and in so compromising a manner, that Monsieur d'Alincourt, the French ambassador, was obliged to interfere : " Say to the husband," wrote Marie de Médicis to Monsieur d'Alincourt, " that their quarrels are a shame to their house, that they are doing harm to their children, and are injuring their own reputations. Admonish the wife to do everything in her power to give satisfaction to her husband, making herself humble, respectful, and obedient to him, that he may have no reason to give her other treatment than that a husband owes to his wife." By way of response, Sforza begged of Marie de Médicis the ribbon of the Saint-Esprit, and the Duchess wrote the Queen a long letter, full of good advice, in which she pointed out how she ought to conduct herself, what she ought to do under given circumstances, and how to render herself a good Queen. Marie was furious. " Having read about half your letter," she returned, " I found it so full of misunderstandings and confusion, that I did not wish to see the rest and threw it into the fire. There is no need for any one in Italy to give me rules or lessons upon the manner in which I should demean myself in France." With unexpected assurance, the Sforza replied expressing their desire to make a journey to Paris, at the expense, of course, of the King and Queen, who however replied that they had no wish to see them, and that they might remain at home. The Sforza, disappointed, took a high tone about it ; they clamoured and railed, and talked of " taking steps." The Queen replied that these menaces left her indifferent. They proposed that their son at least should go to Paris ; the Queen refused. Some little time later, they vainly solicited an increase of their pension, and, hearing that the Duke of Santo Gemini was receiving a similar annuity, addressed bitter reproaches to their royal cousin. " Henry IV. was much annoyed by your missive," Marie drily replied : " the King is at liberty to favour whom he will, and this manner of procedure with him is extremely unpleasing and disagreeable."

This couple, of whom she could never entirely rid herself, were by no means alone in their importunities upon Marie. Many others tirelessly besieged her with demands, solicited money, and claimed honours. Though princes and noblemen, many of these cousins " from over the mountains " proved themselves, indeed, but mean-spirited beggars.

CHAPTER VI

THE QUEEN'S FRIENDS—LÉONORA GALIGAI

MARIE DE MÉDICIS enjoyed few friendships, for the gulf between a Queen of France and her subjects was too broad to permit of their readily sinking instinctive reverence in favour of frank friendliness. Moreover, the wife of Henry IV. did not possess those qualities of sincerity, impulsiveness, a warm heart, and intellectual sympathy, which inspire devotion. Her intimates were thus limited to no more than four or five persons, her friends for as many reasons. Yet, while almost invariably these were women of the highest position at Court, princesses for the most part, one of the few was of far humbler origin. This one, perhaps because nature abhors inequalities, certainly made good the balance in herself, for seldom surely has favourite enjoyed such exceptional and continuous favour, or led a Queen more blindly to her ruin—a curious anomaly that requires elucidation or explanation.

First among the Queen's friends was the old Duchesse de Guise, widow of that hero of the League who was murdered at Blois—a personage high in the King's esteem and ever certain of a welcome in the royal apartments in the Louvre. A gay and laughter-loving person with somewhat easy manners, her rank, age, and history alike licensed deportment and conduct in which none but herself would have dared to indulge; nor would their Majesties have pardoned such manners in any other than the old dowager, in whom they found them amusing. Critics of his imprudent confidence were never lacking, but were he weary—and, of course, failing the presence of Madame de Verneuil—Henry gladly unbent in her company. The imprudence of this action did not lie in the dangerous qualities of the widow of Henry III.'s sometime foe, but in those of her children, who were somewhat unreasonably accused of " continual indulgence in the most dangerous foreign customs." Saint Simon was particularly strong upon the point. "The King's friendship for, and confidence in, Madame de Guise do not admit of easy justification. This friendship is based upon no apparent cause or reason." Sully, writing to Marie, finds its real cause in those qualities of the Duchesse already described.

The Queen, seldom far behind her husband in love of a jest, was so far from withholding a welcome to the genial princess as continually to require her presence and company. Madame de Guise had survived several reigns, and her position at the Court of the last Valois had not failed to store her memory with a wealth of crisp tales, upon which she was in nowise loth to draw. If her reputation were not unspotted, this is a subject into which we need not probe, and one which Henry IV. found of quite secondary importance where there was question of a really amusing companion. For this cause she enjoyed his confidence, and the Queen's letters to the Duchesse have preserved for us a specimen of the conversation in which these friends delighted. These epistles are full of wit, life, and mockery, pointed with a characteristic familiarity but also with affection. To the Queen's customary " My Cousin," Madame de Guise responds with " Our good Queen ! " To keep the cousin as near as possible to her person, the Queen allocated to her an apartment in the Louvre, on the second story and above her own, and here she was to abide in so far as she could. Madame de Guise, none the less, maintained her own establishment in a fine hotel in the Rue de Grenelle, where her brilliant receptions were attended by all the Court and the cream of the city. Hither she invited the Queen, organising especial gatherings in honour of her guest, and certainly the Duchesse was not averse to playing hostess in the elegant rooms which she had made one of the most select social centres in all Paris.

The duties of friendship, however, attached her closely to Court, and it is only fair to say that this duty was passably rewarded with privileges, favours, and allowances. Foreign ambassadors sometimes attributed the Queen's friendship to deep political motives, but Marie's mind was simpler than such suggestions presume. Nor was the relation without a cloud. Troubles arose, and the temper of Balafré's widow was outrageous. The Queen refused to see, and her blindness was so frequent and so prodigious that Henry came to wonder whether the influence of the lively princess upon his consort were not for evil rather than good. They talk overmuch ; the Duchesse's eye is not quite single—in respect of Madame de Verneuil, she coquettes with either side and then betrays them impartially ; to Henriette d'Entraigues she is sweetness itself until the Queen comes on the scene, when she " breathes fire and brimstone at her." Having warned Marie to place no further reliance upon her, he urged a test, to be made in the form of a fictitious confidence, under pledge of secrecy. Thereupon the Queen confided to the Duchesse a plot by means of which the Marquise de Verneuil should presently find herself spirited away to the Ferry of Argenteuil. No one was to hear breath of this, but Madame de Verneuil was fully informed before the day was out.

Richelieu's Memoirs assert that the Queen and Duchesse were constantly quarrelling, and he makes an especial point of a case in 1613, when a certain gentleman met his death in Rue Saint Honoré at the hands of the dowager's son, the Chevalier de Guise. The Queen was for dealing severely with the Chevalier, and the Duchesse, defending her son with asperity, " did not stint her words, and permitted herself such freedoms that the Marquise de Guercheville bade her beware by reason she was no less a subject of the Queen than any others there present, none of which sayings assuaged but rather increased her fury. One retort of the Duchesse, indeed, caused some sensation, as being plainly infect with the League, to wit, ' I own no mistress but Our Lady, the Virgin ! ' "

The double-dealing which provoked the King's resentment was not so much that of the Duchesse as that of her daughter, the Princesse de Conti, little less intimate than her mother with the Queen. As this lady, then Mademoiselle Louise Marguerite de Guise, was some twenty-four years of age on Marie's arrival in France, the couple were of an age. Blessed with her mother's spirits and, possibly, an even less trammelled tongue, much wit, and more cynicism, " she owned a pleasant humour," and readily amused at the expense of third persons. She had been the object of some attention on the King's part—at one period he even spoke of marrying her. But Marie de Médicis was no sooner landed at Marseilles than Mademoiselle de Guise paid her assiduous court. Whether by calculation or natural sympathy, these attentions served, and the pair were soon fast friends, the Queen's feelings responding readily to attentions that were long to hold her— invariable amiability, delicate and discreet devotion upon all occasions, the prudent art of always sharing the Queen's opinion, of being ever on her side. Marie's sympathy thus assured, Mademoiselle de Guise readily gained an influence upon her, but Malherbe dealt in exaggeration when he afterwards wrote, "the Princesse de Conti rules the Queen."

Mademoiselle de Guise soon had her own apartments in the Louvre, on the entresol floor, hard by that of the Queen, to whom she henceforth acted as Lady in Waiting, and at times as secretary. She also it was who, on occasion, read aloud from some book or letter in the Queen's evening circle. Important letters were taken down by her from Marie's own dictation, while in lesser matters she served her mistress confidentially, being the channel through which the small talk, scandal, and gossip of the Court came to her ears. She was particularly fond of literary people, but never forgave any against whom she bore a grudge. Her reputation was none of the best, and it was somewhat late in 1605 before—being then in her twenty-eighth year—she was married to a widower of forty-five, the Prince de Conti, half-brother of Henry IV., a poor, deaf old man, who stuttered horribly and was very stupid. Having had by her a daughter, who died before she was weaned, he faded out of existence in 1614 at St. Germain des Prés, of which he was titular abbot, and where he lived in retirement on the ten thousand crowns which he derived from the monastery and the twenty thousand crowns allowed him by the King. From this time forward the Princesse de Conti followed her own inclinations, with the result that during the ensuing thirty years her name was freely coupled with that of many men, among them Bassompierre, who boldly asserts: "She was the cleverest, most intelligent and capable Princess that ever I met." The Princesse had received a brilliant dowry on her marriage, and subsequently inherited a large fortune. Henry IV. could seldom refuse her anything when it was a question of gifts; she obtained the privilege of farming the office connected with the salt monopoly at Marseilles; and, at Fontainebleau, a present of "a square and lane hard by the Grand Hôtel Ferrare;" and further an assignment of twenty thousand livres from the general

imposts of the Province of Brittany. But notwithstanding
his generosity, towards the end of her life the King would
hardly speak to her, reproaching her " with her incredible
slyness " in regard to Marie de Médicis, and alleging that
" she poisoned the Queen's mind." Being, however, a
man of little courage where affairs of the household were
at issue, he never mustered enough spirit actually to dis-
miss his wife's bitter-tongued and dangerous friend.

Calmer and more reliable by far was another friend of
the Queen's, the Duchesse de Montpensier. In her case
Marie de Médicis undoubtedly made the first advances,
subsequently safeguarding their friendship with peculiar
care. The reason for this was obvious enough : Madame
de Montpensier's only daughter was the richest heiress
in France, and the Queen, like a prudent mother, had
marked her for her second son. The Duc de Montpensier,
a Bourbon of the Montpensier branch of the fifteenth
century, was destined to be the last of his race. Like
the Prince de Conti, his intelligence was of the feeblest,
although he was a brave soldier and had done good
service against the League. His wife, Henriette Catharine
de Joyeuse, an amiable and sweet-tempered lady but
always ailing, was a woman of great sense and modesty
who cared little for dissipation of any kind, and was by
no means enamoured of the tumult of Court life. Her
brother, Cardinal Joyeuse, Archbishop of Rouen, owned
in virtue of his office the beautiful Château de Gaillon,
built by the Amboise family, where he often and gladly
received the Duchesse. Marie de Médicis, who corre-
sponded frequently with Madame de Montpensier, was
wont to allege herself disturbed by the fragile health of
the latter. She therefore insisted upon regular bulletins
being sent to her, and was always pressing the Duchesse
to return to Paris. It is not altogether easy to decide
whether this anxiety was real or assumed ; but whenever
the Queen found herself about to lie in, she would send
her squire, Rubantelle, with a pressing summons if so be
that Madame de Montpensier could possibly come to her.

As the smallest incident always gave Marie de Médicis an excuse for professing the greatest interest in all that concerned her friend, a little outbreak of fire at Gaillon moved her so that she could not rest until she heard all about it. "I was extremely sorry to hear of the unfortunate fire which has troubled you at Gaillon ; what damage has it done to the furniture and the buildings ? " The " disaster " was fortunately unworthy of that name, and no human being was in the least injured, so that the Sovereign's anxiety cannot be held free from the charge of a certain want of proportion, a failing yet more noticeable when the daughter, the most precious heiress, is in question. Really little Mademoiselle de Montpensier, born at Gaillon in 1605, was in 1617 somewhat young for her youthful graces to win such enthusiastic praise on the part of the Queen. Yet Marie de Médicis was conscious of this affection from the hour of their first meeting, after which the child is so dear that she must be called " our daughter." Not a letter of the Queen but demands news of the child, so that afterwards the daughter of this very Mademoiselle de Montpensier— herself that other Mademoiselle de Montpensier who played so notorious a part in the history of the Fronde— could write in her Memoirs : " Marie de Médicis, the Queen, my godmother, bore me far greater affection than ever she displayed for her own children." This love was a consequence and a pale reflection of that godmother's tenderness for the writer's mother.

On January 14, 1608, the infant bride being then two years old, a contract of marriage was drawn out and signed between herself and the Duc d'Orléans, the miserable and sickly first bearer of the title. The contract cannot fail to arouse interest through its citation of all the belongings of the ancient house of Bourbon—" The Duchies of Montpensier and Auvergne, of la Combraille and les Dombes, of Saint Fargeau," and so forth, and all without mentioning the rest of the child's fortune and expectations. Exactly a month later her father,

Monsieur de Montpensier, died of the after-effects of a terrible wound received at the battle of Dreux, while only three years later her unfortunate husband died. But Marie de Médicis had long foreseen the latter contingency, and the same letter which announced the little Prince's death to the uncles and tutors of his child wife, the Duc de Joyeuse and the Duc d'Épernon, contained a formal demand for her hand for Gaston, his younger brother. This marriage so long and jealously prepared—it finally took place in 1626, when Marie de Montpensier was twenty years of age—proved an unfortunate union, for only a year later the young wife died in childbed.

No princely families of France were more closely related to the royal family, or stood nearer to the throne, than those of Guise, Conti, and Montpensier; in choosing her friends from among them, therefore, the Queen certainly did not overstep the ordinary bounds within which her choice was confined by etiquette and the natural order of things. Madame de la Châtre, however, stood on a lower level, being a Chabot, daughter of that Guy de Chabot, Baron de Jarnac, whose name became known through his duel with La Chataigneraie. Her first husband was the Baron de Givry, Comte de Tancarville, but being early left a widow, she soon married, in 1564, Claude de Châtre, Baron de la Maisonfort, nominated a Marshal by the League, and confirmed in that title by Henry IV. Madame de Châtre, always known as " La Maréchale," was no longer in her first youth, but was an amiable and worthy old lady, who made an excellent and most serviceable friend. She could never endure Madame de Verneuil, and had even taken so bold a stand against her before the arrival in France of Marie de Médicis, that Henry IV. was compelled to banish her from Court at the special instance of Henriette. This was quite possibly one reason why the Queen took her into favour, and always remained her constant friend. Monsieur de la Châtre, as Governor of Berri, usually resided at Bourges or at the Château de la Maisonfort; La Maréchale, however, always remained at Maisonfort, supervising like a good housewife her possessions, woods, and hen-roosts. The friendship between her and Marie de Médicis was of that excellent kind which finds expression in the exchange of letters between a lady resident in Paris and one who remains in the provinces, varied now and again by a gift from the Parisian shops or some delicacy for the table fresh from the country. Madame de la Châtre was never, when in Paris, allowed to reside anywhere but at the Louvre. " I shall give orders," wrote the Queen, " that you are to have two rooms in the Louvre, so that we can see each other with convenience." The prospect of so great a journey was, however, an undertaking to decide upon which the dweller in the country required no less exceptional an event than the Queen's in-lying. " Dear Maréchale," runs an affectionate letter from the latter, " in twelve days or a fortnight I must remove to Fontainebleau, whither I trust you will come to bear me company. I beg you therefore to make up your mind and prepare to come to me directly I arrive there."

Marie de Médicis never failed to provide her friend in Berri with a present from the annual fair of Saint Germain, nor was she less prompt on the occasion of the New Year. During the rest of the year the Queen's favourite offerings seem to have been perfumed pastilles, while, whether the poultry of Berri enjoyed a special reputation at this time, or that those from Maisonfort appealed particularly to the Queen's palate, Madame de la Châtre's presents to Marie de Médicis were always "pullets." The recipient invariably finds them "fat and delicious," and again, " your chickens are so good that I feel I am growing fat upon them." Apples, hares, fruits— there were few products of her farm that Madame de la Châtre, that most matter-of-fact friend, did not send to Paris.

The husbands of these ladies were clearly of no account in the Queen's friendship ; she found them either too old, too ill, or too stupid. Whether because she had no taste for their company, or as a young woman always in the public eye was careful of her reputation, one may almost say that not a single man was to be found among the Queen's more intimate friends. When such a one does appear, he was usually of the vaguely sympathetic type like Bassompierre, that typical fine gentleman of the period, very much a dandy, a " devilish quiz," full of conversation, spirits, and the zest of life. His success was great with the ladies ; he was a gambler, a duellist, always ready to fight, and afraid of no man. Though he was the one man about whose relations with the Queen gossip might have been busy, no word ever appears to have been breathed in this respect. For his introduction into the royal circle, indeed, Henry IV. was himself responsible ; the young man's humour was of the kind that appealed particularly to the King, being frequently quite beyond bounds — very French, in fact. The King held him in such esteem and so enjoyed his conversation that " he would ever, so to speak, have had me by his side." While extremely frank, Bassompierre was also a courtier, and did his best to cultivate this connection : " I was always a servant of those who rule," runs one entry in his journal, witness of his appreciation for " the quarter whence the wind blew." He held faithfully to his friendships, a characteristic which was later much appreciated by the Queen in her days of trouble, and which won him her staunch championship in 1613, when the dandy and the sister of the Marquise de Verneuil tried conclusions in a case before the Parlement de Rouen. Bassompierre had given this young woman, whom he loved, a written promise of marriage, and failure to carry this out was the cause of her citing him before the Parlement de Normandie. Whether or no her friendship for the young man was heightened by dislike for a family to whom she certainly owed little, the Regent put incredible pressure upon the magistrates, writing several letters apiece to the First President, Monsieur Faucon de Ry, to the five Presidents, the Prosecutor General, and the twenty-two Councillors. Moreover, she sent Marillac to Rouen, not only charging him to deliver the letters in person, but also to use all possible additional pressure when so doing. The Maréchal de Fervaques, Lieutenant General at Rouen, was to take like action in respect of each magistrate ; further, an ex-officer of the Guards, Montbron by name, was even sent to observe matters upon the spot, and to compel the First President to hear the case with closed doors. Bassompierre, however, insisted upon a public hearing, whereupon the Queen invited other personages, such as the Bishop of Evreux, to add their influence to her own. When the affair came on, the Public Prosecutor of the Estates of Normandy, Monsieur de Brétignières, Bassompierre's advocate, made a most eloquent speech. Better cases have failed in the face of less odds, and Mademoiselle de Verneuil lost her case. " I promise you my good offices," the Queen wrote to Bassompierre at the beginning ; she certainly kept her word.

Next to, and sometimes among, those with whom the Queen was on terms of friendship we naturally find many Italians. Thus one, Ottavio Strozzi, " the which I did bring with me when I came into this realm," she first commended to Monsieur de Vie, Governor of Calais, for instruction in " the bearing of arms," and next endowed with " the priory of Solesmes, in Maine." In the case of the Ruccellaï, until indeed one of them was advanced to an important post at her side in 1617, she was rather concerned with furthering the fortunes of this family in Italy, recommending to her uncle, the Grand Duke of Tuscany, Domenico Ruccellaï, " an old and necessitous gentleman whom, being blind and with a family to support, I would have elected to some magistracy or place in the city of Florence, the which would be an act of charity." " The constant affection in which I have ever held this house " was, further, the Queen's reason for inviting the Ambassador, Monsieur de Brèves, to extend his protection to every member of it who dwelt in Rome. Her patronage of yet another Italian family was even more extraordinary, for the part played by the Concini in the private affairs of Marie de Médicis is only matched by their notorious share in the entire story of the Regency.

The Grand-ducal Court of Florence, naturally anxious to surround the future Queen of France with as much Italian influence as possible—in which effort it succeeded so well that Paris severely reprimanded the Ambassador, Sillery, for his undue complaisance—had included among the Princess's "Italian ladies," although in the humbler guise of *cameriera* to the Queen, Léonora Galigaï, for seventeen years the faithful and lowly companion of her mistress. For Marie entering, as she was, a new country in which she was as yet without a single friend, and of the language of which she was wholly ignorant, this inclusion in her household of the devoted and affectionate friend of her youth would have seemed no less fitting than natural, even had Léonora not been a woman of many parts. She had not, however, grown in beauty with years, though it is but fair to remember that the following portrait is from an unfriendly pen : "Her figure was thin and her features expressionless, her hair that of a Medusa, pale as tow, a forehead as smooth as a stone . . . green eyes, the proboscis of an elephant, protruding teeth, a harpy's hands, the feet of a lobster, a body scraggy as an old cow's, and a mouth as narrow as that of an oven." Her complexion was sallow and freckled, and her face a mass of wrinkles. But her wits were keener than ever—" of a subtle understanding," a contemporary says, while a letter from Sully to the Queen avers : " I have always found Madame Conchina the most honest and the most reasonable of all those who have access to you." [1] Marie herself, also, told Monsieur d'Alincourt that she really cared for none beside this friend; and her uncle, perfectly aware of the intimacy and hoping to find in her a useful political tool, warmly

[1] This letter is dated 1604.

supported his niece in her plea for Léonora's company, while he carefully explained to the companion that she must now constitute herself her mistress's devoted guardian and marry some gentleman approved by Henry IV. Thus, thanks to the league between his prospective wife and the Grand Duke, Léonora Galigaï was the first, as she was the sole, person who was frankly permitted to follow her mistress with the assurance of a permanent post in France. She was not popular there. Bassompierre found her "no flatterer," but the position of a companion was, after all, too lowly for so insignificant a personage to attract any particular criticism.[1]

The prospects with which Concino Concini entered France were at the opposite pole to those of his country-woman, for he came prepared to return to Italy should fortune withhold her smile. In spite of popular reports, he was neither the son of a carpenter nor a draper, but a scion of one of the best Florentine families. His grandfather, Bartolomeo, a distinguished and able lawyer, rose from membership of the rota of Mantua to the position of ambassador at the Court of Maximilian II. Having, in this capacity, skilfully obtained for his master both the style and the patent of a Grand Duke, he was subsequently for a long period First Minister and the right hand of Cosimo I. The career of his son, Giovanni Battista, was little less remarkable, for as Senator and Supreme Auditor to the Grand Duke Francesco—that is, Superintendent-in-Chief of the Imports of all Tuscany—he occupied one of the highest ministerial posts in the State. Belisario Vinta, his brother-in-law and successor in office, was Secretary of State at the time of the French marriage. As Vinta's nephew, Concino Concini came of a stock which had controlled the destinies of Tuscany through three generations, and succeeded but little less notably in the more personal matters of excellent marriages with the best Florentine

---

[1] Canestrini (*Negotiations*, i. 415) calls her, in so many words, "La fanciulla che di presente acconcia la testa alla regina."

families, and the securing of appointments for all its members.

Concini's early years were scarcely marked by the promise naturally to be expected in a member of such a family. His career at the University of Pisa was remarkable rather for its failures than successes, for he did not even become proficient with weapons. Such success as attended his efforts on leaving the University did him also but little service, since a few years saw his fortune dissipated and himself so notorious that Florentine society unanimously closed its doors in his face. At this juncture, when the despairing family was preparing to expel him from Tuscany, and he thought of retiring, if report be true, into a monastery, the French marriage inspired Vinta with the brilliant idea of ridding himself of this undesirable nephew by attaching him to the Queen's train. The Grand Duke Ferdinand was not friendly to the idea. He disliked the young man, whom he considered a braggart and untrustworthy, and declined to place his name before the French Government. A consultation with the Florentine envoy at Paris proved equally unpromising. If his family were bold enough to imagine this worthless youth a suitable candidate for a post as one of the King's Gentlemen, Giovannini assured them that he was not so. Concino was effeminate, poor, greedy, and ignorant, while " the King's Gentlemen in Ordinary go ever booted and spurred, follow the King in his hunts, and suffer the most distressing fatigue. Court life is, further, inordinately expensive, and Concino would be valued by the depth of his purse." [1] Vinta, however, declining to be snubbed, was presently able to interest the Grand Duchess in his suit. Thus, though afterwards to write to Concino himself : " May I never pardon the Grand Duchess and Vinta for inducing me to let you pass into France before I knew your genius ! "

[1] As a "gentleman" was required to be of three paternal lines, have a sufficient following, six horses, of which four shall be coursers, &c., Giovannini's report to the Grand Duke certainly did not underrate the qualifications.

Ferdinand yielded. Vinta informed Henry that his nephew was "full of the best qualities." The young man joined Marie's train; and the King, uninformed as to his real character, accepted the arrangement without committing himself either to a promise or a refusal as to future possibilities.

That "Concini has his faults but is no fool" was Bassompierre's early verdict. The same critic records that his knowledge of French was as poor as the manner in which he spoke it. "Par dio, mousu, je me ride, moi, delle chose de ste monde." Nevertheless, the future Maréchal d'Ancre was certainly intelligent, though excitable and not always reliable, and if he really answered a friend who, in the moment of his departure, inquired what he meant to do, with "Die or make my fortune!" this mood may explain his success. In person he was not without distinction, having somewhat angular features, a full, high forehead, aquiline nose, a slight moustache curled elegantly upwards, large eyes, arched brows, and a regular mouth—a face, in short, fine until altered by the permanent unrest and constant bad temper of later days. His character was nervous almost to excess, being ardent, sharp, irritable, and impulsive. Ordinarily, however, he was an extremely easy companion, full of kindliness and always ready to bestow a service with every appearance of willing affection, so that he soon obtained a following, and this not the less that his frequent fits of temper when any detail went amiss—and never man was more quick to see that detail—presently invested him with an authoritative, almost compellingly authoritative, manner. Outwardly a light, intriguing, and boastful Italian whom Ferdinand was to reproach with never conversing with Marie de Médicis "except upon rumours, gossip, and petty matters unworthy of her rank, thereby making her to seem other than prudent or stable," Concino Concini's southern blustering, extravagant dress, and more extravagant speeches and boasts, concealed a calculating, cynical, avaricious, and most supple ambition. In this complex character the faults outnumbered the virtues, and when, all considered, we realise that the whole brilliant political career of that man was focussed upon the single end of amassing a fortune by honest or dishonest means, the only possible verdict must place him in the category of the great adventurers.

So soon as his departure in Marie's train was licensed, Concino obtained an introduction to the Queen through Baccio Giovannini, sometime groom to the family, but a man of such parts that, perceiving his quality, Concino's father and grandfather had pushed his fortunes, and not in vain. Baccio certainly proved his knowledge and perspicacity in this case, for he presented Concino to Léonora as well as to her mistress. Never behindhand where his fortune was to be made, Concino at once lavished all his graces and attentions upon Marie, and when she proved obdurate, upon the little companion. Unused to so fine a gentleman, Léonora fell into the toils, was dazzled, and lost her heart. Perceiving his success, Concino redoubled his attentions with as much sincerity as was to be expected. "He made love to Léonora," wrote Princesse de Conti—"I do not say was in love with her, for really she was a woman impossible to look at!" Such a man does not, however, make love through the eyes. Léonora was interested, and through her he might go far. He went, now, as far as he might, and the long progress through France, offering every opportunity for propitious intercourse, the pair were betrothed to each other when halt was called at Avignon. Here, however, Marie de Médicis hesitated, although, Léonora being Léonora, Concini was a match indeed. The Queen was too young and inexperienced to perceive to what quarter the young man's sails were trimmed. Léonora's wits were sharp enough to understand her own game, but she was deeply in love, and her young countryman counselled her wisely in what manner to bear herself towards the King, how best to handle his ministers. The woman with her quick southern nature divined the cleverness of the man, for did she not also dream of fortune ? Heart and brain were thus one in her, and passion swayed her till the Court was almost scandalised and her reputation hung in the balance. Concini falling sick at Lyon, she would have constituted herself his nurse had not public opinion risen in arms. Later, holding themselves betrothed, their conduct toward each other caused such scandal that Henry IV., already annoyed by earlier rumours, lost his temper, and bade Concino go—or, rather, marry Léonora and begone with her, unless of course she would marry a Frenchman. This was the first storm : the lovers found shelter in obscurity. Léonora had requested a place as Mistress of the Robes,[1] but at Paris Henry signified that he would have none of her in such a capacity, gave the appointment to the Comtesse de l'Isle, and informed the Italian that he would give her a sum of money, have her married to Concini, and the pair of them out of the kingdom as fast as he might. Ruin thus staring them in the face at the very moment when they had counted on opening the game, the two adventurers took counsel with themselves, and found their solution to the problem in a master-stroke.

Seeking out the Marquise de Verneuil, Léonora explained that the Queen was particularly incensed against her— which was indeed the case—and this in so active a fashion that Henriette was likely to feel Marie's wrath to some purpose. Thanks, however, to her influence with the Queen, Léonora was able to mollify her mistress, and would do so if Madame de Verneuil would in return persuade the King to grant her the coveted post of Mistress of the Robes, sanction her marriage with Concino, and obtain permission

---

[1] Henry IV. was so determined not to give this place to Léonora that he offered it to Madame de Richelieu, before appointing the Comtesse de l'Isle, " but at Marseilles the Queen declined to accept her." Pressed to accept the Galigaï, Henry retorted that none but nobles could enter the Queen's coach, which Women of the Chamber must do. To this assertion of Léonora's want of nobility, Vinta replied that she was " *cittadina*."

for their residence in France. Henriette accepted, and the astute *cameriera*'s plan succeeding at every point, the Queen for a while modified her frowns, and the King yielded to the double solicitations of the Queen and his mistress. Those who knew were, of course, loud in their indignation. The King's weakness was incredible—yet this was no news where his inclinations came into play— while Marie was taken to be an inconsequent if not eccentric person, light in any case, and as feeble in judgment as in will. Opinion regarding the remaining actors in the little drama was plainly spiteful ; Giovannini, the Florentine envoy, fully conversant with all Concino's manœuvres, wrote home to Vinta that Léonora Galigaï was now so much a creature of Madame de Verneuil that, did they wish it, the Grand Ducal Government would find it difficult to recall the precious couple. Thanks to the intervention of his mistress, the King's attitude was now completely reversed, for had he not discovered how to accommodate duty with desire, and to hold his wife while retaining absolute freedom in respect of Henriette d'Entraigues ? He therefore lent himself to the intrigue without reserve, presented Léonora with twenty thousand crowns on her marriage, and even mentioned Concino as a possible Gentleman of the Chamber.

In the same year (1601) the marriage of Léonora, now Mistress of the Robes, was celebrated at Saint Germains with the strictest privacy. Thus began the career of " the Sieur Conchino and Madame Conchino," a career in which the first step was successively to remove from the French Court those fellow-countrymen who were too well aware of their characters to be comfortable companions, too ambitious not to be jealous of their success, and finally their diligent detractors at home. Subtle machinations soon made the position of the Italians untenable, and the Grand Duke, exhausted by the complaints, intrigues, and quarrels consequent upon the struggle, wrote to Concini : " You seek to be rid of all the Italians against whom you bear a grudge, you ruin their credit by your plots, and you drive out of France those who came thither without means, but under the Queen's protection and purposed to be her sincere and devoted servants." But the Grand Duke was far away and raged in vain. Concino, fully aware of his wife's strong hold upon Marie, lost no time in pressing every advantage, heedlessly, imprudently, rashly indeed, but— thanks to a happy star—successfully.

As Mistress of the Robes, Léonora Galigaï had a right to an apartment in the Louvre—in this case, three rooms on the second story directly above those of the Queen, sufficiently well situated to suit any taste, and presently, as fortune began to smile on her, magnificently furnished. Her antechamber and bedroom she hung with fine tapestries, worth from eighteen hundred to two thousand crowns, displaying the varied stories of Lucretia, Jacob, David, and Saint Paul. The posts of her bedstead were covered with embroideries "in little gold points and silk, the chairs with velvet cramoisy bound with cloth of gold." Against the walls stood great cabinets of Indian woods or German work, above them mirrors in frames of rosewood or ebony : the floors were covered with Eastern rugs in many tints and of many kinds. The tablecloths were all of value, " silks in the manner of China and of many colours, velvets in full violet cramoisy, picked out with gold filigree, or yellow velvet on a silver ground." Cushions and pillows " of violet velvet, embroidered with gold," lay everywhere amidst a profusion of the richest stuffs—" velvets in the tones of dead leaves bound with gold or silver lace ; cloth of silver embroidered with gold and silver, bound at the edges with velvet of tan-cramoisy, also embroidered with silver and gold ; stuffs flowered with nosegays, as yellow fleur-de-lis upon a ground of tan colour ; " brilliant counterpanes " of blue velvet built upon a ground of silver doubled with blue taffetas," or " crimson doubled with plush in the tones of dead leaves." Twenty coffers in the recesses contained as much or more of stuffs for the display of which space did not serve, with change upon change of gorgeous furnishings waiting their turn to decorate the bed ; the wardrobes were crammed with garlands, valances, canopies, bed-curtains, and coverings for bedposts. The number of bibelots and gold and silver objects was beyond count—candlesticks of gold, baskets, and little panniers of silver, agate chalices mounted in silver gilt, cockboats of silver gilt, crosses, reliquaries, vessels for holy water, ewers of gold and silver, vases in silver-gilt and plates of gold—to a value which the Maréchale d'Ancre, at the time of her impeachment in 1617, estimated at no less than from fifteen to sixteen thousand crowns.[1]

As a lady in the fashion, Léonora's personal adornments did not lag behind those of her chamber. Thus her purveyor of linen, Jehan de Wolf, delivered to her in a single day seventy-seven ells of Holland cloth for sheets at four livres and ten sols the ell ; two dozen chemises at one hundred sols apiece, further two dozen at six livres apiece, and yet others at twelve livres, likewise one dozen embroidered coifs at thirty sols.[2] The inventory of her wardrobe taken at the time of her impeachment further adds to our view of its extent : " fourteen dresses, nine cloaks, thirteen petticoats, four vests, three capes, two doublets, two mantles, &c.," were all from her stores in the Louvre alone, whereas her apartment in the palace was but one of many places in which her possessions were collected. Her costumes were equally luxurious : " of satin cramoisy sewn with pearls and diamonds," cloth of silver, silk broidered in gold and silver, and " furred with grey plush," satins— white, blue, yellow, black, any and every colour indeed, and " gauze figured with flowers in gold and silver."

This almost outrageous luxury notwithstanding, Léonora's prudence kept her in comparative obscurity. She

[1] Léonora's valuables are given in this detail, as her secretary's inventory, made at the time of her impeachment, is a document of unique value upon the minutiæ of contemporary luxury.

[2] 12 deniers = 1 sol (sou) ; 20 sols = 1 livre (1 franc) ; the purchasing power of the livre was about six times that of the modern franc.

seldom left her own apartment and eschewed assemblies, either because she really disliked them or because she desired to avoid the public eye, feeling that her gradual rise in favour was too well watched and the cynosure of envious eyes. Another and yet better reason for this retirement will presently appear. She maintained it consistently, entertaining no more frequently than she accepted the hospitality of others, and keeping her apartment so well that even that constant frequenter of the Louvre, the Queen's purveyor of perfume, could state in 1617 that he had not seen her within the last four years. Such aloofness necessarily kept her in ignorance of Court usage : "she was unacquainted with those among whom she nominally moved, and was quite unused to the customs at Court." [1] When abroad, she remained always in her carriage, and went masked according to the fashion prevalent among great ladies of the day. This carriage was a magnificent equipage, upholstered in crimson velvet cramoisy embroidered in gold, its imperial furnished in like style, and "the harness of its horses of velvet cramoisy, bound with gold and silver." To the Queen she paid daily visits at times when they were sure to be alone together, as a rule late in the evening, at the hour of Marie's retiring. These visits were regular little councils, at which the Queen's Mistress of the Robes sometimes discussed her special province of the royal toilette, but more usually men and things—above all, matters of State. Léonora, however, had not dwelt long in the Louvre before the earlier stages of her disease restricted these visits. From daily events they became limited to three or four evenings a week, and when later she could no longer descend to the Queen's apartment, Marie herself paid bi-weekly visits to her friend on the second story. Léonora Galigaï now dwelt alone day after day, a strange existence which may claim attention.

"Hasty, difficult to serve and ill-tempered," Léonora led the life of a crazy and superstitious old woman,

[1] Tallemant.

wearing out the lives of her two servants—Marie Brille, wife to the major-domo of the Concini, and an Italian housemaid, Marcella. Employing her mornings in attending masses and visiting the churches, she confessed and communicated frequently, having for spiritual director a decayed Carmelite, Père César, while in the afternoons she would cause the Bible to be read aloud, or "would sit and string pearls, chaplets, and such-like," or arrange and handle her rings. She adored music, and would often play the guitar or sing to her own accompaniment on this instrument, but her chief and especial occupation was the amassing and direction of her property.

Having originally desired lands and houses in France, Léonora subsequently inclined to the thought of one day retiring to Italy, and therefore limited her investments in real estate to a town-house and another in the country. In addition, she conferred upon her husband the use, or rather gift, of a house at the corner of the Quai and Rue d'Autriche, the street upon which opened the main gate of the Louvre—a modest dwelling built upon the lesser garden of the palace. Léonora obtained this house for Concino, whom, since he was not admitted to his wife's apartment in the palace unless as a visitor, she desired to have within call. Over it she placed the Italian, Fabiano Cosimo. For her own town-house she first hired the Hôtel Pecquigny in Rue Tournon, but subsequently purchased it of Monsieur de Liancourt for the sum of fourteen thousand crowns. Dissatisfied, however, or rather taken by the whim to build, she levelled her purchase and entrusted its re-building to the Italian architect and sculptor, Francesco Bordoni. Of the exact details of his work no record has survived, but the new hotel included a chapel, and its several rooms were lavishly adorned with pictures and sculptures. Though Léonora seldom occupied it for long—usually for a week at a time, when the Queen was away from the city—it was in this house that she entertained her patron with dinners and concerts. It was also her storehouse for such valuables as she could not house in the Louvre, and the place in which was her strong-room. In 1616, on the occasion of the arrest of Prince de Condé, the reputed work of Concini, the Prince's servants from his house hard by in Rue Neuve Saint Lambert, broke all its windows and forced the doors with balks seized from the forges of the Luxembourg, then in course of construction. They were gutting " this house in which was furniture to the value of above two hundred thousand crowns," and had even begun to wreck the building itself when a rescue was effected by the opportune arrival upon the scene of several companies of the Gardes françaises. For her country estate, the Château de Lésigny and its lands and various re-buildings, Léonora paid to Baron de Lésigny and his sister, Madame de Réaux, more than one hundred thousand crowns, but being closely tied to Paris derived even less enjoyment from this property than she did from the Hôtel Pecquigny. She negotiated for, but never acquired, an estate at Chévry on account of which she advanced twelve thousand livres, another at Luzarches, and two houses at Bordeaux, of which she spoke of making a house for the Minimite Order.

Such extensive business affairs, even had Léonora not engaged in numberless and most complex financial ventures, necessarily required assistance, and we therefore find her the centre of quite a little group of business and financial personages, to whose services she was deeply indebted. Her first secretary, Monsieur Lecomte, claims no particular notice, but his successor, Rafaello Corbinelli, was as skilful as he was secret, and well versed in all things monetary. Coming to France in 1597, at the early age of fifteen, this man was first attached to the staff of Monsieur d'Attichy, Intendant to the Queen, passed thence into the service of her favourite, and finally returned to the Queen as her secretary after the arrest of the Maréchale d'Ancre. Equally involved with the Maréchale, was Louis Dolé, Advocate General to Marie de Médicis, with whom, no less than with the ministers, his remarkable intelligence and knowledge of all problems of procedure obtained for him the highest consideration. History does not reveal the details of this man's career as fully as we might desire, but there seems reason to believe that Dolé's influence was far deeper and more extensive than the records attest, and that Concini largely owed his astonishing political fortunes to this man's supple duplicity and masked assistance. Nevertheless, not all the Advocate's experience and strength of character obtained for him such influence with Léonora as was exercised by the little Italian priest whose talent with the guitar and lyre had first attracted her notice. André de Lizza, Abbé de Livry, was the chief influence in her career, and from all appearances his powers of fascination cast a spell upon her.

Born in the Kingdom of Naples about the year 1579, André de Lizza came to France with Cardinal Perron, whose almoner he was for six years. At the close of this period, being about to return to Italy, the accident of his taking part in a concert which she was giving at her hôtel in the Rue de Tournon caused Léonora to retain his services, although to compass this she was compelled to appeal to Marie. The Queen having insisted, nay commanded, that he remain in France, and having even written to Cardinal du Perron when he raised objections, the young priest yielded. Attached to the Mistress of the Robes as almoner, he was made first Abbé de Livry, and then Abbé de Hautefontaine in Champagne. His duty was to celebrate morning Mass for his mistress, but this done he would remain closeted with her for four and five hours together, as the servants testified ; by his own admission at a later date, " within the chamber of the future Maréchale until eleven P.M., or even until midnight." Contemporary gossip naturally noted these confabulations, but it never aspersed their propriety any more than it censured Léonora's dealings with other men. Questioned at the impeachment of the Maréchale d'Ancre, Abbé de Livry replied, " That their discourse

was of the Maréchale's private affairs, the conduct of
her house, her investments, her building operations at
Lésigny, of the which he had charge, as also—at times—
of Italy, whereunto she would sometimes say she would
retire." Trusting him completely, Léonora no doubt
consulted him with regard to her investments, her
affairs, and the conduct of her household; but it is
equally certain that the Abbé had obtained such a hold
upon her as to isolate her from all other influences.
Lodged by her in a tiny apartment in Concini's house
upon the Quai, " he was daily in the said Maréchale's
chamber, by night no less than by day, nor did withdraw
until such hour as the gates of the Louvre were closed."
Matters came to such a pass that her household and
friends were presently unable to see her unless by his
leave, " wherefore did they which were about the said
house murmur greatly," and his power increased in that
such " as had to do with the said Maréchale addressed
themselves to him." His isolation of her was so effectual
that, on occasion, André de Lizza found himself obliged to
perform the duties of servants whom he had driven from
their mistress, while the indignant doctor Alvarez asserted
that Léonora's own husband was compelled "to address
the Abbé in respect of a certain matter wherein he desired
somewhat of his wife." " Finally he served the Maréchale as secretary, major-domo, and cook, indeed as
every kind of servant by reason that she had dismissed
them all."

On the testimony of these servants, André was a most
uncommon individual, with a mind, priest though he was,
to mock at religious ceremonies and ridicule fasts and
festivals. He had a taste to jest with the men-servants
and maids in the offices, and to tell crude tales " and use
most licentious discourse." A friend of Concini calls him
a man who gives one an impression of viciousness. None
the less, this André de Lizza possessed unrivalled knowledge of all Léonora's acts and ways, and—thanks to his
detailed replies to her judges in 1617—it is he who has

left the clearest record of her influence upon Marie de Médicis.[1]

The problem of this extraordinary influence is usually solved by reference to a reply alleged to have been made by Léonora when she was under examination, but the base saying, " My influence was that of a clever woman over a fool," is apocryphal. The real reply was, " I have been honoured by the Queen's liking because I was her companion from youth, and I have won her goodwill by serving her well, and because I was ever very diligent to follow her and to do her mind." " Being interrogated as to whether he were cognisant of the source of the said Maréchale's influence with the Queen, and whether he did not know, or had not heard, that she was used to practise spells or other extraordinary devices to the end to govern the will and understanding of the said Queen Mother," André de Lizza " replied that he had never observed nor heard of her having used such means, and that he believed the said influence to issue from her long familiarity with the said Queen Mother, the which was from youth upwards, and from her great devotion to her." André, however, added : " The Maréchale's character exercises great influence upon less robust minds," and it is this reply which was distorted into the apocryphal " fool," the saying being drawn from current gossip in which Léonora was alleged to regularly use this term when speaking of the Queen. The real propagator of the allegation is Tallemant des Réaux, the only contemporary writer who records it, and those who quote him have

[1] We are well informed about André de Lizza, thanks to his own replies under the interrogatory of 1617, the testimony of the usher, Desdiguières, and of the doctor, Alvarez, who enjoyed special opportunities for observing him. On his arrest in 1617, after the murder of Concini, he was somewhat severely treated, despite his age (sixty-eight), being imprisoned in For l'Evêque " with much hardship, having no conveniences, no, not to hear a mass." Without reflecting on his orthodoxy, we may remember that such a point did not greatly trouble his mistress, for it was she who caused to be brought from Florence that Cosimo Ruggieri, whom she made Abbé de Saint Mahé, in the diocese of Léon in Brittany, who died an atheist, answering to every question put to him upon the tenets of the Church the one word, " Superstition ! superstition ! "

overlooked his addition : " But I doubt that she said it," a qualification which in his mouth is tantamount to a denial.   Richelieu and Pontchartrain allege that Léonora currently used this term of the Queen, but such a lapse would be too extraordinary in so clever a woman, even had her conduct under examination been less careful. That Léonora's influence was no riddle to those who were able to observe it at first hand is clear from the testimony of Vincenzo Ludovisi, Concini's secretary, who declared his belief, " that the great influence exercised by the Maréchale upon the Queen Mother proceeds from the long intercourse and particular familiarity that the said Maréchale has from the age of ten or twelve enjoyed in respect of the said Queen Mother."   This early tie, adroitly strengthened by a boundless devotion, ready zeal, and passive obedience at every moment, a warm affection—whether feigned or real; above all, a capacity to amuse, that made their long talks seem as necessary as they were agreeable, finally erected between Léonora and the Queen one of those relationships that long habit makes indestructible.   Towards Marie de Médicis she thus came to stand in some such position as is enjoyed by an old confidential servant whom semi-familiarity makes almost a member of the family—the ally to whom an old woman clings above all others, and from whom she can never separate herself, though the result be quarrels and even separations between relatives, the instigator herself escaping without blame or even less than blame.

Marie de Médicis was wholly blind where this friend was concerned.   Do or say what she would, the Queen could see nothing but as she directed, nor act otherwise than in her interest, so that those whose position enabled them to see clearly could only regard the sovereign as a woman vexatiously imprudent and feather-brained, and almost wholly wanting in decision of character and consistency of action.   The Grand Duke of Tuscany, who had so built upon his niece's marriage, and dreamed of the political combinations to issue from the alliance, finding that Marie was beyond his control, thanks to the counsel of that egoistical creature—the ungrateful *cameriera*—wrote to the Queen in terms of the liveliest spite, not untinged with a somewhat provincial and ridiculous sense of being duped. "Thus far you seem to have interested yourself in nothing but Léonora, as though the fortunes of this nobody had been the sole end of an alliance made good in the face of the gravest dangers, the fruit of all my labours, and indeed at ruinous cost to my purse. I could easily have made you Duchess of Braganza, an obscure exile in a corner of Portugal. Yet when, without a thought for my eight children, I lavished my treasure to make you Queen of France, your indolence and ingratitude have changed all my prospects in that quarter at the moment in which I looked to reap the fruit of my disinterestedness." [1]

As well aware as any one of her real power over the Queen, Léonora, for some reason, let slip no opportunity of impressing the world with its existence, as though the power should grow in proportion to its place in the public eye. Alvarez was astonished to hear her say, " before himself and before several ladies of the Queen Mother, that no one could so influence the said Queen as she." The King's secretary, Monsieur Chalange, has left on record : " Madame Conchino wished us to feel all her credit, and that she was in a position to obtain her every desire of the Queen." Cumulatively persuaded in this fashion, the world came to hold that Léonora's influence was preponderant, and with one accord flocked to the only certain agent. " Whosoever would obtain aught of the Queen Mother," affirmed her own equerry Desdiguières, " must approach her (Léonora). In the first three years of the Regency, she was courted by every sort of person, Princes, Princesses, and Officers of the

---

[1] "Odious and scandalous" was the description applied by the Grand Duke in speaking of Marie's favourites, but those who denounced them to him did not certainly try to create any other impression. Thus Giovannini wrote of *Questa insipida e damnosa passione*, while Botti spoke of " Her Majesty's most extraordinary friend with whom she seems, as it were, enamoured."

Council and of the foreign Courts." Ludovisi confirms this testimony : " Seekers for place or profit paid their addresses to the Maréchale, and to her were returned thanks for whatsoever favour the Queen Mother might accord." An anecdote, indeed, seems to show that Louis XIII. himself was perfectly aware of this, for his nurse, having on one occasion solicited his intervention on behalf of a wretched woman condemned to death upon suspicion, the recorded reply runs : " Bid the Marquise d'Ancre, Doundoun, speak to the Queen, my mother, and incline her mind to do this grace." If Saint Simon, suspect as he is, may be added to the list of witnesses, Léonora was known to send word that Louis should abate the noise, when incommoded by the royal pastimes on the floor above her own.

André de Lizza, interrogated at a later date upon this very point : " Whether or no all affairs touching the State, as the distribution of imposts, pensions, and gifts, were made under advice and counsel of the said Maréchale ? " replied that this was so, and that " the list of pensions was brought to the said Maréchale, and without her advice and counsel was no gift or gratification accorded." Abbé de Livry has a long list of those who owed their preferment to Léonora, in the Royal Household alone—the equerry, the major-domo, the intendant, the secretary, the three comptrollers, and, last and most illustrious, the Grand Almoner of Anne of Austria, " Armand Jehan du Plessis de Richelieu," whose Memoirs certainly do not magnify the fact of this compromising protection. Even the Duchesse de Bar solicited the favourite when seeking place in the Royal Household for a person whom she was protecting, while no sooner was it whispered that a Household was to be formed for the King's brother, the Duc d'Orléans, than the Bishop of Angers, and Présidents Miron, Jambeville, and Chevalier, evinced a remarkable unanimity in addressing Léonora as the first step towards obtaining the office of " Monsieur's " Chancellor. The remarkable Lady in Waiting herself informed Alvarez that not only did she draw out the lists for the entire establishment of Anne of Austria, on the occasion of that Princess's first arrival in France, but that every member of it was her own nominee. The personality that exercises this minute detail in household matters will not be satisfied with a lesser share in the great issues of politics. On this point the testimony of André de Lizza is again explicit.

Léonora, de Lizza asserts, exercised a preponderant influence in the preliminary negotiations for the Peace of Loudun. Informed by Dolé of all that passed, Ludovisi, Concini's secretary, was the channel through which she transmitted her opinions. " He would come to no decision," says the Abbé de Livry, " unless with her counsel, and in this matter she was served by the Maréchale's secretary, Sieur Vincent (Ludovisi), who verbally bore her advice and counsel to the Queen Mother." This affair of Loudun saw the beginning of Léonora's anger against Villeroy, " for that having been commanded, at the time of the conference at Loudun, first and before all else to treat of the matter of Picardy on behalf of the said Maréchale d'Ancre, he (Villeroy) did not so do, but made treaty as he would, wherefore was she greatly enraged against the said Sieur de Villeroy." Léonora's subterranean influence completely foiled the ministers ; disgrace was the immediate consequence of resistance or protests, as Sillery and Villeroy were not slow to learn. Having frequently told André that " she desired to change the chief ministers and officers of State in order to replace them with men of parts, complaining in especial of Monsieur le Chancellier and Monsieur le Commandant (de Sillery), of his brother and of Monsieur de Villeroy, in that these were not of her friends nor yet good servants of the Queen Mother, and particularly the Sieur de Villeroy as said," Léonora finally procured their removal. Their successors, her creatures, were Barbin, whom she had brought forward and caused to be named successively Intendant and Comptroller ; Mangot, Richelieu, and Du Vair—all remarkable and honourable men, excellent selections, and perhaps a little sore at heart to owe their advancement to so unwelcome an influence. Having twice written to offer the seals to Du Vair, then President of the Parliament at Aix—to which matter André added that he was well able to testify, having himself written the letters at her dictation — she sent her confidential emissary, de Barbin, to bring him to a decision. These changes effected, " Well, and what is it that they say ? " she asked. " You will see that the King's Council will be much more efficient with our ministers." Her equerry was able to confirm this testimony of André de Lizza, since she had not feared to dwell upon " my establishment of the ministry " in his presence. Of this, nevertheless, she must have repented in at least one case—that of the venerable and upright Du Vair—for a little while afterwards she said : " You see what trouble I was at to establish him in office, and yet I cannot obtain a single courtesy from him. Truly he is ungrateful for the good that he has received at my hands." The rest were more malleable.

That Léonora effected her changes in the ministry [1]

[1] Léonora's choice of ministers was certainly most judicious. Richelieu included, she seems to have set herself to select none but men of the highest capacity. Barbin, a nobody who had "arrived," thanks to a brilliant brain, was deeply versed in matters financial, a little rigid in his outlook, of a sure and upright judgment, active, resolute, an easy and authoritative speaker, "of much good sense and most judicious, whose hands were clean and who did not spare himself." Thanks to the patronage of Jeannin, who appreciated his quality, he became Director of Finance and Intendant in the Household of Marie de Médicis, from which post he was elevated to the ministry. He was a strong ally of Richelieu. Mangot, the son of a famous advocate, was himself a man of learning and probity, the father of a numerous family, and had enjoyed a brilliant and rapid advance due to great merit. He had been Master of Requests, Counsellor, and First President of the Parliament of Bordeaux. His success was so rapid that it frightened his friends, with whom he was extremely popular, and even made him nervous on his own account. When nominated minister, his inclination was for refusal of the advancement. Guillaume du Vair, Bishop of Lisieux, First President at Aix, was one of those personalities who force themselves to the front when their hour arrives. Though a most admirable and worthy man, his intellect was scarcely as supple as those of his colleagues. With the sole exception of Richelieu, who was able

single-handed, and without the least help from Concini, is formally and unanimously asserted by those who were in a position to know the facts. André de Lizza affirms that in this matter Léonora acted " of her proper motion and authority," that she did not write to her husband on the subject, and that he had no knowledge of it. André should be correct on this point, because he added that " he read all such letters as Léonora received from the said Maréchal, and wrote all such as she addressed to him." Interrogated on the same point, Concini's secretary testified " that the whole of the said matter was by the will of the said Maréchale d'Ancre and not by that of her husband, and that the aforesaid Maréchale would not that her husband knew aught of it." Léonora was to all intents omnipotent. An adventure which befell Monsieur Antoine Allory, " burgher, dwelling in Rue Saint André des Arcs," will afford a better illustration than anything else of the exact position of Léonora at this moment—towards her mistress, the ministers, or the private citizen.

In October of the year 1613, one Monsieur Antoine Allory, Seigneur de la Bornerie, obtained the lease of the Five Great Farms of the Kingdom. This lease was granted to him in due form, at the Louvre, in full Council by the King under the Presidency of the Queen, " the which, on the snuffing of the candle " did with her own mouth, and in the presence of many persons, adjudicate the said lease to Allory for the sum of eight hundred and eighty-six thousand livres. Arriving at the Louvre next morning, in company with his associates and guarantors —the names of whom he had given on the previous evening to Jeannin, Comptroller General of Finance—he purposed to sign the lease at the day's Council of Finance;

---

to regain his place, all these men suffered for their patronage by Léonora. Compromised by their association with her, they were swept away before they were able to stamp history with the record of their real worth, or to render to their country the services which she should have received at their hands.

this being Saturday, President Jeannin caused it to be made known to Allory that the Council would not sit by reason that the King was leaving for Fontainebleau, and that the ministers must accompany His Majesty. The farmer having followed to Fontainebleau, the embarrassed Comptroller finally " expressed his regret for his case, that there were those which purposed forcibly to oust him from his lease, and that it was the intent of the Queen to grant it to a certain person recommended to her by the Maréchale d'Ancre." Allory, much surprised, proceeded to call upon the Chancellor, who said : " Monsieur de la Bornerie, my friend, I well understand that evil entreatment is purposed for you, and to take from you that which we have adjudged to you. But in this matter you must not yield, but must speak to the Queen, and make appeal through your friends." Much put about, the lessee arranged with Monsieur de Guise to present him to the Queen ; and on the Tuesday following, Marie de Médicis having come out from the palace to walk in the gardens in company with the Princesse de Conti, Monsieur de Guise, and certain other persons, Allory approached as, having come to the Fountain of Tiber, Her Majesty was leaning upon the balustrade. " Madame," then said the Duc de Guise, " behold before you one of our friends, who has prayed me to present him to Your Majesty, and whom I pray you hear ! " The farmer having knelt, and the Queen as soon bidding him rise, he briefly opened the matter in hand. " See the Marquise," exclaimed Marie with small interest, " and arrange the matter with her." Monsieur Allory at once sought out Léonora, to whom, having developed his argument, and understanding with whom he had to deal, he insinuated " that he was come to the Marquise to understand what might be her desire." In no way disturbed, Léonora quietly discussed the value of the Five Grand Farms, and valued the probable profits at two hundred thousand crowns a year. Allory, much disturbed, assured her that she was misinformed. The ministers had fixed the lease after a minute inquest at the four stations of Paris, Amiens, Nantes, and Lyon. None the less, he was prepared to offer Léonora ten thousand crowns "for pin-money." This offer constituting "a laughable mockery of herself," the Lady in Waiting dismissed the unfortunate farmer. After a consultation with his associates at Paris, Allory consulted Jeannin, and following his advice again sought audience with the Queen, this time in her apartment and under the introduction of Monsieur de Montbazon. Telling the Queen of what he had done, no less than of the ten thousand crowns offered to the Marquise, Marie promised to see "and to speak of it with her." Allory then insisted "that the act of justice which he sought imported greatly to the King's honour, that of his Council, and that of the Queen Mother, who had herself adjudged the lease." Marie de Médicis repeated that "She would see and would speak of it with the Marquise."

On the following Thursday, Allory learned that the name in the lease was changed by authority, so that it now stood in the name of Monsieur Pierre de la Sablière, agent of one Monsieur Giovannini. Thoroughly aroused at last, he determined to resist this perversion of justice by every legal means, and entered a protest against this fraudulent lease before the King's Council, the Chancellor even licensing his appearance in person before the Council, "to the end that all men might know the injustice that was doing, and whereto he, the Chancellor, might in no way afford relief." The objection was notified to the Recorder, to Dolé as Grand Auditor of France, and to the Comptroller of the Great Seal, and so referred for examination to the Chamber of Accounts. Allory, approaching Léonora for the second time, learned from her secretary that Giovannini, his favoured rival, had promised the Marquise twenty thousand crowns, together with an annual payment of ten thousand livres for so long as the lease ran. He therefore offered the Lady in Waiting twelve thousand crowns at once, and twenty thousand

from the profits earned, but this tardy amendment was
disdainfully rejected. Allory's temper vented itself in
furious threats : he " would use his pistol on whosoever
should rob him of his lease, which was his by right, and
whereupon he had spent much, having made inquiry
and sent his agents throughout the regions of the Farm
that so he might learn the value of those Farms." The
Queen's circle finding this pother irksome, President
Jeannin was commanded to advise Allory to make terms
with Giovannini, accept a forfeit of four thousand crowns
" and abate his objections." He declined, unless the half
of the lease should be assured " to him and his associates," and renewed his offer to pay the Marquise ten
thousand crowns, together with one-half the annual payment offered by Giovannini. She refused, and he renewed his appeal. It was admitted by the Chamber of
Accounts, and a delegation from the Court—a President,
the Procurator General, and the Reporter in the case—
waited upon the Government at Fontainebleau in order
to enter notification of their action. The Queen's reply
was a command that the Chamber should ratify the lease
as amended; and on December 12, 1613, a Decree of
the Council " in form of an injunction, commanded the
Chamber forthwith to execute the Lease, all opposition
notwithstanding." Léonora Galigaï was thus affirmed
mistress of the ministry, a sovereign Court, the law,
equity, and public opinion.[1]

No more evidence than is afforded by this story need
be adduced to prove that Léonora's first and especial
use of her power over Marie de Médicis was for self-
enrichment. " Her vision was limited to money," writes

[1] Allory's deposition before Léonora's judges is our authority for this
account. The Chancellor and Jeannin both opposed the injustice with all
their influence, but were powerless before the favourite. Further, Giovannini
was allowed a rebate of sixteen thousand crowns on the price of the lease.
Allory had offered the King a loan of one hundred thousand crowns, to run
for six years free of interest. The public, also, was fully aware that "great
rebates had been allowed in the matter of the Five Grand Farms, and that
large monies had been given to this end in diverse quarters."

Michelet, and André de Lizza admitted that his mistress " did ever so design her counsel that her power might be increased with the Queen, and herself thus acquire the means to enrich herself." The aim of her accusers in 1617 was, therefore, to prove that " being come into France destitute of all worldly means, the riches of the said Maréchale could not have accrued to her otherwise than through extraordinary and illicit channels, as the receiving of money on all hands, taking of bribes on account of leases of the Farms of the King's Realm, and corrupt practices of every sort." Naturally, " interrogated as to whether she had not profited by all such appointments, she replied that she had never so acted," but her operations were no less systematic than their proportions were surprising. Every part of the administration was so controlled that it should yield her the highest possible returns—a veritable system of highway robbery.

Of gifts proper, from hand to hand, Léonora seems to have received few from the Queen, although, over and above her annual salary and perquisites, the Mistress of the Robes enjoyed a yearly pension of four thousand crowns. Léonora, however, did not exactly want for presents of jewels from her mistress, for adding these to such as she had herself purchased, and others that came to her from various sources, she estimated her possessions in this kind at no less than two hundred thousand crowns. Yet, although Marie consented to indemnify her in the sum of a hundred thousand crowns [1] on the occasion of the pillage of her house in Rue de Tournon, direct gifts were not the source of her fortune. This was chiefly the fruit of speculation. Vincenzo Ludovisi deposed that " the Maréchale had frequently told him that her receipts were not due to the liberalities of the Queen Mother, but to enterprises upon which she staked her credit, or

[1] Apart from this one hundred thousand crowns, sums up to 352,600 livres are to be found on record, but their nature is not clear, and it does not seem certain that they were gifts. In respect of Léonora's pension of four thousand crowns, Concini habitually forged the receipts and turned the monies to his own uses.

whereof she had particular advice." Her grand resource was the taking of bribes. "There was no matter, howsoever small," declared Germain Chalange, Secretary of Finance, "wherein she was not set to benefit in whole or in part, by a bribe at the least." Every important appointment, concession, or lease, brought in something. "Of posts in the King's Household, in that of the Queen or that of the royal children, in the Judiciary or other high services, there was none conferred but it paid tribute to the Galigaï." The jeering populace finally called this "spitting into the basin," "and the public mock hereat, as the broadsides printed in her despite, were current throughout the Kingdom."

The creation of new posts by the sale of which she should gather in profits, and the general devising of a thousand means by which to shake gains from the folds of a tangled financial system, compelled Léonora to retain the services of quite a staff of clever rascals—Germain Chalange, Secretary of Finance, Dolé, Feydeau, more often Feydeau's brother, whom she made Abbé de Marmoutier and Archbishop of Tours. But her chief ally was Vincenzo Ludovisi, an Italian from Treviso who, having "come to see the land" in 1605, had been engaged as his master's secretary by Concini's major-domo. Until they quarrelled, he was for several years chief agent in amassing his mistress's fortune, but the entire band spent most of its time in devising methods for the ingathering of gold. Outraged by their actions, Messieurs d'Argouges and d'Attichy, Marie's financial advisers, "ofttimes took counsel together if so they might devise a means to warn the Queen that snares were laid for her, and her name misused, for the extortion of so much gold," but their courage was never quite equal to the task.[1]

---

[1] Ludovisi was thirty-eight in 1617 ; he was incarcerated at For l'Evêque after Concini's death. Léonora's lawyer was one Antoine Arnauld. The equerry Desdiguières deposed that, during their tenure as ministers, Barbin and Mangot also gave financial advice, but that Richelieu always took care to hold aloof. The future Cardinal readily foresaw a catastrophe in the extreme unpopularity of the Concinis, and was not seen at their house above twice

The number and variety of Léonora's peculations were certainly large. To secure the reversion of an office for a son, or a rebate on a lease, the hands of the Lady in Waiting did but need to be crossed. She was a pensioner of the Farmer General for the Collection of Subsidies, compelled the Receivers of Customs to compound with her for their authorisations, for the sum of fifty-four thousand livres consented to procure the re-establishment of the offices of the Two Treasurers of France in each of the great administrative divisions (*generalités*), and arranged this transaction, before a notary, with Chalange, who paid in cash and did not fail to make his investment good. For the sum of a hundred and twenty thousand livres she similarly revived the two offices of Comptroller General for the Taxes upon Salt and upon Grain. Two hundred thousand livres was the price at which she extended her protection to the representatives who, in certain provinces, had collected an impost of five sols and pocketed the difference between that sum and the lawful tax of two sols six deniers, while the Farmers of the Salt Tax in Languedoc agreed with her in the sum of one hundred and twenty thousand livres for the privilege of assuming to their own uses " eight deniers in the livre on the impositions extraordinary made under the Edict of 1611." Her judges, endeavouring to clear up all these transactions, cited fifteen heads under which she had profited to the extent of nearly two million livres, among them a payment of a hundred thousand livres by Monsieur Duret for renewal of his lease of the farm of the ancient demesne of Navarre, eighty-three thousand paid by Monsieur d'Argouges in 1613, and an advance of sixty-three thousand by Barbin through the intermediation of Monsieur Feydeau. Six other persons had found occasion to hand to her sums amounting in the aggregate to four hundred and forty-eight thousand livres. All these affairs

during the three or four months immediately prior to the murder of the Maréchal d'Ancre.

came to light rather through the papers of the Maréchale and her husband than the information given by Chalange and other associates, although Léonora, greatly confused, asserted that her memory failed her, that they were not exact, or that they applied to matters of the Queen's business. When also, having denied everything, she was confronted with proof, the accused spoke of her gains as gracious gifts made by her mistress. In the matter of Antoine Allory, already related in detail, she averred that "she well remembered that one named Giovannini would have had her receive eight thousand crowns for the Five Great Farms, which monies she refused, but afterwards accepted by desire of the Queen Mother." In the beginning, however, she had firmly denied all knowledge of the affair, swearing "that this was the greatest untruth ever imagined, that never had she heard mention of this affair, and that she could well believe that President Jeannin and Giovannini would not bear out a word of it ; that the whole matter, in short, was witness suborned to her hurt." She repeated that "she had never received monies but by express desire of the said Queen Mother," but her judges concluded that "she had disposed of the finances of the King as of her own property, and for the payment of her own affairs."

Léonora Galigaï carried ever upon her own person the key of the strong-room in the house in Rue de Tournon, but she was too wise a woman to hoard her wealth. She cherished dreams of a time when she should leave the Kingdom, and she was well aware of the instability of a fortune amassed by suspicious means. All her wealth she therefore secretly invested outside France, the great banking house of Lumagne, at Lyon, being her agents to place it in Antwerp, Cologne, Frankfort, and especially in Italy. She herself confessed that she had two hundred thousand crowns invested in the Monts de Piété, excellent investments bringing in twenty per cent. The bank of the Grand Duke of Florence had a balance of yet another two hundred thousand to her credit in 1617. In France, where she had bought bonds of Monsieur de Guise, and had negotiations with the Comtesse de Soissons, the Maréchal de Souvre, and the Princesse de Conti, she calculated her investments as worth a hundred thousand. The confiscation of all her possessions decreed by the Parliament of Paris, prior to her condemnation, gave rise to some pretty squabbles in respect of these Italian investments, for the governments of the Peninsula alternatively maintained that such confiscations accrued to the governments within whose jurisdiction the possessions were situate, or else that since French law did not run in Italy, the Concini were to be held dead and intestate, their possessions therefore reverting to their relatives and their sovereign.

Léonora's foreign consignments were by no means limited to money. Numerous large cases figure in the list, and Lumagne stated that he consigned numerous bales and cases to Amsterdam, thence to be forwarded by sea to Leghorn. In the beautiful simplicity of the custom-house declarations, these cases were marked " kitchen utensils only " !

Speculation and corruption not sufficing, the immense fortune of this adventuress was increased by yet other methods. Swindles and actual robbery were specified at the trial. Antonin Mesnillet, " furnisher of tapestries and the storeroom to the King," thus deposed that he had, on one occasion, journeyed into Flanders with his partner Marcellot to bring thence certain tapestries of Lorraine, purchased for the approval of Henry IV. and Marie de Médicis. Unfortunately they did not please their Majesties, but when he would have removed them from the Louvre, Léonora notified him that not one should go out thence unless she should receive as a gratification one " in which was represented the history of Saint Paul." Marcellot further testified that this was not the only occurrence of the like kind which had befallen him, for having once sold to the same lady " nine pieces of tapestry containing the History of Lucrece,

o

fine-woven of silk with gold and silver thread," in value twenty-four thousand livres, Léonora had paid him seventeen thousand and declined to render another sol. He was followed by Decomans and La Planche, " adventurers in the manufacture of the tapestries of this realm," who deposed that the Lady in Waiting had offered her mediation in the matter of a pension of nine thousand crowns promised to them by the sovereign, on condition that they should present her with a tapestry setting forth the history of Solomon. They delivered this, but were duped for their pains, hearing no word more of the matter.

Questioned by her judges in respect of a certain Book of Hours, the property of Catharine de Médicis—a remarkable volume still extant, adorned with miniatures of all the Kings and Queens of France in the sixteenth century—last seen in the royal hands, Léonora denied all knowledge of the precious volume, though all averred that none but herself knew where it might be. Her denial in this matter caused her to be confronted with letters detailing many larcenies of an equally sordid kind, but her denials were so sustained that public opinion presently began to doubt if she were really the culprit. She admitted, under pressure, that she had more than once obtained articles, silverware in particular, at the Queen's expense under pretence that these were " furnished for the service of the Queen Mother," but where Concini alone was involved in such affairs it is admitted that he frequently forged his wife's name in order to rob her of money.

Active and able as was this woman whose existence was passed so darkly at the very heart of the State, this Mistress of the Robes whose mysterious influence embraced, controlled, and regulated such manifold matters, Léonora was a daily victim to a most painful and incurable malady, in the throes of which she would lie shrieking and in contortions for hours together. The symptoms leave us no room in which to doubt that she was a victim of the most advanced hysteria. Servants found her " seated in a chair, bent backward, and in such condition that she was unable to utter a word." It seemed to her " that she was in travail with so great a ball that the pain thereof caught her in the throat until she was as one strangled." Being " as one frenzied with her pains," Léonora adopted her strange habit of seclusion, being liable to seizure at any moment and in any place. A steady gaze was her great horror, and if any one stared at her she was seized with the terrors of sorcery. She became " crossed and melancholic in her humours," averring that her throat was swollen. She supplicated the court which tried her " to consider her infirmity in that she was swollen and in danger to become dropsical ; also that she was ever in fever, which things she did tell us with tears." She spoke of pains " now in her head, her stomach, or her legs." She was considered mad at one time, a maidservant having seen her " wandering all over her chamber at night, stark naked and bearing in her hands little lighted candles." She was found " moribund " one evening, and considered upon the point of death, but she was " walking in the Tuileries " next morning. This malady which declared itself early, almost at the date of her first arrival in France, never left her.

Understanding nothing of her illness, the doctors tried all sorts of devices, " bringing to her two nurses to suckle her," placing her upon a diet of goat's milk—without success. To try a change of air, she would sojourn in one of the Queen's houses at Chaillot, bought her house in Rue de Tournon, and afterwards Lésigny. When the French doctors failed to cure her, she turned to Jewish practitioners, being assured of their greater subtlety— a matter which was bitterly charged against her and Concini at a later date. For this, the Queen's perfumer, Emmanuel Maren, long a resident in Portugal, introduced her to two Portuguese Jews, Montalto and Alvarez, the latter of whom was entrusted with the special care of Léonora, receiving the title of Doctor in Ordinary to the

Queen. He was soon convinced that his patient was "crazy": she cried out that all the world was conspiring to cast a spell upon her, drove away all who would approach her, and thrice slammed the door in the face of her new attendant. On one occasion when her husband was present, she having declared that Alvarez could cure her if he would, Concini followed the doctor into the anteroom, seized him by the throat, and swore to destroy him if he failed to cure his wife within five days. The terrified doctor stammered out that Concini had no right to treat him thus, but the Italian drew a dagger, renewed his threats, and added that he would cast the doctor's body into the moat of the Louvre. The wretched man retired to his house, took to his bed, and was compelled to call a consultation of four fellow doctors—Petit, Duret, Pìètre, and Seguin. At nine the same evening the enraged Marquis forced a way into the room, where were assembled the doctor's wife and seven children, and another lady. Terrified by the dagger which he held under his cloak, Madame Alvarez fell upon her knees, beseeching him to spare her husband's life, and to have compassion on herself and her seven little children. Cursing them all, the Marquis commanded that the doctor should attend at dawn next day, and cure his wife, failing which he assured them that his "credit and power" were sufficient to find Alvarez wherever he might hide, but the appearance of the latter, when he did attend upon the next day but one, was such that Duret ordered him back to bed. Somewhat later, Léonora besought his pardon for these scenes, and that he would kindly consent to continue his care for her, but she none the less drove him from the house on at least two other occasions.

Montalto had more success. Tarrying in Paris on a journey from Flanders to Italy, he was presented to the Lady in Waiting, for whom he prescribed a sufficiently simple treatment. She was to fast and abstain from all but plain diet, to enjoy quiet and complete solitude, not to see her husband for forty days, pray and do alms, and take "certain ordinary medicines" thrice or four times in the week. A sensible benefit resulted, and the delighted Léonora would have had him remain with her. Unfortunately the Government was at this time renewing its measures against the Jews, and Montalto was compelled to withdraw to Venice, until, being in worse health a few years later, Léonora procured his return, and by " permission of the pope " made a royal doctor of this clever, philosophical, and amusing talker. The Lady in Waiting was henceforward unable to live without the society of " this most charming man "; but a long sojourn with her, during which he endeavoured to keep the entire household at a distance, caused a domestic revolt. His death in 1616 was " wept and bewailed " by " the Maréchale in a most extraordinary and violent manner, for she said that her life was taken from her, and she would rather have lost all her goods—her two children no less. She said that she could not possibly survive him for six months, that she would give a hundred thousand crowns to find another doctor but half so wise," and much else in the like kind. Failing to find this " other," Léonora called in all sorts of quacks, causing " to come out of Normandy a certain shoeing smith, who boasted that he could cure the quartan fever." As he was unable to cure her, he assured the Lady in Waiting " that she was undoubtedly bewitched, seeing that he had cured so many others."

Sure as she had always been of this, Léonora was now positive on the point. The doctors could not be expected to help. She invoked God that the devil might thereby be vanquished. Mere churchgoing was not enough : masses must be said for her at the Churches of the Cordeliers, the Carmelites, and the Augustinians. The shrine of Our Lady of Loretto was unfortunately too distant ; she had perforce to content herself with pilgrimages to Chartres and Bonshommes. La Passitea, the holy woman of Siena whom Marie de Médicis had consulted in her youth, was brought from Italy, but although her multitudinous prayers were at first credited with some effect, a relapse followed. " Passitea was not allowed to be seen, being alleged a saint. She was therefore ever covered with a great veil while at her prayers and orisons, nor would she consort with any but a sister of religion, which was her companion."

Certain Ambrosians at the Convent of Saint Nicholas at Nancy were in great repute ; Cardinal de Lorraine had derived much benefit from their prayers. Marie de Médicis, therefore, deputed Monsieur de Champvallon to bring them to her friend, but their two months' sojourn in Paris only injured Léonora's reputation, for their methods of prayer were extraordinary. Conveying relics from the Convent of Saint Victor into Léonora's room, they placed them upon a white napkin between two lighted candles and two torches of white wax ; reconveyed them thence to the Chapelle des Spifames in the Convent of the Augustinians, and there celebrated nones. Having sent Concini to obtain leave from the curé of Saint Sulpice to bring their patient thither at seven in the evening, they remained there for three hours, the doors shut and entry forbidden to all others. Led by curiosity, Marin Poret, sacristan of the church, effected an entry ·despite Concini's close watch, and discovered Léonora upon her knees before the Holy Sacrament, her hair down. One Ambrosian was seated beside the altar, while his fellow read aloud. This continued for the space of two hours. To Poret's questions, Monsieur Lemarie, the curé, replied that " this was to a good end," Concini having explained that his wife was subject to " frenzies," for which cause, the better to avoid the public gaze and to conceal her attacks, the priests had brought her thither at this abnormal hour. The scenes in the Chapelle des Spifames were even more curious. Léonora's Augustinian confessor, Père Roger Girard, obtained leave of entry into the church for the Concini, with closed doors. For greater security, the ceremonies were enacted behind the high

altar, and this was again surrounded by " a screen of
wood." No brother was to approach, and the com-
munity said prayers in the chapter-house. Whether
the Concini arrived at seven in the morning, remaining
to ten or eleven, or came at night, they left their carriage
at a little side door in the cloister, and the vehicle at once
drove home. The Augustinians, though no less mystified
than their brethren of Saint Sulpice, were only able to
remark that the two Ambrosians were " plain as plain
can be," and that they took possession of every stole in
the House. Under plea of ringing for matins, Brother
Ambroise, under-secretary of the convent, finally succeeded in locking himself in the tower, whence he observed the scene. Léonora, apparently " very feeble,"
was laid upon cushions and covered with stoles. Robed
also in stoles, the Ambrosians took up their books and
" made several mental orisons," after which Brother
Ambroise heard " terrible cries," Léonora screaming and
the priests chanting. The entire convent was forthwith
aware that here were magic and sorcery. There was
afterwards a question whether a cock had not been killed
at this moment, but the judges at Léonora's interrogatory could obtain no evidence upon this essential point.
Explain as the accused would that exorcisms and " little
liturgies " peculiar to Italy were all that then took
place ; that she cried out on account of her pain, that
" all this story of the monks was mere foolishness, and
herself had done nothing but pray," she was of course a
witch, and as such no credence could be placed in her
words. This was the terrible charge which was to seal
her fate, and the suspicious scenes in this place, together
with Montalto's imprudent actions, were the chief points
on which her accusers obtained their verdict.

Montalto applied his curious and recondite learning
to discover in certain Hebrew tomes symptoms of his
client's malady, and their cure. Dissatisfied with his
treatment, which he considered insufficiently successful,
he took counsel with his renegade co-religionist, Philippe

Daquin,[1] who had studied with the learned Gaulmin de la Guyonnière, criminal lieutenant of Moulins. Their collaboration unearthed from the Royal Library " certain fair and rare prescriptions, which Montalto caused to be copied by the said Daquin." Three of these Hebrew volumes were unfortunately discovered in Léonora's house in 1617, " the one very small and bound in violet calf, the second in octavo bound in red basane,[2] the third a quarto bound in red basane, much worn." On the evidence of these—the *Arbaah Turim Quatuor Ordines* of Rabbi Jacob Ben Ascher, and the *Synagoga Judaica* of Johann Buxtorf—the judges clearly discovered a plot to use sorcery. Both volumes were imprinted at Hanover in the year 1610, and Montalto had presumably bought them as novelties out of curiosity. Alonzo Lopez, " sometime agent and embarked in business with the Moors," had been his intimate, but could only reply to questions on the point that if Montalto had practised magic it was without his knowledge. " Being extremely secretive, he said, Montalto spoke little of details, and made known his actions to none, no matter who it might be." Charles Garcia, another Aragonese doctor, averred, though with some confusion, that Montalto had made search for clever sorcerers, had inquired of him whether he could not recommend any such, and meeting him later in the Rue Dauphine had informed him that he had found his man in the person of Alonzo Lopez, a Moor. Léonora's household found the Portuguese Jew " a great magician because he made use of Hebrew characters, did things both extraordinary and admirable, and predicted the future by a system of judicial astrology." All this was, of course, hearsay. Léonora herself denied that her physician had ever spoken of magic. Concini probably believed that Montalto's Hebraic studies must inevitably

[1] Daquin's Hebrew name was Mardochée Cresque. Born at Carpentras and having studied in Piedmont, he was baptized at Avignon in 1612, whither he had returned to marry. Passing hence to Paris, he attached himself to the Bishop of Comminges and studied with Gaulmin.

[2] *Basane*, a variety of sheepskin treated with a tan of bark from oak-trees.

lead him into seeking in the Kabala the magical means of curing Léonora; for that wise physician was no sooner dead than he invited Daquin to join himself in further study of the Hebrew texts, adding " that he knew well that the Jews by virtue of their science of the Kabala, or magic, were able to cure the sick, and had power to appease the fury of the demon which troubles and devours men." Daquin hesitated, but Léonora, being one day in a fit of contortions, Concini insisted upon the attempt. First asking Daquin to read a psalm aloud in Hebrew, he suddenly imagined that his wife was pointing her finger at something at the bottom of the bed; he therefore removed hastily into the next room the crucifix hanging above the head curtain of the bed, and likewise a certain amount of the furniture. This done, he caused Daquin, who had no idea of what was taking place, to wash his hands and also to read a fragment of parchment covered with Hebrew characters which Montalto had left. Daquin could make nothing of this, and meanwhile the condition of Léonora underwent no amelioration. The Jew, highly disquieted at the turn matters were taking, begged Concini to excuse him from further attendance, and departed with a fee of ten pistoles, firm in the intention of not resuming such practices. The chief endeavour of the magistrates being to establish Léonora's magical practices, and that these were due to Montalto's influence over her, they subjected the witnesses to a minute cross-examination on this head. Desdiguières was compelled to aver that Montalto had injured the Maréchale's intellect, causing her to abandon her former religious practices. Alonzo Lopez deposed that Léonora's protection of the Jews, and her deliverance of such of them as were in prison, were due to Montalto's instigation. The public, making no distinction between Jews and magicians, and hating the former, were equally enraged against Léonora for her protection of both.

But as there was really nothing in all these details, the judges found themselves compelled to rely upon the fantastic stories reported by more imaginative witnesses. Louis Dubois, who was present at the sack of Léonora's mansion in Rue de Tournon in 1616, swore that he had seen in one of the upper passages in the home of the Concini a bier of gilded wood covered with a pall of black velvet, having for lid a plate of glass, on which was stretched a linen cloth about the size of a handkerchief, and all round this bier were placed gilt wooden candlesticks containing lighted wax candles. Looking through this glass he had perceived a man lying upon his back, his legs crossed, and with black hair and beard ; " he did not know whether that which he saw were wax, flesh, or other matter." The said gallery being closed by three great iron bars, Dubois entered it " through a window by means of a gutter under the eaves." Extraordinary as is this tale of Louis Dubois, that of a Sergeant of For l'Evêque is even less convincing. This man, Melon Charton, deposed that he had found in the courtyard of the hotel in the Rue Tournon books " containing incomprehensible characters and figures within a triangle." " The painters employed to gild the Queen's apartments in the Louvre have seen the said respondent, having in her hands seven or eight little candles crossed one upon the other, wander shivering through the rooms of the palace." Léonora's reply to this was " that she must have been crazy." The judges were also curious to know why the Maréchale " hath no liking for basted meats," to which Léonora replied " that she ate of all alike."

Parchments found in Léonora's lodging were covered with characters round Hebrew letters ; bullets of wax " about the size of the head of a great pin " ; " a little box of pinewood, lozenge-shaped, wherein were three circular pieces of velvet silver-worked, and a fourth in the form of a heart." Having opened these, the astonished magistrates discovered " portions of the *Agnus Dei*, leaves of the olive-tree, of the palm, a fragment of incense and a fragment of crape." André de Lizza vainly endeavoured to explain that the Italians are wont to carry leaves of the olive-tree and palm, which have been blessed, and a portion of the *Agnus Dei*, as charms against thunder— his explanation was not listened to. As a matter of fact, Léonora never practised sorcery ; Alvarez the physician, who had known her well, was vehement in affirming this in his testimony, while Léonora herself indignantly repudiated the ridiculous accusations, saying, " How is it possible for such sinful fables to be invented about me ; " repeating, " May God punish me if I know from whence come these stories of bullets of wax ; may I die if I have seen such nonsense as this story of a coffin." Despite the violent hatred that she earned, public opinion never believed the stories of magic. " No one ever believed that she was a sorcerer," said Bassompierre, " and she never in any way appeared to be one." Léonora protested that " never did she commit in France any action to lend countenance to the opinion that she had practised magic," and that Marie de Médicis " would never have suffered her company so long if she had been as had been alleged."

It was, however, for her subtle intrigues and her continual abuse of the inexplicable power she exercised over the Queen that the friend of Marie de Médicis was condemned in 1617. If, however, her judges did not state their real reasons as openly as they should have done, and even withheld their hand at certain stages of the inquiry, the clear explanation is that through the Queen's friend they struck at something higher and more out of reach. What exactly this was we shall shortly discover.

CHAPTER VII

ARTS AND ARTISTS

ALTHOUGH never artistic in any real sense, a youth spent
in that Pitti Palace, which her father's taste had filled
with such treasures of the arts, had taught Marie de
Médicis to appreciate beautiful things. Her patronage of
the arts has left nothing by which she may claim rank with
other famous and royal collectors : instead, as one who
was naturally somewhat heavy and lacking in intellectual
subtlety, she was a Princess inclined to magnificence—one
who amassed beautiful things with no particular heed
to number or quality, rather than a woman choosing her
possessions with delicate understanding. While, therefore, Marie proved herself a true scion of the Medici in
her desire to play Mæcenas, to build and to patronise
artists, she never evinced a real personal taste except in

the matter of precious stones, of which in early youth she
had become a skilful judge.   Artists, again, did not receive
the fewer commissions from her on account of that trait in
her character which loved to exhibit " our greatness and
liberality " in the gifts which fell from her hand.   Works
of art of every kind—pictures, statuettes, silks, tapestries,
silver plate and ewers, she must have about her, no less than
she must have her coffers filled with brilliants.   With these
the Louvre must teem, and they must be showered upon
the ladies of her household, her friends, acquaintances,
near or distant, strangers sojourning in Paris, the Princes
and Princesses of England, Spain, Germany, and Italy.

For these two reasons Marie had frequent relations
with the artists of her time : either sufficiently explains
why she never influenced their work, and why seventeenth-
century art owed nothing to her patronage.   Buying
artistic objects as a rich woman may buy any other article,
she only once sought to define the style of what she
ordered.   The Luxembourg was to be enriched with a
monument modelled on one in that Pitti Palace so dear
to her sentiment : the artist ignored her and produced a
work essentially French.   For the rest, French art, at the
moment chiefly remarkable for the diversity of its style and
of the influences to which it responded, was original and
cosmopolitan, as yet seeking rather the form in which best
to express itself than developing on fixed lines.

Of the goldsmith and jeweller no Queen of France was
ever so good a patron as was Marie de Médicis, nor need we
wonder when a glance at contemporary Florentine portraits shows us the school in which she had been reared.
The taste was indeed but the fashion of the day and if,
at the Dauphin's baptism at Fontainebleau, in 1606, the
Queen's dress was sewn with " thirty-two thousand pearls
and three thousand diamonds," the *Mercure François*
records the appearance at a reception in the Louvre, six
years later, of Queen Margaret of Navarre and the Comtesse de Soissons " so laden with jewels that the stuff
whereon they were sewn might scarcely be perceived."

Jewels, again, were a favourite form of investment, and this not without reason in an age of such political uncertainties. A little case of jewels, hastily snatched at the moment of flight, may contain the equivalent of much treasure, difficult both to collect and to transport. But Marie de Médicis, in her purchases of jewels, went beyond both reasonable precautions and the needs of a princess.

The Queen's bills, receipts, and records of exchange, would alone furnish us with an almost complete list of the chief goldsmiths and jewellers of the Pont aux Changeurs at this time—Louis de la Haye "at the sign of the Little Mill"; François Dujardin, Pierre Courtois, Jean Subtil, a particularly happy and subtle craftsman; Mathieu Lescot, Claude Bourdon, Claude Couturier, Jean Chancel, Nicolas Chrestien, Paul Louvigny, Paris Turquet, Claude de Cambrai, Martin Bachelier. Most of these opened shops in the Faubourg at the time of the Fair of Saint Germain —their especial season, at which the Queen never failed to buy lavishly for herself and her friends, and also on account of the raffles dear to her heart. The Pont aux Changeurs did not, for all this, enjoy her exclusive patronage. Corneille Roger, a jeweller of Rue Saint Honoré, and François le Prestre, trading in the Gallery of the Palais, knew her well, while a certain clever goldsmith, Luc Roiset of Châtellerault, being mentioned to her, was shortly attached to the household with an honorary title. Again, notwithstanding that there were at this time at least three hundred goldsmiths in Paris, Marie, in her search for the finest diamonds obtainable, had correspondents throughout the Continent—first among all, Hélie Fruit, the Fleming. Georg Langraf, Johannes Pitten, Gilbert Hessing and Hottman in Germany; Nicholas James in England; Andreas Fioravanti in Italy, and Giovanni Castruccio, an Italian resident in Prague, were others. All these, none the less, either maintained an office or a correspondent in Paris. Finally, not content with daily visiting, or receiving in her own apartments, those goldsmiths who reported a new treasure, the Queen retained Nicolas

Roger, one of the cleverest jewellers of the day, who, as titular valet of the chamber, was engaged solely on work for her, and to keep the keys of her treasures no less than to keep those same treasures in repair. This Nicolas Roger, a confidential servant indeed, who gave his advice almost as one of the household, and was more than once employed on semi-political missions, obtained the royal confidence to such a degree that Louis XIII., in 1616, created him first valet of the wardrobe and " keeper of the keys of the jewels," while Henrietta, afterwards Queen of England, desired to have him as her personal " goldsmith-jeweller." This post he actually filled between the years 1622 and 1625; his son, Vincent, succeeded him as valet of the wardrobe in 1631.

Portraits of the earlier part of the seventeenth century show that pearls were the precious stones most in vogue, even excessively so. Diamonds were, however, the grand extravagance which ruined Marie de Médicis—a taste in which the inventory of the gifts taken to England by the Ambassador Sully proves that Henry IV. agreed. Thus, having one day sold to her two diamonds for twenty-one thousand livres, Hélie Fruit returned next day with four others, "cut and fashioned as pendants," for which he asked thirty thousand three hundred. Monsieur Florent d'Argouges, Treasurer General of the Queen's Household, vainly observed that the Chamber of Account would raise the question of such abnormal expenditure upon stones. Marie declined to hear a word, and signed a paper setting forth both that she had commanded the purchase, and her desire that the Chamber should pass the account. It is, perhaps, well to recall that, a year later, the bill for the first pair was still unpaid. Jean Subtil's ingenuity in mounting explains his preference for selling set stones. Among the trifles that he supplied to Marie we find three dozen little gold buttons, set with brilliants, for nineteen hundred and fifty-three livres, a *rivière* for thirteen hundred and fifty, and a diamond nosegay valued at three hundred. Earrings like grapes, an enamelled fillet of flowers for the hair, a nosegay of gold and enamel flowers, frosted with brilliants, were other products of his ingenious taste. The Queen at times suggested ideas for these things, as on one occasion when she supplied two great diamonds as centres for a pair of earrings.

Marie certainly liked variety in her acquisitions, witness another pair of earrings, value two thousand livres, consisting of two great diamonds " set in circlets of brilliants " by Charles Godin ; another pair, garnished and enriched with diamonds, which Paris Turquet delivered to Madame de la Châtaigneraie ; " a fair case of portraits enriched with diamonds," and a ring set with a fine stone, for one of her almoners. Two of her rings are well known. One of these Fioravanti, who offered it, valued at eighteen thousand livres ; Marie was most eager to possess it, but dared not spend so much money, and the jeweller, with an unexpected but doubtless premeditated gesture, presented it to her : it contained a specimen diamond set in fine chased work. The other, bought of Gilbert Hessing in 1613 for one thousand and fifty livres, enshrined the portraits of Louis XIII. and the Infanta of Spain, Anne of Austria, set in gold under a large stone with bevelled facets. Her personal ornaments were extraordinarily rich. Apart from Henry IV.'s famous wedding gift of a collar of pearls valued at one hundred and fifty thousand crowns, Melchior Dagières supplied her with a necklace of eight almond-shaped pendants of graduated diamonds. François le Prestre's bracelet, of gold set with seventy-two brilliants, cost all but one thousand livres, but another—the extra-ordinary whim of a heedless woman—a diamond oval enclosed by four picked stones, with the device *Titani lumina vesper* in the centre, cost three hundred and sixty thousand.

Marie had a taste for crosses. One of these, of gold set with ten great diamonds, cost eighteen thousand livres ; another, more modest, adorned with two hundred and fifty rose diamonds, was the work of Corneille Roger, jeweller of the Rue Saint Honoré. She was equally well furnished with fillets : Jean Subtil supplied one of great gold beads, picked out with brilliants, and finished with a little enamelled cross also set with stones, for three thousand six hundred and thirty livres, while the English jeweller, James, supplied another, twice as rich and twice as costly by reason of the finer quality of the stones in it. Her presents were on the like scale. For the Princess of Mantua, Pierre Courtois supplied her with a magnificent " ensign "—a pendant for the neck—formed of a ruby surrounded with brilliants, for fourteen thousand four hundred livres ; for her daughter, the Princess of Spain, with a golden chain encrusted with a hundred little stones, and for a Castilian gentleman, returning to Spain, a watch in a gold case set with brilliants. Watches of this kind were much to her taste, and she herself owned several, on golden chains pointed with diamonds. A set of works from Blois were enclosed for her, by Pierre Courtois, in an oval case for two thousand one hundred livres. " Repeaters " were, at this time, a speciality of the craftsmen of Blois, and Marie's chosen watchmaker in that city, Salomon Chesnon, supplied her with " a repeating movement to fit a golden box crusted with stones," for one hundred and eighty livres. Nicolas Norry, also of Blois, " by reason of his great experience in the art," shared with this Chesnon the honour of the title " Watchmaker to the Queen."

The Queen's craze for diamonds was not satiated by the wares of professional dealers, for no sooner did she hear of a fine stone than its possessor, whoever he might be, was pestered to sell at any price. Jean André Lumagne, the banker, was thus driven to sell to the Queen, for eighteen thousand livres, a fine cut stone in the year 1612 : in 1614 he obtained payment of half this sum, but only after endless applications. Sebastian Zamet, having sold Marie a fine brilliant for seventy-five thousand livres in 1605, was compelled ten years later to hand over to her a second, valued at fifteen thousand. This was too much for the King and his Chamber of Account, but on coming into power the Queen compelled the Treasury to conclude the

P

purchase. More than once she stooped low in order to secure a desired treasure. Francis de Grimberg, a German gentleman in the suite of Archduke Maximilian of Austria, owned two diamond rings which excited her cupidity, and although she had not a crown in hand, the Queen agreed to purchase the pair for twenty-eight thousand eight hundred livres. Grimberg, doubting her ability to pay for them, Marie—Queen Regent as she then was—was constrained to " command " Messieurs Barbin and Florent d'Argouges, the Intendant General and the Treasurer General of her Household, personally to " back her bill." In this connection, a request of the States-General of 1614 is distinctly amusing : " That all recovery at law be withheld from merchants who have sold jewels or goldsmith's work on credit, sales between merchants excepted, and that it be forbidden to all persons, unless by especial exemption by your Majesty, to wear pearls, diamonds, or other jewels ! "

The matter of Monsieur Harlay de Sancy's diamonds, the " Sancy " stone in particular, forms an interesting chapter in the history of the Crown jewels. De Harlay, deeply in debt and seeking a market for his stones throughout Europe, sold one to the King of England for one hundred and ninety-two thousand livres. Sully took one at twenty-five thousand, and Marie de Médicis a third for three times this amount. Her desire to obtain " the Sancy " was shared by the King, but he was too cautious to pay the price, and although this diamond was afterwards acquired by a successor on the throne, Marie had to suffer the mortification of realising that it was beyond her means.

Besides diamonds the Queen bought almost any other jewels. Although, as already said, she had no great taste for pearls, Fioravanti sold her a fine pair of round specimens for twelve hundred livres in 1614, and Martin Bachelier six more for eighteen hundred. Castruccio, a Florentine of Prague, " supplied three square pictures of diverse sizes, fashioned with fine stones inlaid, like Bohemian jasper, to represent figures in landscapes." Nicolas Roger sold her a fine ruby in a ring for six hundred, Jean Pitten mounted ten emeralds on a golden cross, and Jean Subtil a remarkable sapphire in a ring. Hearing that turquoises were readily procurable in Turkey, she ordered Baron de Salignac, Ambassador at Constantinople, to send "two or three pounds' weight in the rough " for chains and circlets. A cut jacinth from Germany was sold to her for two hundred and forty livres. Agates were in high favour at this time and the Queen bought agate vases enriched with gold, and, of Mathieu Lescot, a chain of seventy-one agate beads linked together with gold.

The Queen's desire to possess the works of the goldsmith was only less acute than her desire for jewels. The Béarnese present of a golden cow, with inscriptions in Latin and the language of that country, valued at twelve thousand livres, did not, perhaps, excite her unduly. Her own commissions to the goldsmiths were of a different kind. Pierre Lepoivre was to supply a finely chiselled statuette of Saint Anne, and elegant little boxes of silver. Of Jean Chancel and Nicolas Chrétien, who had their stall every year at the Fair of Saint Germain, and were her favourite workers, she ordered a Veronica of gold and enamels, a statuette of Saint Jerome of the same to serve as a reliquary, a ewer of worked silver and dishes for fruit of pierced silver. Nicolas Roger, more goldsmith than jeweller, seems to have enjoyed the best of her patronage to judge from a multiplicity of bills and complaints at their non-payment. Besides chains, rings, and reliquaries, he furnished such trifles as three hundred silver soldiers for the little King, a little service of silver, other gifts for the King's brother, the Duc d'Orléans, candlesticks of silver gilt and silver andirons. An artist of many talents and much taste, his splendid ingenuity is well displayed in the account for over thirty unpaid items presented in 1612, constantly ordered to be settled, and still open a year later. Worse than all, Marie borrowed from him hard cash in order to pay other debtors. His work would certainly repay study could we identify it. The andirons mentioned above cost eight thousand six hundred and nine livres, while more interesting still would be the splendid golden chain, cost two thousand eight hundred and thirty-five livres, weight ten marks and one ounce, to which was attached a medal bearing the portraits of Marie de Médicis and Louis XIII. But neither this nor any other work by Roger has come down to us.

Madame Hotmann supplied the Queen with a great quantity of silver plate—gold plate also for her own use—for which, in 1615, one payment only amounted to ten thousand seven hundred livres. Hotmann does not, on the whole, seem to have lost by her dealings with the Queen. Thus, in the matter of a certain exchange, Marie, for over three hundred and forty-six marks in weight of old silver, plus seven thousand six hundred and seventy livres in cash, obtained new silver to the weight of only four hundred and sixteen marks. The list of her purchases might, indeed, be extended almost indefinitely, and this in the matter of trifles adorned with imitation pearls no less than more genuine articles. The Queen's desire, whenever and wherever possible, to embellish all her possessions with diamonds remains, however, the prime indication of her tastes.

The opening years of the seventeenth century, and particularly the reign of Louis XIII., are marked by a certain revival in art and architecture, as may be seen by the Supplement, published in 1639, to Du Breuil's *Théâtre des Antiquités de Paris*, first issued in 1610. To this movement the Queen contributed, first by subventions, later by herself becoming a builder. Her seven years of real power, 1610–1617, were too troubled for her to touch the Louvre on which Henry IV. had spent so much, or she might have carried out his great design of raising the ground between the Tuileries and this palace, and throwing out wings until they joined on either side of this space. She had not, indeed, any real leisure to spend upon her architects except prior to Ravaillac's crime and after the murder of Concini and her own fall from power. An exception was the tomb of Henry IV. at Saint Denis begun by Métezeau in 1613 and still incomplete in 1618.

Her chief claim to remembrance rests on the fact that she attached to her person the most illustrious architect of the age, Salomon de Brosse, who towards the close of the year 1608, received the title of " Architect and Overseer of Buildings to the King and Queen." Long family traditions had prepared the future creator of the palace of the Luxembourg for his career of grand achievements. After an education at Verneuil-sur-Oise amid the plans of the splendid château which was being constructed there by his uncle Jacques Androuet du Cerceau and his father Jean, the former had introduced him as his successor into the royal household. In 1613 Marie de Médicis caused him to build the aqueduct of Arcueil in order to collect the waters of Rongis and provide Paris with drinking water, while at the same time putting an end to the disastrous floods of the Bièvre. Later she entrusted him with the reconstruction of the château of Montceaux-en-Brie.

This château, the work of Primatice, had been built by Catharine de Médicis, who was fond of it and converted it into a palatial residence. In 1596 Henry IV. bought it when the estate of Catharine was distrained and put up for sale, and presented it with royal lavishness to Gabrielle d'Estrées. She furnished it with great magnificence, as the inventory taken on her death bears witness. Gabrielle once dead, Henry IV. regained the estate in consideration of a payment to the heirs of the Marquise, and removed the furniture. Then Marie de Médicis became Queen of France, and when, on September 27, 1601, she gave birth to the Dauphin, the future Louis XIII., the royal father in his happiness made her a present of Montceaux. This edifice of Primatice was greatly to Marie's taste, but despite its dimensions, with the exception of a few royal apartments, it was not, as Bassompierre says, habitable, at least for a numerous company. The Queen's first care was to furnish it. When money failed, Henry IV. had recourse to shifts. He created new councillors in the Parlements of the kingdom. Marie, meanwhile, loving Montceaux from the very first, set to work to adorn it with all splendour. After procuring costly tapestries and furniture, she turned her attention from the year 1602 to the architects and masons who were to restore and complete the palace.

The directors of the work were the Cerceaus, the royal architects, but their precise share in the restorations is not now easily determined as the château has disappeared. They seem to have repaired it without modifying the general design, and to have added detached buildings on the demesne, which Marie had increased by the purchase of one hundred and thirty acres. The courtyard, the captain's quarters, and the terraces were rebuilt ; a deep moat was dug between the house and the courtyard, and the outbuildings were repaired. In 1602 Salomon de Brosse, who had taken charge of the work, constructed a tennis court, an indispensable adjunct in the reign of Henry IV. to every prince's residence, and even to every gentleman's. He built, moreover, on the home farm, huge stables capable of receiving the fifty or sixty horses of the Queen's establishment, restored the chapel of the lower court, and built a new chapel in the château.

The Queen's expenditure at Montceaux was heavy. The budget of 1612 provided thirty thousand livres for the work and a hundred thousand must have been spent between 1615 and 1617, the annual expenditure being approximately the same as in 1612. Moreover, the Queen's income was constantly exceeded and her Treasurer General was forced to advance money out of his own pocket. Salomon de Brosse proceeded vigorously. At the end of one year, 1610, Marie de Médicis was able to write to Queen Marguerite : " You will find such changes at Montceaux since you have been there that you will no longer recognise it." Yet the changes appear to have consisted for the most part in restorations and the ancient residence remained substantially the same. To the monotonous work of restoration de Brosse apparently devoted all his time, and we see him, with the honourable title of Sieur de Brosse, supervisor of buildings to Her Majesty, passing his days in the verification of carpenters' and masons' accounts. He was, says the Queen in her memoranda of expenses, particularly fond of Montceaux.[1]

The Queen came to the château and resided there for weeks at a time. She maintained there a captain, a kind of manager, M. Guillaume du Bois de Condren, who had held the same office under Gabrielle d'Estrées. He was replaced by Bassompierre in 1616. The captain was subordinate to the superintendent of buildings. There is a list of the staff of the château, which was exempt from the *taille*. During the crisis of 1614 the inhabitants of the town took refuge with their movables in the château.

Marie passed her time, surrounded by her little court, in making good cheer, playing for high stakes, and devising comedies and ballets. The gardens, in which she loved to walk, had been designed in 1595 by Claude Mollet, and were kept up by her gardeners, Louis de Limoges, Jean Marchant, and Santi Vallerani. The last was an Italian, brought to France in her suite, to whom on one occasion she gave as a marriage-gift a sufficient sum to enable him to build a mill. Marie was lavish of invitations to her friends to visit her. She took a lively interest in the fences she was building, in the plants she was cultivating, and even had seeds sent from Florence for her use. She had a menagerie there, and, in short, Montceaux was her favourite residence, the scene of her experiments in amateur estate-management.

She longed to have other such estates. The quiet of Montceaux doubtless not satisfying her, she had, in 1614, thought of buying the château of Anet, " in order to

---

[1] Th. Lhuillier is in error when he says that Salomon de Brosse's name appears at Montceaux for the first time in 1615. M. Palustre is even more in error when he writes that he did nothing there. In the chapel which he built, de Brosse placed twelve white marble pillars bought in Italy, with bases and capitals complete, and conveyed in boxes to Rouen by sea, and thence up the Seine to their destination on the boat of "Toussaint Dieppedalle, carrier."

possess some place a little removed from the noise and bustle of Paris, whither I may withdraw when my affairs will permit." Was it a question of temporary residence or was she really thinking of abdication ? The château of Anet and the barony of Ivry were then for sale by auction ; hostile bidders appeared. She asked Mademoiselle d'Aumale, who had the right of hereditary redemption over the estates, to resign them to her, but nothing came of the matter.

But after the death of Queen Marguerite she bought the house called *l'Olympe* at Issy, with the parks, gardens, and other hereditaments and appurtenances, situated in the village of Issy, which belonged to the late Queen. Marguerite had purchased them in 1606 from the goldsmith Roger de la Haye, in order to escape from Paris, where the plague was raging. It was in May 1615 that Marie secured the estate. It was a plaything for her ; she used to arrive in a coach or on horseback, lunch, hunt, and return in the evening. Being but the end of a short excursion which could be made easily in a few hours, the upkeep of this estate cost little, three hundred livres a year. The old watchman and caretaker, Etienne de Bray de la Haye, who had been there in the time of Marguerite, looked after the house and took care of the swans in the parks. It does not appear that the Queen did any building here, and we do not know whether or not the paintings still to be seen on the walls a few years ago were ordered by her. Marie had also a château at Chaillot, which we have already had occasion to mention.

The most important architectural enterprise undertaken by the Queen was, of course, the building of the Luxembourg. Upon her arrival in Paris in 1601, Marie de Médicis established herself first in the Hôtel de Gondi, situated in the upper part of the Faubourg Saint Germain des Prés, a quarter " very agreeable," say the contemporary writers, " by reason of the conjunction of vast gardens and vast palaces, which unite the pleasures of the city to those of the country." The house of M. de Gondi was reputed to be the most beautiful in Paris after the Louvre, and there it was that the King lodged foreign princes and ambassadors extraordinary, the latter being the result of the fact that the Gondis were hereditary introducers of ambassadors. Marie de Médicis was well pleased with the place and frequently returned there for recreation. After Henry IV.'s death, the Prince de Condé, who had taken a fancy to the place, asked and obtained from the Queen-regent, then under the necessity of conciliating her nobles, the sale or grant of the hotel to him.

To provide for the future accommodation of ambassadors, the Queen now cast her eye on a house in the immediate neighbourhood, that of the Duke of Luxembourg, which was in the Rue Vaugirard, opposite the Rue Garancière, a modern mansion of considerable size, dating from the sixteenth century. The Queen had first thought of securing a residence in the Place Royale for the entertainment of ambassadors, and, in August 1610, the first request to lodge an envoy was addressed to M. de Luxembourg. The latter, who was surnamed de Piney, had been Ambassador at Rome. He was now persuaded to rent his house to the Queen, who afterwards often visited it, and liked it so well that in 1611 she bought it for her own use. The contract of sale was signed on September 27, and the price is variously estimated at ninety thousand livres, forty thousand crowns—by Bassompierre—and eighty thousand crowns. Appreciating the healthiness of the palace in its airy and lofty position, she used it for her children, whom she sent to the Rue Vaugirard with their attendants whenever they were ill. Unfortunately the house was inadequate in size for these requirements, and it was necessary to rent small and unhealthy rooms in the neighbourhood.

What followed may thus have been the result of a desire for more room, or on the other hand it may be conjectured that Marie de Médicis foreseeing the majority of Louis XIII., or rather the day when his eventual marriage would force her to surrender her tenancy of the

Louvre in favour of the Queen-regnant, desired to have in Paris a dwelling worthy of herself and quite her own.

One thing is certain ; ever since 1611 she had been contemplating the erection of a vast palace on the site of the old Hôtel de Luxembourg. At the same time, either to recall the memories of her youth, or owing to some special admiration for the architectural details of the Pitti, she had conceived the idea of reproducing this Florentine palace in the Faubourg Saint Germain des Prés. She wrote to her aunt, the Grand Duchess of Tuscany, under date October 6, 1611, to send her " the complete plan with elevations and perspectives." The Florentine envoy, Matteo Botti, had already told Vinta of the Queen's intentions, and so great was her impatience in this matter that (October 14) she even sent Clément Métezeau, then thirty years of age, to prepare personally " the designs of the Pitti Palace."

Meantime she bought up several pieces of property in the neighbourhood of her Hôtel de Luxembourg, including the house of Champrenart, at the foot of the Rue de Tournon, and it was on the site of this that the "Queen-mother's Palace " was really built. She purchased also the house bearing the sign " A la ville de Bresse," a farm belonging to the Paris hospital, which cost five thousand livres, and other property. These purchases were not all effected with ease, as appears from the remonstrance addressed to the Queen by Chartreux. For elms and cypresses with which to make the alleys and clumps, in the fashionable " quincunx " pattern, in the gardens, designed by Nicolas Descamps—appointed on April 6, 1612, with the style of "Gardener in ordinary for the gardens and parterres of my residence and palace of the Luxembourg "—Marie sent everywhere—to Doullens, Orleans, Clermont.

Four years passed before her plans could be executed ; the particular cause of delay being the want of funds. It has long been asserted that the creator of the Luxembourg was Jacques de Brosse, but it was in fact Salomon de Brosse, architect to the Queen since 1608, who undertook the great work upon a formal contract concluded between Marie de Médicis and himself. It has been said also, and is still said, that Salomon conceived the plan of the Luxembourg under the inspiration of the Pitti Palace, but we have just seen the reason for this belief, in Marie's original intention of constructing a replica of the Pitti in Paris. In point of fact, the architect considered neither the plan brought back by Métezeau nor the ideas of his mistress. Not a trace of the Pitti is to be found in the Luxembourg, but if we compare the views of the château of Verneuil with those of the Luxembourg, we are struck by the similarity of the two buildings. Salomon de Brosse was inspired by the structure produced by his uncle Androuet du Cerceau, the building on which his father had laboured and which he himself during his youth at Verneuil had had continually before his eyes. Verneuil is a French work, and no less so is the Luxembourg. All the features in which Italian influence has been thought to appear—cupola and embossment, for example—are common in French buildings of the sixteenth century. Good architect and skilful workman though he was, Salomon de Brosse was but the follower, and a follower, too, not free from faults, of the French artists who had preceded him.[1]

When the plans of the Luxembourg were complete and Pierre le Muet had executed "the model and relief-plan of the buildings," Marie laid the corner-stone of the palace on April 2, 1615. Then the work began under the direction of the masons Gamard and Biterne, the carpenter Scellier, and the tiler Regnauld. The sculptor Guillaume Berthelot undertook to make the statues destined for the façades.[2]

Owing to political troubles, but still more lack of

[1] There are grounds for thinking that Métezeau brought back from Florence a plan based on the Pitti, but that this was rejected in favour of de Brosse's design. It seems that de Brosse, on Marie's invitation, examined the mansion of Rambouillet.

[2] Pierre le Muet, "architect to the King," received three hundred livres for his work. When she laid the first stone, Marie placed three medals engraved by Régnier in the foundations. Salomon de Brosse removed from the Rue Vieux-Augustins to the Rue Vaugirard. The materials from the chapel of the Valois at Saint-Denis were used for the Luxembourg.

money, the work progressed rather slowly. The *Topo-graphie historique du vieux Paris* says that the Luxembourg was almost finished in 1620, but the contrary is proved by the report of " the examination and regulation of the work on the Luxembourg Palace, begun June 23, 1623, in virtue of an order agreed upon between the attorney general of the Queen-mother and the directing architect of the said buildings, Salomon de Brosse." This document shows that at this time the main building which was roofed over had only its four bare walls, while one of the wings was not begun, and yet the total expense already amounted to seven hundred thousand one hundred and thirty livres, six sous, six deniers. It was not until a later date that Marie de Médicis was able to resume and complete the structure.

In the Queen's relations with painters, the idea of art for art's sake, as we conceive it nowadays, hardly appears. What the princess desires is a picture which shall be a fitting object of presentation ; if it is a portrait, the like-ness must be conspicuous ; if a *scène de genre* or religious piece for convent or chapel, it must be in keeping. Occa-sionally but rarely, she is pleased to desire that the picture be " very pretty and well done," but her desires on such subjects are always vaguely expressed. It is, however, a matter of pride with her to give her commissions invariably to the best artists of the day.

Jacob Bunel, the "painter valet de chambre " of the King, who was employed on the small gallery—our gallery d'Apollon—had already been employed by Henry when he was King of Navarre. He had been commissioned to paint the portraits of the Cardinal d'Armagnac, de Vaudoré, Saint-Gelais, and we have already seen that Concini had com-manded from him a duplicate of his portrait of Henry IV. in the little gallery of the Louvre. In 1612, when he ranked among the celebrities of the hour, he painted, by the express command of the Queen, " a great picture, on canvas," representing the Annunciation, with life-sized figures, the whole eight feet high and six wide, with an open heaven whence descends the Holy Spirit in the form of a dove, and clouds on which are portrayed a number of small angels. This picture, valued at six hundred livres by M. Donon, Comptroller General of the royal buildings, was presented to the Capuchin monastery at Paris.

Except for Bunel, Marie de Médicis seldom employed the "painters in ordinary to the King," such as Marin le Bourgeois and Ambroise Dubois, author of the paintings in the oval room at Fontainebleau, though the latter received in 1606 the title of "first painter to the Queen." Marie had artists of her own, whom she admitted to her household with definite titles and functions. Such were Claude Bourcier, Jacques Berthelot, François Pulinat, and Louis Beaubrun, the last a member of that dynasty of court-painters which began with Mathieu and Claude Beaubrun, valets to Henry IV. as early as 1589, and which was continued in the persons of Henri and Charles Beaubrun into the reigns of Louis XIII. and XIV. Pierre Courtois received the title of "painter and enameller in ordinary to the Queen" and later became a valet de chambre with a pension of ten livres. But the Queen sought also for foreigners, such as David Baudringhien, "a Hollander by birth," whose "great skill in his art she realised from the painting which he had executed by her command and in her service." These dependants rank as "painters in ordinary." Finally she employed English artists, such as Peter Oliver, among other commissions, for seven portraits in 1611, for which the payments were forty-five livres apiece.

It was, indeed, portraits that Marie de Médicis had greatest pleasure in ordering. They were a fashion of the day, and were exchanged almost annually, especially with the English court and the princely houses of Italy. In 1603 the portrait of Marie was sent to London, in 1604 another was entrusted to the care of the ambassador, M. de Beaumont, in 1605 the Queen of England presented her own, and Marie replies that she will shortly send by way of acknowledgment a new portrait of herself, in addition to those of her husband and children, when the latter shall have been completed. Generally group portraits of the entire family are sent. Full-length and bust pictures, simple miniatures, all kinds indeed, abound. In 1606 Concini on a journey to Italy takes with him a box in which, as Marie writes to her cousin, "are our portraits, which I send you to refresh your remembrance of us."

Quite a long list of portraits of Marie de Médicis might be made, for few queens have sat more often to the painter. Though very few artists of merit have failed to leave us pictures of this Queen, one of the most remarkable, François Porbus, whose precise and careful work furnishes the student of faces with priceless documents, chanced— with the exception of a brief period in 1606—not to be employed until 1610, the year in which he settled definitely in Paris, and at this date financial and political troubles were beginning to restrain Marie's passion for portraits.

In addition to the very fine portrait painted in 1606, when Porbus came from Mantua, where he had been painter to the Duke, in the train of the Duchess on the occasion of the Dauphin's baptism, the accounts furnish the date of but few of his pictures of Marie. On December 31, 1616, he received one thousand six hundred and thirty-five livres for six portraits, of which four represented the Queen-mother. Again, on December 17, 1617, Marie de Médicis orders that one thousand five hundred livres be paid to François Porbus, painter in the service of the King, "our most honoured lord and son, for three portraits of ourself, one of large size to send to our very dear daughter, the Princess of Spain, and a small one to be placed in a locket."

Numerous also were the Queen's portraits of her children ; the little princes and princesses reared in the château of Saint Germain were depicted repeatedly and in every known manner. Oil-paintings, pastels, crayons, wax, bronze, and clay statues, and medallions all abound.

Portraits of the Dauphin were, of course, especially plentiful, and were sent by the royal family into all quarters. Between 1602 and 1611, for instance, we note the names of the artists so employed. On January 16, 1602, when the child was three and a half months old, Marie commissioned Charles Decourt, "painter to the King," to "execute a crayon drawing" of Louis, to be sent to the Grand Duchess at Florence. A month later a Flemish artist, whose name is unknown, is called on for another portrait, and after the lapse of one month more, on March 27, François Quesnel, the celebrated artist whose excellent designs are still preserved, receives instructions to "draw the Dauphin at full length" for the Duke of Mantua. Charles Decourt begins a second crayon portrait on July 25, and yet another picture by an unknown artist is required on November 7.

In one year, then, Marie de Médicis had five portraits of her son made, and she continued to do this, though less often, in the following years. In her letters accompanying canvases or sketches, the Queen takes little heed of the artist, and her judgment of the work is brief. "Although it appears to me," she writes to the Duke of Mantua, concerning a picture, "that the painter has made the face a little swollen and puffed out, and that he (the Dauphin) is more beautiful than this portrait, I shall not fail to send it to Mantua as being a tolerable likeness." The artist for her was but an artisan, and this although in 1604 he bears the name Dumonstier, Daniel Dumonstier, son of Côme, the former valet of Henry III., and soon he will be a Dupré or Porbus.

In 1604, also, Charles Martin paints the child's portrait, as do Decourt and a certain Paolo, who is hard to identify, and who "models him in wax," evidently with a view to sculpture, the destination of the work being still Italy. Claude Mallery and Guillaume Dupré were also engaged. Dupré's fine medals of the royal family are well known. This artist did not, however, confine himself to medals. On September 21, 1604, he came to Fontaine-bleau to take the likeness of the Dauphin for reproduction in a statuette of enamelled porcelain. On March 10, 1605, he returned, and this time modelled the prince in wax for the purpose of making a small statue in bronze, which was also done by another statuary, a Fleming, resident at Florence—possibly Pierre Franqueville. In 1606 Marie de Médicis had her son's portrait painted once more by Charles Martin, and later by the child's drawing-master, Fréminet ; in August by Porbus himself. The next year Decourt undertakes another crayon, while Dupré at Fontainebleau is at work upon a new medallion.

On Friday, February 11, 1611, Jean Héroard wrote in his journal, "At three in the afternoon, Porbus, a Fleming, an excellent painter, made a full-length drawing of him" (the Dauphin). Porbus, then forty-one years old, was in his prime, and the portrait executed on this occasion, which is now in the Uffizi at Florence, is one of the best likenesses of the prince.

Though they were not so well treated as their brother the Dauphin, the other children of Marie de Médicis were quite as often painted, and especially Elizabeth, the eldest daughter. Ambassadors, and especially M. de Bressieux, ambassador to London, prided themselves on taking with them, on their return to their posts, portraits of their sovereigns as presents to the Courts to which they were accredited. Thus in 1609, M. de Bressieux suggested to Marie the idea of having a portrait of Elizabeth painted for the English Court, and the Queen gave her consent. Porbus painted this princess in 1611, at the same time as he painted Louis XIII. A letter from the Queen-regent to Madame de Monglat, governess of the children at Saint Germain, informs us that the Grand Duke of Tuscany had ordered this particular painting through his envoy, the Marquis de Botti. The Flemish painter's portrait of Elizabeth is now in the Uffizi at Florence, and, as is the case with the portrait of Louis XIII., displays the exact skill of the artist, who, though lacking the ability of a Van Dyck or the breadth of a Rubens, had the excellent technical qualities of a worker of the first rank. The Archduke and Archduchess, regents of Flanders, asked for the portrait of Elizabeth in the same way in 1611.

It is certain that many other pictures were commanded
by the Queen. Those which have been mentioned will be
enough to illustrate the zeal and taste of Marie de Médicis.

This taste was equally displayed in respect of another
form of art, tapestry. This was in great request at the
period. "We see," writes the tapestry - maker, Pierre
Dupont, in his *Stromatourgie*, "that every one has in his
house at least a small tapestried chamber." Gorgeous
hangings, pieces of the highest finish, often worked with
silken threads and with gold, displaying biblical scenes or
mythological incidents, with figures of more than life size,
splendidly adorned the guest-rooms of the royal palaces.
The great hall of the Louvre, on the first floor, which had
a ceiling adorned with sculpture and carvings, was hung
with tapestries. The bedchambers of the princes were
usually decorated in the same way, and when the King, the
Queen, or their children went on a journey the decorations
of their rooms were borne in carriages with them, as well as
the bed in sections and the necessary furniture, in order to
adorn in a homelike manner the rooms of all of them.
Marie de Médicis, when she caused her apartments at the
Louvre to be refurnished, had preferred to place panels of
carved and painted wood on the walls. But she managed
to introduce tapestries there, and had many in her other
houses. She supported Henry IV.'s efforts for the development of this industry, which had hitherto been
essentially Flemish. He had introduced the tapestries of
the north and had played no small part in the growth of
the firm of the Faubourg Saint Marcel, the first Gobelins.
He had assisted the Dubourgs, "designers of excellent
pieces, which were adorned with gold and silver thread,
gold and silver cloth, gold and silver canvas, and gold
fringes of all sorts." Marie de Médicis granted a pension
of nine thousand crowns to Marc Decomans and François
de la Planche, "masters of the manufacture of tapestries in
the Flemish manner in this kingdom," whose fortunes in the
Faubourg Saint Germain have been related by M. Guiffrey,
and who hold so prominent a place in the history of

tapestry in France at the beginning of the seventeenth century. It is true that the embarrassed finances of the Queen resulted in the irregular payment of this pension, but the two owed much to Marie, who was a frequent customer of theirs.

She kept in constant employment in her household, under the title of " tapestry-maker to the Queen," a certain Antoine Mesnillet, who was commissioned, as we have already seen, to find tapestries for her. Did he make them himself ? In any case he travelled constantly in search of rare tapestries which were announced as being for sale, and he brought them to the Louvre where the King and Queen selected from them. Mesnillet also bought and sold on his own account, and Decomans and la Planche also bought tapestries for their own collection. Louis XIII. continued to the tapestry-makers the protection granted to them by his father ; in 1624 Mesnillet was tapestry-maker to this king. In order to encourage the industry in France, the importation of foreign tapestry had been forbidden by Henry IV.

Marie de Médicis occasionally appears in her correspondence as busied about the transference of tapestries from one château to another ; to her they were precious treasures, and when she removed one from one residence, she felt bound to give a discharge under her own hand to the caretaker or governor of the place whence the piece was taken. So well did she realise the value of these goods that when she got up a small fête at Saint Germain, on the occasion of a comedy to amuse her children, she wrote to the superintendent of buildings that he should remove the valuable tapestries which were in the hall, and on account of the danger from accident or from fire, he should use only common pieces taken from the lumber-room. At this time, and the detail is significant, this superintendent —the Duc de Sully, who succeeded M. de Sancy and was succeeded by M. de Fourcy—bore the title of "Superintendent and Comptroller of the Buildings and Tapestries." There are interesting signs of the value of these rich tapestries at this period and of the rivalry for their possession in the letters of the Nuncio Bentivoglio.

Works of sculpture do not appear to have interested Marie de Médicis to the same extent, though, as was the case in all other departments of art, she did not wish to be thought indifferent. We can only mention in passing the wood-carver whom she summoned to her Cabinet to let her see him make carvings in wood such as chaplets of Saint Francis, which she gave away to the princesses and to her ladies. But just as she took pleasure in sending portraits of members of her family abroad, so, though in smaller numbers, she sent busts and statuettes. We have alluded to the statuettes of her son, the Dauphin, which were executed at her orders in enamelled china, bronze, or gold. In the same way she ordered busts of Henry IV., especially directly after his death, and sent them to her Italian relatives by the makers themselves. It is unfortunate that at this time the secretary who wrote the Queen's letters in most cases neglects to give the name of the artist, but contents himself with calling him " very excellent at his art." Many other sculptured figures were ordered by Marie for presentation to convents. In 1611, the " master sculptors," Nicolas de Cambrai and Georges Allemant, received one thousand four hundred and seventy livres from her " for making and supplying ten wood figures, which they carved and adorned by our orders," says Marie de Médicis, " that is to say, two large and eight moderately sized which we have given and presented to the Church of the Order of Saint Bernard in the Faubourg of Saint Honoré in this city to ornament and decorate it."

The sculptor who enjoyed the highest and most constant favour from her was Pierre de Franqueville, a Fleming, born at Cambrai, who went to Italy and was there trained under John of Bologna, a member of the Florentine academy of sculpture. He had attracted the attention of Henry IV., who had summoned him to his side and lodged him in the Louvre and employed him. Marie de Médicis shared her husband's high opinion of this artist, and commanded a number of works from him, notably an equestrian statue in bronze of the Dauphin, which is now at Florence, and her interest in him bordered on tyranny. When Franqueville wished to go to Italy in 1607, the Queen would only give him leave on his declaration that he wished to " settle some personal business." He left his wife and children with her, but even so in her letter of recommendation for him to the Grand Duke of Tuscany, Marie added that he was to be sure " to give strict orders to Franqueville to return as quickly as possible in order that he may get back to work on the matters which he has begun." If any one offered the Queen a statue to buy, and knowing her tastes they offered every kind of works of art, it was Franqueville who was instructed to go to inspect the article. A case in point was the statue of the Virgin in marble which the nephew of M. de Souvré, Baron de la Flotte, had in one of his houses, called Bellefille, near Le Mans, and which he offered to Marie as " a rare article, excellent in make and the work of a very distinguished person." Franqueville went to see if it was really worth the great reputation which attached to it.

No one was better able to induce the Queen to appreciate the bronze statuettes of John of Bologna, his master, which Cosimo, Grand Duke of Florence, sent in 1614 for her and her son. On this occasion there came to Paris with Pesciolini, who brought these statuettes, some Florentine artists, whom Marie received graciously and to whom she gave large presents.

Florence, John of Bologna, and Franqueville, these three names are associated in the most important episode in the relations between Marie de Médicis and the sculptors of the period—the history of the equestrian statue of Henry IV. at the Pont-Neuf.

The Pont-Neuf, projected in 1577, was carried forward by Henry III. to the extent of completing the arches over the small arm of the Seine and the sinking in the main stream of piles of great size. It had been resumed by

Henry IV., who had carried it so far, under the direction of Guillaume Marchand, that in 1604 the public were able to cross the river. Quays were built, the Samaritaine, a force-pump surmounted by a clock, the work of the Fleming Lintlaer, was set up. Yet there was certainly still more to be done, since the municipality of Paris still paid, in 1607, fifteen thousand five hundred livres as a tax for the completion of the bridge.

It was in 1604 or 1605 that Marie de Médicis, in order to finish the bridge from the artistic standpoint, thought of presenting to the city of Paris an equestrian statue of Henry IV., to be placed at the end of the Ile de la Cité, on the open ground which divided the two sections of the bridge. The idea originated in Italy; at Florence the Grand Duke Ferdinand had caused a bronze statue of himself on horseback to be made by John of Bologna, and had erected it in the Piazza della Signoria. Marie declared her project to her uncle Ferdinand, who suggested to her the employment of the same artist.

The Queen eagerly embraced the suggestion. Then, feeling doubts, she wrote to the Grand Duke that John was very old—he was actually eighty-one—that he would work slowly, and she might never see the work completed if it was entrusted to him. However, as she was very anxious that the statue which she intended " to place on the site prepared for it on the Pont-Neuf at Paris, which is nearly finished," should be executed by this artist, she suggested to Ferdinand the following arrangement. The Grand Duke should give Marie the bronze horse which was already made, and on which Ferdinand's own statue was seated, this statue should be removed and in its place John of Bologna should set a statue of Henry IV ; so John might perhaps finish the work in time, and the statue for the Pont-Neuf being thus completed, he could at his leisure make another horse for the Grand Duke.

This proposal was not to Ferdinand's taste. But he suggested a middle course ; that the moulds which had been used for casting the horse should be brought into service once more and a new statue thus made. Marie agreed. The Grand Duke, filled with zeal, then determined to have not one but two bronze horses cast, and to send his own statue to the King of Spain as he was sending the King of France his.

John of Bologna had spent much labour on the horse in the equestrian statue of Cosimo I., but very little on that for the similar statue of Ferdinand. Sauval, much later, found very little to admire in the reproduction of this at the Pont-Neuf, and considered the horse to be like a Neapolitan charger, too large and out of proportion. According to Germain Brice, though Henry IV.'s horse was by John of Bologna, the figure of the King was the work of Guillaume Dupré ; but this is an error. Franqueville made a model of the prince's head for John of Bologna, and he must have done so with skill, as the statue, when in position, was declared "the living image of the King, and one of the most remarkable likenesses of this great prince which we possess." There is no doubt that the horse was not that of the statue of Cosimo, as has been asserted ; a letter of Marie places the matter beyond dispute.

It was not without reason that the Queen had feared John of Bologna's delays : it seemed as if the work were never to be completed. Marie showed impatience ; the present, she declared, which she wished to make to the city of Paris would be more acceptable the sooner it came. It was held back for nine years. Twenty times Marie asked for it ; in 1606 she sent Luigi Bracci to John of Bologna to arrange for the payment for the horse, as if that was already completed. But Bracci was disgraced and degraded from his post, as a result of his intrigues with Madame de Verneuil, and was forbidden to return to France. He was even thrown into prison, where, on various pretexts, he was kept until 1607. In his place Marie sent Concini, who was instructed " to settle the price with John of Bologna for the horse of bronze," " and you shall inform yourself," added the Queen, " of the means of transporting it hither, and shall order the said John of Bologna to complete with the greatest possible speed the figure of my lord the king which is to be placed on the said horse." At the end of two years, nothing had been completed. M. d'Ocquerre, son of M. Blancmesnil, the Queen's Chancellor, starting for a tour in Italy, according to the custom of young men of family of the period, was ordered by Marie to see what was the state of the work, of which she had had no news, and to visit the Grand Duke and come to some arrangement with him about the matter.

Meanwhile the Place Dauphine was built at Paris, and the architect of the Pont-Neuf, Marchand, arranged the open space on which the expected statue was to be set up. Then John of Bologna died ; as Marie de Médicis had foreseen, he had been unable to complete the work. Had he made any real progress with it, even supposing that the horse was finished ? It is hard to say. Letters were exchanged between the Queen of France and the Grand Duke Ferdinand as to the steps to be taken in consequence of this event, and it was resolved to entrust the completion of the statue to the sculptor, Pietro Tacca. " I have no doubt," wrote Marie at a later date to this artist, " that having, as you tell me, put the finishing touches to this work, it will be worthy of him whom it represents." Pietro, who was a faithful pupil of John of Bologna, worked for three years at the statue of Henry IV. after the death of his master. It was not until 1614 that the end of this great undertaking was reached. In his turn Tacca, to whom, according to a letter of Matteo Bartolini, a payment of seven hundred crowns had been promised, had to wait patiently for two years for the settlement of his account.

The conveyance of the statue to Paris was a momentous undertaking. The Grand Duke had entrusted the affair to his diplomatic agent, the chevalier Pesciolini, with whom was associated an engineer, Guidi. The statue was embarked at Leghorn for Havre. When it had almost reached its destination, the ship was wrecked on a sandbank ; the vessel was sacrificed, and the statue itself recovered from the bottom of the sea.

In was on June 2, 1614, at four in the afternoon, that the young King Louis XIII. laid the first stone of the pedestal of the statue. Franqueville had complete charge of all the work connected with this. In consequence of the threatening political outlook, the King and his mother soon afterwards left Paris for Brittany, and it· was in their absence, in July 1614, that the work of John of Bologna and Tacca, enclosed in wooden packing cases, arrived. Marie de Médicis wrote, on July 31, that the erection and unveiling of the statue was not to be postponed until her return. On August 23, took place this solemn ceremony, which consisted in placing the statue on its pedestal. At it there were present the Commissioners charged with the building of the Pont-Neuf; the first Presidents of the Parliament and of the Chamber of Accounts, MM. Verdun and de Nicolaï ; the Attorney General, M. de Bellievre; the Civil Governor, the Treasurers General of Paris, the Provost of the merchants, M. Miron, and his four secretaries ; and Pierre Franqueville, in his character as " first sculptor to their Majesties."

In the belly of the horse was placed an inscription painted on vellum, enclosed in a lead casket with powdered charcoal for its better preservation. This inscription, the work of M. Gilbert Gaulmin de la Guyonnière, stated that the Grand Duke Ferdinand of Tuscany had ordered the statue from John of Bologna and had caused it to be finished by Pietro Tacca, " his sculptor," in memory of Henry IV. Was the statue of the Pont-Neuf, then, a gift from the Grand Duke ? It might seem so. " As soon as you learnt," wrote Marie to her uncle at the beginning of the business in 1605, " that I was anxious to have a statue of my lord the king made on a horse of bronze, you determined to have the said statue made in Italy by the hands of John of Bologna and to send it to me ; you wished to do me this courtesy." When the Regent returned to Paris, some days after the unveiling, and had admired the statue, which she could see from her apartment in the Louvre, she wrote to the Grand Duke of Tuscany to thank him " for this handsome token of your courtesy and goodwill. It is a present," she said, " which is particularly agreeable to me." Probably doubting whether it was a present herself, Marie, as we have seen, sent to Florence to settle the bill for casting the horse, and two years later the Florentine envoy reminded her that she had not yet paid Pietro Tacca. These facts reduce the courtesy of the Court of Florence to more modest proportions.

It remained to adorn the pedestal, which was a long and difficult work also. Pierre de Franqueville took an interminable time about it, and, even so, did no more than supply the plans, leaving others to carry out the work. He proposed to place at the four corners figures emblematical of the four quarters of the globe, and on the sides to have bas-reliefs illustrating the battles of Arques and Ivry, the capture of Paris, the sieges of Amiens and Montmeillan, with inscriptions, laurels, and olives, the whole lacking nothing in the way of beauty and magnificence, and comparing well with the pedestal of 1818.

Franqueville was unable to execute his design. There had already, even before the statue had been unveiled, been some question of removing him. The commissioners and directors of the buildings of the Pont-Neuf were opposed to him and wished the bas-reliefs to be undertaken by another artist. Franqueville wrote to the Queen, and sent his son-in-law, Bartolomeo Bordoni, to her, and Marie answered that he need feel no anxiety, that she did not wish " that any one but himself should touch this work, as he had already made the plans and the model." The commissioners had the last word, if not ostensibly at least as a matter of fact, since Bordoni, the son-in-law, made the four statues for the pedestal, which were very poor and as thin as skeletons ; while as to the bas-reliefs, which in 1635 were still uncast, Richelieu ordered them from Bordoni, Michel Bourdin, and Barthélemy Tremblay. They were better than the statues.

The interest which Marie de Médicis showed in the arts
appeared also in various other forms. A certain Jean Biot,
called Mercure, was skilled in the preparation of enamels
which were like marble, jasper, or "chalcedony." The
Queen "wished to give a present to the said Mercure and
to encourage him and inspire him to produce examples of
his skill and cunning." She allowed him to search at his
leisure through all the lands of her demesnes in Bourbonnais "for minerals, both metals and others, which
would serve for this purpose, and also to gather ferns and
other useless plants in the woods and forests in her possessions which would be useful to him." And she gave him
in advance all that he might find.

Another worker, Etienne Sager, was skilled in the
imitation of Chinese lacquer. Marie attached him to her
person at a fixed salary to make for her "with lacquer gum
and gold decoration, in the manner of the same country,
cabinets, chests, boxes, panelling, ornaments for churches,
chaplets, and other small articles and Chinese goods." She
even placed a seller of Chinese goods in the gallery of the
Louvre, where she also set an artist who worked well in
ebony, Laurent Septabre, the best known of workers of
this kind at the beginning of the seventeenth century.

There were retained in her household, under the title
of craftsmen, a certain number of artisans of all grades ;
the situation was good because of the privileges enjoyed,
the orders received, and the fixed annual income secured.
Every Queen of France had such men : Marie de Médicis
increased the number, and in place of the twelve whom
Louis de Lorraine, wife of Henry III., had had by her,
she had as many as forty-three. Doubtless it is of little
interest to us that she had in this company a seller of
curiosities, a maker of wicker baskets, a shoemaker or a
linen-draper, a barber or a lace-maker, but it is not without interest to know that she enlarged the number of these
artists. We have already mentioned her jeweller, Nicolas
Roger, and her architect, Salomon de Brosse ; in the list
there also appear two engravers, Danfrie and Pierre

Turpin, to whom she entrusted the work of engraving her seals ; two clockmakers, a publisher, Jacques de Heuqueville ; four painters, Ambroise Dubois, Daniel Dumonstier, Guillaume Dumée, Nicolas Duchesne ; and we should know of still more had it not been that the persons entrusted with the drawing up of the accounts thought it not worth while to give the names of the forty-three privileged persons. One of the valued privileges was the right to receive a lodging in the great gallery of the Louvre, which was constructed by Henry IV. to join his palace to the Tuilleries ; the first story was retained for the use of the King, but the ground floor and the mezzanine were left to the artists. Of the eighteen persons who were the first invited by letters patent of 1608 to enjoy the honour of this royal favour, almost half were artists dear to the Queen ; the proportion showing that Marie shared in the measure taken by the king.

As to foreign industries, her interest is strange. There was a certain Fleming, called Pierre de Brun, whose business was to sell in France " rare paintings, pictures, and other valuables which he brought from foreign and distant lands." Pierre de Brun frequented the market of Saint Germain in particular, but as he did not wish to take any of his stock home again, he never left the kingdom to undertake a new buying campaign elsewhere until he had disposed of all that he brought. Marie employed him in the great cities, Bordeaux, Orleans, Rouen, to make the sale of his " rare merchandise " easier. De Brun put his goods in a lottery. The Parlements, anxious to protect local industries, prohibited these lotteries or *blanques*. The Queen asked the King for mandatory letters commanding the judicial bodies to withdraw their opposition, and wrote to the first Presidents of the Parlements to request them as a personal favour graciously to hasten the carrying out of the definite commands which the King had sent to them.

Marie de Médicis was devoted to embroidery. Thus she personally selected that for the cloaks and mantles of the archers of the guards. She had in her household some selected French embroiderers : Nicolas de Vaudray, Jean le Boiteux, Jean Michel, Louis Boucherot, Nicolas Desforges. She affected oriental embroideries and caused to come from the East a whole group of workers, male and female, who formed a curious little colony entirely devoted to this type of work. A Turk, to begin with, was lodged at the Luxembourg ; M. de Brèves, Ambassador at Constantinople, had brought back with him a clever Levantine, a Pole by birth, called Anne Ossache, who had married an artilleryman, Laurent Cosson ; the Queen had in addition " three ladies of the Turkish nation, whom we have caused to come to this kingdom," she wrote, " to do much work for our service," and to whom one hundred and twenty livres a year were paid as wages. They were engaged in embroidering silk, which was supplied to them by the merchant Decreil ; their elaborate dresses were regarded as " the most beautiful things in the world," to quote de Malherbe. Above all Marie included in this company two Greeks, Adrienne Theodoran and Marguerite Thamary, at the same wages of one hundred and twenty livres, to whom she appears to have given special attention. She supported them ; on one occasion, when there was no money in the Queen's coffers—she was always short of money—the Treasurer General of the household, M. Florent d'Argouges, was forced for three years to advance the money for their support, and at the same time to pay their wages. She lodged them, up to 1615, no doubt on account of their youth, with the sisters of Saint-Ursula, to the superior of whose convent, sister Marie de Sainte-Croix de l'Incarnation, three hundred and sixty livres were paid for the cost of the support of these two girls. After 1615 she placed them with Anne Ossache ; and when she had married her artilleryman, Adrienne Theodoran, for her part, wedded in 1617 a quartermaster of the household of Anne of Austria, called Jean Guillot, and received for her wedding present from the Queen two thousand four hundred livres. Both of them went on as before, working embroidery in the manner of the Levant. As for Marguerite Thamary, she became a Carmelite and a sister at the convent of Sainte-Croix. The merchant, Jean Henriot, delivered to " the Greek girls " the " loosely woven cloth " on which they embroidered, and the painter, François Bénard, " drew the outlines on the cloth on which they worked."

Finally, Marie de Médicis gladly devoted herself to the work of assisting savants and artists of every kind who wished to go to Italy to complete their education in the peninsula to do so. She recommended them to her princely relatives, to her friends. Such an one was " the son of a cultivator of medicinal herbs to my lord the king, who some years since began by his command a garden at Paris for various rare shrubs, herbs, and simples, collected from distant provinces. Now he wishes to go to Italy," she wrote, " to see what rare things he can find there. I beg you to consent to allow him to see your gardens and that if you have any simples of which he can bring us cuttings or seeds, that you will permit him to do so." Another similar case is that of a young man of Blois, Jean Mosnier, who went with the Archbishop of Pisa to the land of Michael Angelo ; Marie de Médicis paid the expenses of his journey and promised him a monthly pension of forty-five livres which he was to receive from the goldsmith, Nicolas Roger, the valet de chambre, that he " might be able to study his art of painting in Italy." It would appear that the Queen was unwilling to omit any of the various acts which distinguish the protectors of the arts in the judgment of history.

CHAPTER VIII

THE QUEEN'S PURSE

French sovereigns in the early seventeenth century not free disposers
of the State revenues—Rigorous scrutiny of public accounts—
Henry IV. fixes his consort's income at four hundred thousand
livres yearly—Minute appropriation of this income—The Queen's
disbursements at least double this sum, chiefly on account of
jewels purchased—Anger of Henry IV.: his meanness—Sully
obstructs a settlement—The King's complicated transactions to
meet the Queen's debts—"Freedoms" and edicts for creating
offices rendered nugatory by opposition on the part of the
Treasury—The Queen's desperate expedients: shipping, broking,
company promoting, pledging, loans from her dependents—
Severity on the part of the Treasury—Marie de Médicis, as
Regent, increases her income by the revenue from her dowry
—She speculates in land, but the deficit increases until it
reaches one million francs per annum—"Secret affairs"—The
Queen's resources—Bribes: depletion of the treasure-rooms of
the Bastille—Arrangements with creditors—Prodigality—Foreign
investments.

In common with all those of unlimited caprice and limited
means, Marie de Médicis, luxurious and extravagant in her
tastes, experienced all the trials which result from an inadequate income. She knew what it was to be in debt,
to be reduced to petty and even sordid shifts. At the
beginning of the seventeenth century, the rulers of France
did not enjoy absolute freedom in the disposal of the whole
revenue : receipts were appropriated to meet definite expenses : a systematic audit was enforced. Does the King
wish to divert to his own use some portion of the revenue
of which he has not ordinarily the disposal ? He is met
with general, if passive, resistance. Auditors will not
obey, sovereign courts will not register, boards of control
protest with vigour and strike out of the accounts the

sums diverted, leaving the agents of the treasury personally responsible. The King has no choice but to discover new sources of income—a more legal course of action, but infinitely more difficult.

What the King cannot do, the Queen is obviously still less able to accomplish. Mistress of no compelling power, she could not give orders to the treasurers of the State. Has a favour to be gained from a superintendent of the finances ? She must make application to him almost as a private person. In the annual budget of the State—the contemporary " General statement based on an estimate of expenditure "—the Queen was allotted a definite sum to cover the expenses of her palace, her maintenance, and her pleasures. Beyond this amount, she had no right to anything. Is her allowance exceeded ? She must beg from the King a royal present to make good the deficit. He would take this money from the portion of his income intended for largesses—the so-called " petty cash ; " or would discover an extraordinary source of revenue : or would debit the sum to the account of the princess. In the last case, she would find herself in the debt of her own treasurers for amounts which increased from year to year ; an unhappy state of affairs from which Marie de Médicis made her escape when she became Queen Regent by deliberately using her absolute power to make good the deficits of the past.[1]

The failure of the Court of Florence to understand the severity with which accounts were audited in France had greatly amused Henry IV. at the time of his marriage. Convinced that with an Italian comptroller Marie de Médicis would be more completely mistress of her privy purse, that Court had desired the King to allow a Florentine financier to be attached to the princess, assuring his majesty that the future Queen was " an excellent house-

---

[1] A detailed account of the financial organisation at the beginning of the seventeenth century and of the history of the finances under Henry IV. and Louis XIII. has still to be written ; at present we have but fragmentary and confused scraps of information.

keeper," *una buona menaggiera.* Had he his doubts ?
Had he already good reasons for disbelief ? His answer
was diplomatic, but he forthwith appointed a conscientious
Frenchman, M. Florent d'Argouges.

Parsimonious by nature, and anxious, with Sully, to
preserve the greatest possible order in his finances,
Henry IV. was careful to provide for the most exact
settlement of the Queen's privy purse. Having given the
matter his most careful attention, he devoted to it an
annual sum of four hundred thousand livres. But the
Queen was by no means free to spend this money as she
pleased.

For centuries, in fact since the Middle Ages, it had been
definitely established that the accounts of what was then
called " the Queen's hostel " should be drawn up in the
greatest detail. Minute provision was made beforehand for
every expense. In the matter of maintenance, the details
had to be specified " with scrupulous care, particulars
being entered under different heads, bread, wine, flesh, fowl,
wood, joints, pastry, spicery, fruit, vegetables, salt, wax,
lights ; " feast days had to be distinguished from ember
days and fast days ; an estimate of the number of persons
entitled to support had to be compiled, and the total
verified daily, monthly, annually. In the matter of the
staff, the complete list of the officials of the household had
to be regularly submitted to the Court of Aids, and no one
could be paid whose name did not appear in the official
books. It is essential to realise fully that regularity and
an exact system in the keeping of public accounts existed
in France from the Middle Ages. The same principles
were rigorously enforced in the accounts of the new Queen ;
their management was regulated by the financial ordinance
of 1585, and an infinity of documents ensured an exact
knowledge of the expenditure of Marie de Médicis.

In December the bureaus prepared a rough draft of
the budget for the following year. The statement, after
having been examined and signed by the Queen, was sent
to the Council of Finance. That body carefully revised

it, produced a complete balance sheet, verified each item, and effected such alterations as it deemed advisable. The complete account was then submitted to the King, and, on his passing it, was sent back to the Treasurer of the Exchequer, who was instructed to convey to the master of the Queen's treasury, her steward, at the end of each month, a twelfth part of the sum settled. The head of each department received at the same time a copy (on parchment) of the section of the budget which concerned him. This he was bound to follow strictly, under the supervision of the comptrollers, drawing up with care the list of his expenses, the entry of which was checked at the end of each month.

In the event of deficits appearing, as for instance when a greater number of gentlemen came to the tables than had been expected, or when some unforeseen cause led to an increase of expenditure, the comptroller was compelled to balance his accounts by making use of surpluses, of the excess of receipts secured in another department ; this was a very weighty matter. If he were absolutely unable to make good the deficit, he was forced to admit that the expenditure could not be met, and to request a further grant of supplies under the form of new " appropriations." This was a matter of time, and the procedure was involved and difficult. Finally the regulations anticipated that there might at the end of these transactions be certain credits which had not been used, " casual accretions " ; and for the sums thus economised definite purposes were assigned. They were employed to " the repair of movables," to replace the old, worn-out material.

That all these provisions of the royal ordinance of 1585 were observed is proved by numerous statements of accounts for the Queen's household.[1]

---

[1] It is not intended to do more than to give the figures ; their reduction to their real value is a very difficult task. M. d'Avenel's conclusions have been much disputed ; M. Louis Arnould believes that the value of a livre can be fixed at seven francs in our money. We may mention that a crown was equivalent to three livres, the quarter crown to fifteen sous, and the teston to fourteen and a half sous.

An equally detailed appropriation for expenditure, and the earmarking of receipts in the statement of accounts, made it impossible for Marie de Médicis to divert a single crown of her revenue.

The four hundred thousand livres assigned to her were portioned out under twelve heads.

Under the first appeared the actual expenses of the household, which included both the maintenance of the staff and of Her Majesty, and the supply of necessary household goods : this item absorbed one hundred and fifty thousand livres, and was denominated " expenses of the Treasury." The wages of the staff, properly so called, amounted in all to seventy-two thousand two hundred and thirteen livres, over and above those of the attendants at the stables, which accounted for fourteen thousand two hundred and sixty-four livres, and of the musicians, which were nine thousand livres. To the upkeep of the stables, horses, carriages and so forth, sixty thousand livres were devoted.

For her minor personal expenses Marie de Médicis had the disposal of three thousand livres a month, a total of thirty-six thousand livres a year. This sum appears as not inconsiderable, when provision was otherwise made for all further expenses. The cost of clothes, both for ordinary wear and for state occasions, balls and receptions, ranked with the expenditure for the maintenance of the apartments of the princess, as " ordinary expenditure and expenditure for the person of the Queen," and amounted in all to twenty-eight thousand livres. For travelling expenses Marie was entitled to seventeen thousand five hundred livres, and she was able to use this for the payment of certain fees and the liquidation of certain liabilities. If the sum were insufficient, she was authorised to charge the excess against the sixty thousand livres appropriated for the stable. Finally there appeared as a distinct charge in the budget the salaries assigned to certain individuals— six thousand livres each to a maid of honour and to a lady in waiting, two thousand four hundred to an equerry, and the honorarium, the "spices," presented to the members of the Chamber of Accounts for auditing the Queen's accounts, a sum of one thousand four hundred and forty-six livres.

We possess the particulars, item by item, of the Queen's budget, and when several years are compared it is seen that the figures do not vary ; every new expense appears under a new head. Compared with that of preceding queens the revenue of Marie de Médicis was immense : Anne of Brittany had but sixty-five thousand seven hundred and ninety-six livres assigned to her.

Despite her thirty-six thousand livres " pocket money," Marie de Médicis never had a crown with her when she went out ; when a beggar asked for an alms she would borrow a coin from one of her attendants. In the ten years from 1601 to 1610 she only once succeeded in living within her income of four hundred thousand livres.

This happened in 1602, the year following her marriage ; in the next nine years her deficits reached the most extraordinary proportions. The fact that, after a year of more than ordinary extravagance, she always returned to comparative economy would seem to indicate that the extent of these deficits caused her some degree of concern. Perhaps she was herself alarmed at the growth of her expenditure, perhaps the King showed his annoyance : but in any case the tendency towards something like economy was short-lived ; in the ensuing year the total invariably mounts higher than ever. These annual totals are preserved for us in the archives of the Chamber of Accounts, the figures here found varying somewhat from those which appear elsewhere. In the first year, 1601, the deficit is seventy-four thousand livres, in 1603 it is thirty-five thousand livres, in 1604, one hundred and fifty-seven thousand livres ; in 1605 it is twenty-nine thousand livres, in 1606, three hundred and eighteen thousand livres, and, continuing alternately to rise and fall, sixty-one thousand livres in 1607, two hundred and twenty thousand livres in 1608, one hundred and forty-one thousand livres in 1609, and in 1610, four hundred and seventy thousand livres, showing an expenditure of more than twice her normal revenue! It must be admitted that in this last year Henry IV. died, and Marie de Médicis, now mistress of the State, henceforth hardly kept accounts. She had royal means of finding sources of revenue, and from this moment the deficits visibly increase.

Up to 1610, this increase and development is not found in the ordinary items of the accounts of the palace. The cost of maintenance and of necessary supplies remains stationary ;[1] the staff, as we have seen, is paid at a low rate and is not increased, nor is there the slightest change in the expenses of the stables. It is but fair to say that the sums spent on clothes were not unduly large, and the credit of twenty-eight thousand livres set apart for them was enough. There were a few supplementary expenses ; the Queen, as owner of the mansion of Montceaux, was obliged to put certain repairs in hand and to undertake a moderate amount of building ; but Henry IV. consented to allow her a special credit for this purpose. It was her insensate love for jewels that ruined her.

At every turn we come across lengthy and indeed interminable accounts of goldsmiths and jewellers, and year by year the list increased enormously. The value of the articles and their number combined to make the expense exorbitant. We have already seen the Queen buying, without a moment's misgiving, two diamonds at twenty-eight thousand and four at thirty thousand livres. She had no hesitation in securing possession of many articles at a ruinous cost, for example a cross of gold at eighteen thousand livres, a diamond at seventy-five thousand livres, and a bracelet, studded with diamonds, at three hundred and sixty thousand livres! Account after

---

[1] Marie de Médicis incurred no deficit in respect of her table, differing in this regard from Louise de Lorraine, the queen who preceded her. She left very large debts, and we have in 1604 a "Statement of the debts due to various officials of the late queen dowager for provisions bought and for goods supplied by them and advances made to the household of the said queen."

account comes from the merchants with its list of twenty, thirty articles, the total value of which reveals an incredible extravagance. With a sum of thirty-six thousand livres a year assigned to meet the expense of trifling amusements, how could the Queen afford to buy diamonds at so high a rate and to purchase jewels constantly ? One realises why the income of four hundred thousand livres was utterly insufficient for the gratification of the extravagant tastes of the princess.

Involved in serious financial difficulties as the outcome of her rash expenditure, Marie de Médicis, though Queen of France, was driven to endure lectures from her angry treasurers, who declined to advance money for which they would eventually be personally responsible. She suffered also the wrath of Henry IV., who put every imaginable difficulty in the way of the discharge of her liabilities ; and she came into conflict with an alliance of Sovereign Courts, Chambers of Account, Parlements, Courts of Aids, unwilling to assist the payment of that which she owed. She was herself aware that her resources were utterly inadequate to her needs. " Alas ! " so ran her written lament to an Italian, Giovannini, who requested her to pay him twelve thousand crowns, " to think of being able to expend this sum without the fact becoming known is a thing which my affairs will not permit, since as you are aware the allowance for the upkeep of my palace is inadequate even for that purpose ! I am heavily in debt owing to the many extraordinary expenses which I have incurred and am daily compelled to incur." Giovannini, however, did at least receive a promise of the presentation to one of the next abbacies which should fall vacant. In answer to the complaint of her treasurer, M. Florent d'Argouges, who drew her attention to the accumulation of bills, she cried despairingly, " I know not where to find the means of settling any of these debts." It was apparently at the close of 1604 that her financial troubles began, if not in point of expenditure at least in the difficulty of balancing her accounts.

She did not know where to secure the means of payment because the only door at which she could knock remained obstinately closed, or if it opened, did so merely to mock her. "You know better than any one," she wrote to honest d'Argouges, "for what great sums I am indebted, and how very hard, how practically impossible, it is for me to obtain assistance or accommodation from my lord the King in the work of meeting my liabilities," and she added bitterly, "and so it is that I am of necessity driven to be economical!"

With a jest, but at the same time in all seriousness, Henry IV. definitely and peremptorily declined to increase the Queen's income. If the debts became too pressing and he was driven to make a contribution, he adopted in such a case methods so complicated that Marie de Médicis found it as hard to secure possession of the amounts granted to her as she had already done to obtain the grant itself. Various causes produced this ill-humour on the part of the King. It was due in the first instance to his policy; he was convinced that the regeneration of the State could only be effected by means of a full treasury, and he could in nowise secure this great result except by practising rigid economy himself and by compelling others to do likewise. Moreover, in marked contrast to his wife, he was personally very economical, very careful, even miserly. The trials of his adventurous days had taught him the value of crowns; he knew how to make them go a long way, and hated to see them wasted. Indeed the degree to which he carried his love of saving shocked his contemporaries! "His greed is abominable!" (*abominevole*), exclaimed the Florentine resident. "He is an absolute miser!" was the verdict of d'Aubigné; and foreigners echo the lively annoyance of the public at this extreme economy. Every one in his own days blamed the greed of Henry IV.; the ill-fated Beauvais-Nangris said that the King avoided gentlemen without fortune for fear of their pestering him with requests. But he had his apologists. Fontenay-Mareuil protested that he was prudent rather than avaricious;

and Dupleix adds that while he was indeed too close-fisted, this was the outcome not so much of base greed as of a desire to have the means of paying his debts. The lower classes gave him their approval, and Henry IV. himself said, " I am called a miser, but I do three things which are far from being the acts of a miser ; I make war, I make love, and I build." On the other hand, the States General of 1614 declared that " kings have only hired servants, and their generosity is the measure of the obedience which they receive."

Henry was really annoyed when he learnt that he was currently regarded as a miser. In a moment of vexation he commanded Sully—" to silence gossip "—to publish a list of the debts of the Crown which he had to meet and which he gradually settled year by year. Sully made the total come to over three hundred and seven millions, exclusive of the cost of the treaties of the League, which amounted to thirty-two millions.

As far as Marie de Médicis was concerned, Henry IV. protested with equal vigour against the charge that he had not done enough for her. " What ! " he exclaimed to Sully one day. " I have given more to my wife, I have made more presents to her, both for the ordinary expenses of her household and for supplementary expenses, than any other King of France ever made to his wife ! You know that well enough," he went on. " You ! for you support her, and your wife plays the beggar for her ! " And it is to some extent true that Henry IV. gave his Queen more than had ever been given to any Queen of France before his time ; but the earlier Queens lived less luxuriously, and those who kept the greatest state, Anne of Brittany and Catharine de Médicis, had been richly dowered, and their large private property allowed them to spend royally. The most extravagant of the Queens of France, Catharine de Médicis, was also the Queen who had the richest personal property, as appears from her marriage contract ; yet this did not prevent her from leaving at her death more than ten millions of debts. As to the assertion

that Sully supported the Queen in her demands, and that
the superintendent's wife acted as a messenger in making
known the requests of the Queen, it must have startled
Marie if she heard it !

M. de Sully on her side !   On the contrary the Princess
was humiliated by having to address requests to the
boorish minister, and by being compelled to beg of him.
It shamed her to experience refusals couched in language
which was devoid of consideration and even of politeness ;
to endure his peevish temper.   This cross-grained old man,
with his high forehead, full beard and forbidding expression, living at the Arsenal all alone in his barely furnished
office, adorned with severe portraits of Luther and Calvin,
who was perpetually at work, perpetually busy, was
utterly unendurable !   He received people without rising,
without ceasing to write, without inviting them to be
seated.   He refused their requests bluntly.   " Ah ! he is
a beast ! " (*e una bestia !*) cried an Italian ambassador, as
he left the office in anger.   " It is his general habit to
offend every one ! " said the Prince de Condé, and a
foreigner wrote, " He is so proud, so haughty, so rude and
arrogant, that he no longer heeds any human being ! "
No one returned from an audience with him without showing extreme indignation at his manners.   *Quello animale !*
" what a pig ! " was the criticism of Vinta, the envoy of
the Grand Duke of Tuscany in Paris ; " he is a groom,"
added M. de Gondi, and Giovannini chimed in, " *un monte
di bestie !* "   Henry IV. laughed when his superintendent
was mentioned to him.   " What wouldn't the Grand
Duke, your master, pay to have a minister like him ? "
was his jesting answer to the Florentine agent.   " All the
same," replied the other, " *e troppo terribile, per non dir
altro !* "

The curious pamphlet, " The Financier to the Members
of the States," which was written against him in 1614,
reveals the popular idea of Sully's lack of manners ; and
the despatches of the Florentines supplement this account.
His secretary, M. Arnault, was as unamiable as his master.

And despite his great administrative ability, it is certain that Henry IV., had he lived, would probably have dismissed him in the end, so difficult was it to deal with him. That the King retained him so long was due to the fact that the superintendent was an excellent official, and while he made the most of the revenue of the State, was unmerciful towards peculators. Yet his own hands were suspected of not being " clean." Though he received in his official capacity a salary of sixty thousand livres, the archives of the Hague reveal the fact that he extorted secret gratuities from foreign states. However, for the time being, the King had complete confidence in his judgment ; in the council of ministers the superintendent usually had the last word, and Henry did nothing without consulting him.

M. de Sully had on occasion made use of the mediation of the Queen to seek from the King some favour for which he dared not make a personal request, and it was in this way that he sought the manor of Saint-Maixent, which, however, Henry IV. would not give him, as he did not care to leave a defensible position in the hands of a Huguenot, "who controlled the finances and to whom he was unwilling to afford an assured retreat." Indeed on every occasion on which Marie de Médicis undertook to act on behalf of M. de Sully, the superintendent was invariably disappointed.

Even in the transactions of everyday life, the stiffness of the minister, his ill-will, and his inconsiderate speeches, eventually annoyed Marie. She complained bitterly to the King, and Henry IV. tried gently to console her, urging her to conciliate the minister, to deal cautiously with him, to win him over by amiability. Then the Queen grew indignant. Had she another master besides the King ? Was she to be driven to " pay court to Rosny ? " (*fare la corte a Rosny?*) The fault was perhaps partly on Marie's side, and her lack of consideration was to some extent responsible for the conduct of the superintendent. The Florentine agent wrote, " The Queen complains of Rosny, but at first Rosny was devoted to her, *tutto suo*, and she has repelled and wounded both him and his wife by not showing consideration towards them. She takes advice ill, and does not know how to restrain her feelings. Yet it is extremely important for her to make friends ! " Whether through the minister's intractable temper or from the Queen's lack of tact, the relations of these two were embittered.

The effect of this appeared in the accounts. Sully had many ways in which he could make himself unpleasant to the Queen, which all came, in the end, to refusing supplies. For example, he postponed the payment of the sums due each month on her regular income ; at the end of the financial year he tried to debit her with seven thousand crowns, and the Queen was compelled to write letters to him before the treasurer would hand over what he owed her. When an additional source of revenue was assigned to Marie for the payment of a debt, the princess was accustomed to conclude an agreement with some person who would give her a lump sum on account and arrange to reimburse himself by receiving the proceeds of the new appropriation, the amount which he was eventually to receive being of course greater than that which he advanced to the Queen. Agreements of this kind had to be countersigned by the superintendent, and the superintendent would not countersign them. Two, three months elapsed. The person with whom the agreement had been concluded grew uneasy, and threatened to rescind it. The unhappy Queen was compelled to write begging letters to the minister. " My reputation will be destroyed!" she groaned.

On the morrow of Henry IV.'s death, Marie de Médicis took her revenge. She desired to give nine hundred livres to Madame des Essarts in order to enable her to educate her two daughters at the abbey of Notre-Dame at Soissons. She wrote bluntly to Sully, " I request you to pay Madame des Essarts nine hundred livres," and added, in a dry and dictatorial postscript, " I desire you to cause the said sum to be paid."

When he was once convinced that it was essential to supply Marie de Médicis with money to meet her liabilities, Henry IV. began by absolutely refusing to give her cash. Such a method would have been too easy, as a matter of fact, since the treasurer general of the Queen would only have had to claim the money from the treasury. Vinta sent word to Florence of the way in which the King, becoming confidential for a moment to the Queen's maids of honour, boldly declared the reason for this refusal. " I don't want to give a penny to the Queen," he protested, " because it would all find its way into the pocket of Signor Concini ! " The real reason was that he did not wish to encourage his wife in such requests by making it too easy for her to receive payment, and also that he preferred to keep his gifts of ready money for his mistresses ! On one occasion at least, early in 1605, he resolved to present the Queen with thirty thousand livres ; but the very letter which requested Sully to transmit this sum to Marie de Médicis, ordered him to place nine thousand livres at the disposal of Jacqueline de Bueil, the Comtesse de Moret ! All his ready money went to his lady-loves ; the Queen received for her support sums which could only be raised with difficulty and after running many risks.

At some peculiarly critical moments, Marie de Médicis thought of appealing to the generosity of her uncle, the Grand Duke of Tuscany. She informed him that she made application to him as to her father, and moved by self-interest or sympathy, the Grand Duke consented to hear her petition. Henry IV. learnt this and was filled with indignation and shame, *molta vergogna*. He felt that it was necessary to excuse himself to the Florentine agent by attributing the embarrassed finances of his wife to the ill-will of his ministers, *quei tenaci ministri*, who invariably refused all the Queen's requests. Neither the agent nor the Grand Duke were ever deceived ; and despite the " *molta compunzione e confusione* " of Henry IV., the Florentine agents advised their master to give favourable ear to the prayers of Marie de Médicis.

The supplementary resources which the King agreed to place at the disposal of the Queen were obtained by edicts creating extraordinary sources of revenue which the princess would have to collect. Among the creations of this type there was one which was a traditional right of the Queen's, the institution of masterships.

When an apprentice in any profession wished to become a master, he was obliged to obtain letters of mastership, declaring that he had completed his apprenticeship. He paid a due to the King. As the number of masterships was limited, it was only necessary if money were wanted to create one or two additional masterships in each profession throughout the kingdom; the new master paid a sum varying from eight to twenty crowns, and the total receipts therefore were considerable. Masterships were created for the benefit of the Queen at her marriage and at the birth of her children. On the former occasion Marie de Médicis received two such creations; at the birth of the Dauphin, the future Louis XIII., four, at the birth of each of her daughters one, and at that of Gaston, in 1608, two. In addition to the creation of masterships at these times, the Queen had a similar right to one such creation " in each town in which she stayed," and she visited many towns. In an edict of Henry IV., of April 1597, the resources resulting from this system are set forth, and H. Lemonnier has written their history, while we have the ordinances for all such creations for the benefit of the Queen.

Unfortunately the result, as shown by Fagniez, was that the total number of masterships increased inordinately, and the angry corporations took measures to prevent the purchase of new letters of creation. The King, concerned at the failure of a regular method by which the Queen could secure irregular supplies, determined to reduce the number of masterships at one blow, and in 1608 the letters which had been granted before, but not issued until after, his accession were revoked; but the action proved ineffective. The evil was not cured by such a partial remedy, and Marie de Médicis saw that means of raising money for her, which had the greatest show of legality and which was most convenient, gradually disappear. The States-General of 1614 entered a vigorous protest against such proceedings, demanding that " the pursuit of the said professions should be left free to your unhappy subjects."

All other methods were laborious, intricate, uncertain. They had first to be discovered, and it is evident that a high degree of imagination was required to find unsuspected sources of revenue, to invent excuses for an extraordinary impost. Such inventors, it is true, were plentiful enough. There was a whole class of men of shady reputation, business men of doubtful honesty, who spent their lives in suggesting expedients, out of which they would of course make a commission. In her search for such expedients, Marie de Médicis embraced every suggestion, while the nobles also listened to others of the same nature —to such, for example, as concerned the provinces which they ruled, and they begged the King to carry out the ideas which they laid before him. " Oh ! what a crowd of base and bloodsucking hangers-on ! " was the cry of Sully, who hated these " projectors, informers, sneaks, Court spies, and men who propose to raise money at the expense of the people." A contemporary calls them " courtiers and proclamation seekers, veritable boils on the State, sucking its life blood." Yet the method was not without its advantage, as appears from the quantity of new imposts which were created by proclamation for the benefit of the Queen. As might have been expected, the States of 1614 violently opposed these people, demanding that the King " should absolutely forbid all persons, of whatever rank and position, to suggest and to undertake the creation or revival by edict of any office, under pain of death and confiscation of property as enemies and disturbers of the peace of all your subjects."

But even when a method had been discovered and had gained the approval of Henry IV., an edict had to be promulgated ; and before such an edict, authorising the use of new sources of supply, could receive the signature of His Majesty, it had to be debated in the Council of State—an initial obstacle. The executive difficulties which would have been consequent upon the adoption of the proposals submitted to the Queen, were not infrequently so great that an examination of the matter by the ministers was most necessary, and they were not at all unwilling to answer with an explicit or implied refusal.

Marie de Médicis, trembling before an opposition which was capable of preventing the realisation of a scheme, was driven to make her suit to each member of the Council individually, to press him to decide in a manner agreeable to the Queen's interest, and even to pray him to do so. She sent letters to every one, those to Sully being especially insistent, and almost obsequious, owing to the weight which the opinion of the mighty superintendent carried with it in the Council. She addressed herself to him on these matters with an affectation of candour and confidence. "I do not wish," she wrote to him on one occasion, "this matter to be settled except as you shall decide and consider to be right." When the Council had eventually expressed its opinion as favourable to the idea, a royal edict was issued, and binding force was conferred on it by a proclamation of the same Council.

Another formality had then to be observed. The edicts had to be registered by the Parlements, or the Chambers of Account, or the Courts of Aids, as the case might be. At once insurmountable difficulties arose. The Courts were themselves traditionally opposed to the registration of edicts which provided for a definite increase in taxation. Zeal for the common good, the conception of their duty, a passion for asserting their authority, led them to remonstrate with the King, who stood firm and sent them letters mandatory. The Courts once more refused registration; the King sent more letters, and the matter dragged on for months or years, until one or other of the parties wearied of opposition. Now and then, when the matter was of importance, Henry IV. lost his temper, and the Court which had aroused the anger of the Prince had an unpleasant time. But as a rule he let things slide, and the magistrates eventually got the last word. From the curious journal of Malenfant, Secretary of the Parlement of Toulouse early in the seventeenth century, one can gather an idea of the absolutely extraordinary independence of the Sovereign Courts at this time in their relations with the King. That independence, respectful but insurmountable, was based on "the tradition, practice, and fundamental laws of the kingdom." Thus all grants assigned to Marie de Médicis were met by the most obstinate inertia on their part.

Unfortunately for the Queen, Henry IV. was secretly in league with the Courts. By an ingenious stroke of policy, he so arranged matters with them that when they received edicts establishing an office for the benefit of any one, they still should not register them, despite all the letters mandatory in the world, unless the King or Sully wrote a special autograph letter instructing them to do so. This letter the King and his minister jestingly called "the password." When he was driven to give way to the Queen's prayers, Henry, by means of this understanding, was able to take away with one hand what he appeared to have given with the other. It was in such a case that he remarked to Sully, "You know that I have forbidden the Courts to undertake the registration of any edict unless they have been bidden to do so under my hand or yours, despite any orders which they may receive and all the *lettres de cachet* which may be sent to them."

Poor Marie ! To what purpose, then, was all the labour which she expended in persuading the various bodies to acknowledge a bogus edict signed by the King and sent to them ? In 1605 Henry IV. granted to her all the money that she could recover " from payments in commutation of rents, or of the rights of superior lords, from dues on the sale of lands held by feudal tenure, from the succession duties on the property of aliens, from confiscations, and from other seignorial rights, payable in Brittany for nine

years." The Chamber of Account at Nantes refused verification of the edict ; Marie secured mandate after mandate from the King ; nothing happened. She wrote personally to every one—to the first president, presidents,
councillors—some fifteen letters ; she urged her case
warmly. "Others," she protested, "in days gone by
have enjoyed this right, who have not been my equals in
rank, and whose claims to respect and whose merit have
not been greater than mine !" Unmoved, the Chamber
retorted that it was a primary necessity to submit the
matter to the States of Brittany. Another batch of
fifteen letters from the Queen followed : "but the States,"
so ran her energetic reply, "have nothing to do with this
matter ; it is not their business !"

Then she tried humility, swearing that she had no intention of using this money for herself, that she required it
in order to make gifts to certain persons. Her efforts were
futile ; the King had not sent an autograph letter.

There is a long list of proposals for raising money
suggested to Henry by Marie, and accepted by him on
impossible conditions, and the registers of the Queen's
correspondence are full of letters on these matters, repeated over and over again.

Of all methods the simplest was the creation of new
public offices, but as the salaries attaching to these had to
be paid promptly, and as every increase in the number of
salaried posts reduced the value of all such posts, the
opposition of the corporations, whose interests were
threatened, was easily aroused in this way. The result
was that the securing of this form of revenue became a
matter of extreme difficulty. When it was merely intended—the proposal of Henry IV. in 1604—to establish
two receivers, two paymasters, and two comptrollers of
the revenue in Normandy, it was the Chamber of Account
of Rouen which alone made any difficulty ; yet the matter
only indirectly concerned this body. But the result was
different when in 1605 the King agreed to create two
salaried councillors in the Parlement of Rennes. Marie de

Médicis urged the Chancellor to register, seal, hurry through the edict, and desired that the " matter might be despatched promptly." The Parlement of Brittany declined to permit this increase in the number of the magistrates ; and for a year after the signing of the edict registration was withheld. It is true that in the end it was registered, and that the Queen presented the son of her Chancellor, M. de Blancmesnil, to one of the two offices, but an enormous expenditure of importunity and prayers had been needed. The Parlement of Brittany had not then the reputation of being one of the easiest bodies to manage.

In 1604 the King created on the same terms four salaried Councillors of Requests in the Parlement of Toulouse, nominally in order that the Queen might meet the cost of the repairs which she had carried out at the château of Montceaux. The Parlement in question refused to verify the edict. Mandate after mandate was issued ; messages from the Queen to each of the presidents and councillors were sent to Languedoc year after year ; Marie declaring that this source of revenue was intended to meet the expenses incurred in connection with the château of Montceaux-en-Brie. Three years later, in 1607, these batches of letters were still being written, and the King was still issuing his commands with equal ill-success. " The Parlement," wrote the Queen in 1608 to M. de Verdun, First President of Toulouse, " cares so little for the orders and requests addressed to it, that I am resolved to write no more, but to try my best to secure some other grant in place of that originally assigned to me." But Henry would not make this other grant, and was equally unwilling to fall in with the Queen's suggestion, based on a hint from Toulouse, that the number of councillors to be created should be reduced from four to two. He merely gave way to the extent of sending an eighth mandatory letter, which was wasted labour. In 1612, two years after the King's death and eight years after the signing of the edict, the business was still unfinished.

The matter of the secretaries of Navarre was quite as hard to settle. When Henry of Navarre had become Henry of France, it had been necessary for him to define the position of the ancient, though miniature, Court of Pau, and Marie proposed that the "secretaries of the House and Crown of Navarre" should be elevated to the rank of "secretaries of the House and Crown of France" —a purely nominal change, since both were merely salaried clerks of the Chancery—in return for the payment of a fee which she should receive. It was a matter of twenty thousand livres, and this sum was to be used to pay off the debts due to M. d'Attichy, her superintendent. After raising many difficulties, the Parlement and the Chamber of Accounts granted registration : but the Court of Aids refused to do so. The space occupied in the Queen's correspondence by her innumerable letters on this question is out of all proportion to its importance.

On the eve of his death, April 29, 1610, Henry IV. agreed to hand over to her the disposal of "the offices of secretaries in ordinary of the chamber"—an important matter involving six hundred thousand livres—as well as that of "the reversions of the posts of secretaries of the House and Crown of France, of the masters of audience, the comptrollers of the greater and lesser Chanceries, and their secretaries." The hopes of the Princess were shattered in the same way.

Side by side with the creation of offices properly so called, a strange variety of sources of income was devised to supplement the embarrassed finances of the Queen.

On the suggestion of a certain Jean Coberet, Marie de Médicis was granted the money which might be derived from the fines inflicted on persons found guilty of defrauding the State in respect of a certain due, that of "the sixty and forty sous payable on every hundredweight of salt" put on sale in Languedoc. The Queen was to receive one hundred and twenty thousand livres, and Coberet two thousand livres as commission. In 1605 the King had granted an edict which permitted two persons in each

parish in Normandy to secure exemption from a certain
number of dues and imposts on payment of a lump sum
once for all : these sums were to be handed over to the
Queen. A certain Leclerc appeared and offered eighty
thousand livres for the right to farm this money ; his suggestion was considered and acceptance delayed. Forthwith came a certain Nicolas Pallier, offering one hundred
and sixty thousand livres, double the amount. His proposal was accepted ; the decree of the Council ratifying the
contract with him is preserved, and there is no doubt that
he made a considerable profit.

These suggestions for " farming " were carefully considered, and the man who offered to receive the dues at his
own risk was obliged to give competent security. In this
way Marie de Médicis handed over to Augustin Bonsergent
the proceeds of the dues levied on the notaries and
scriveners of Languedoc and Provence, and to Jean
Viguier those levied on the process-servers and sergeants
of the kingdom.

These process-servers and sergeants, hitherto only entitled to practise in the district attached to their respective
Parlements, now received the right to practise in the rest
of the kingdom on the payment of a due to the Queen.
Notaries, process-servers and sergeants pursued their profession in virtue of commissions granted by the stewards,
seneschals, and provosts who admitted them. It was
decided that they should be given royal letters on payment of further fees, which were to pass into the hands of
the Queen.

The " late receivers and farmers of the *gabelle* in the
district of Lyon " had some balances of accounts to settle,
and possible fines to pay in respect of apparent irregularities in their documents. Marie acquired these re-
mainders.

In 1605 the officials of the bureaus of election were re-
instated in their rights and privileges throughout the
kingdom, and they also had to hand over fees to the Queen.

Over and above this, Henry IV. agreed to give his wife

" the money received from the settlement of the four matters reserved by the letters of pardon which he had granted to his officials in the year 1607, and also the revenue derived from money made by the officials and other persons who were commissioned to recover and receive licences of all kinds." To her he also gave the money " invested in funds resulting from the general or special receipts from the demesne lands, from aids, taxes, tallages, tithes, mortuary dues, the gabelle, customs, and from dues on or off the demesne lands ; from houses and from town halls throughout the kingdom ; for the payment of certain rents, which had been commuted, compounded, or already used in the shape of receipts, or which were no longer due or had become obsolete by disinheritance, forfeiture, and lapse of time." He also gave her the money derived from " exempt persons called *francs topins*," or from " free fiefs and from the additional receipts and acquisitions made by the administration of the taxes and from the revision of the accounts of the receivers of the districts of Languedoc," and so forth.

In fact there was no fiscal expedient, no feudal or administrative right, which the projectors did not inquire into minutely in order to discover some unsuspected source of revenue. A proclamation of the Council of State dealing with the increase of the powers of the official scriveners shows that the money derived from this was needed in order to enable the Queen to liquidate certain debts in the matter of her stables and her silver, on the ground that her ordinary income was barely adequate for the expenses of her household. Queen Marguerite objected to this proclamation, and alleged that she had the right to receive this impost throughout her dower lands, and Marie de Médicis informed her that it should be as she wished, expressing her regret that there had been a dispute on the point. The Queen was in the habit of asserting that these revenues were given to her to assist in meeting the expenses " of our household." They are not here given in full ; the States-General of 1614 demanded the total abolition of offices created since 1576, "except those of payers of pensions and First Commissioners of the Treasury, which are the only offices which the Queen has proved to have been granted to her by the late King ; none the less the suppression of these at the death of the present holders is demanded, since they are a charge on your finances and an injury to your people."

The projectors did more. In 1609 the Spaniards expelled the last of the Moriscoes from the Peninsula by a proclamation of January 10. It was estimated that there were two millions of these people in Spain, and while some of them went to Africa, the rest made their way across the mountains into France. It was the original intention of Henry IV. not to receive them, but when they poured in crowds into the valleys, he was compelled to do so. They were forbidden by him to cross the Dordogne, and he urged them to embark for Africa at the ports of Languedoc. Minute directions were issued to the authorities for the avoidance of disorder, violence and robbery, whether committed by the Moriscoes against the people, or by the people against the Moriscoes, and the whole incident created much trouble.

Some eight or nine hundred thousand of these unhappy beings made their way across the Pyrenees in miserable plight, and spread over the south of France in a condition of absolute destitution. Yet it was suggested that they should pay for this temporary hospitality by the sacrifice of their "clothes, personal property, and gold and silver whether coined or not," and that the profits resulting from this practical brigandage should be handed over to the Queen. Fortunately the Parlement of Toulouse raised an honourable objection to this outrageous robbery.

Whether it was the result of this daily increase of debts, or of the opposition of the Supreme Courts which nullified the King's gifts, all the various methods proved inadequate, and in the end the Queen resolved, without the knowledge of Henry IV., to attempt a more effective increase of her revenues by engaging in commercial undertakings and indulging in profitable speculations of all kinds.

To begin with she tried shipowning. She bought " a great vessel " in the Low Countries, with which she proposed to undertake the carrying trade between the Dutch and Italian coasts. The result was disastrous. The Dutch were masters of the carrying trade of the world, and were anxious to retain their monopoly. Already in 1604 they had declined to allow Henry IV. to fit out ships in the Low Countries, without making any concealment of their reason for this refusal ; and their privateers preyed upon rival merchantmen. In the present instance, the States of the United Provinces, ignoring the lofty rank of the shipowner, laid an embargo on this vessel, on the score of certain technical errors. Marie applied to her husband, but received an unfavourable answer. " Cut to the heart," as she wrote, she addressed herself to M. de Buzanval, the French Ambassador to the United Provinces, and to Aarsens, the Dutch envoy in France, moving heaven and earth to recover her ship. This first essay had turned out badly.

She then tried a different plan, advancing money to other traders. Arriving at Havre, in the course of her travels, she agreed to invest several thousand crowns in four ships going to Peru, being anxious " to venture something " ! A certain M. de Serre was instructed by her to " watch for their return and let me know how much my profit amounts to." When the time came, she told him, " immediately on the arrival of each ship he was to examine carefully what they had brought back, causing them to bring before you in detail their merchandise, papers, and inventories, that I may not be swindled out of that which is my due." Unfortunately, the season was exceptionally bad, and the speculation turned out ill. Not only did Marie make none of her hoped-for profit, but her capital was endangered. " Fortune has been so very unfavourable," she wrote sadly, " that through no avoidable fault, it may even be impossible to recover my principal."

The second venture had met with no greater success than the first.[1]

She then tried to turn some of her ornaments to account. At times of especial difficulty, when she wanted a jewel which was too costly, and when the jeweller would not sell it to her on credit, she went through her drawers, looked up gold trinkets for which she no longer cared, and sold them. As she was descended from accomplished bankers, she knew how so to do this as to avoid suspicion. First of all, she put the gold in the melting-pot ; caskets presented to her by the provinces, gifts from the King, objects of vertu, statuettes, and bracelets. It was then weighed, and sold for cash, as metal. It was thus that she dealt with her old gold plate, and to the melting-pot went " the gold cow, standing on a pedestal decorated with small jewels," presented to her by the district of Béarn in 1602, and " valued at four thousand crowns in all."

She had recourse to an Italian pawnbroker. The history of the incident is long and obscure. Many years before her time, the French kings of the sixteenth century, when in need of money, had borrowed it from Italian bankers, to whom they had handed over their crown jewels as security. One by one these jewels had gone to Rome or to Florence, where they had often been sold in fault of redemption. The Ruccellaï had been the chief agents in this business. In 1576 M. de la Rocheposay, the French ambassador at Rome, had been officially employed to place the crown diamonds in the hands of " certain Italian princes and states." The history of these jewels is not very clear. We have an inventory of the crown jewels in 1570, and six years later Rocheposay had pledged some of them, as is evident from " A list of the crown jewels

---

[1] The nobles at this period were allowed to engage in wholesale though not in retail trade. The public was, however, aware that "the greatest and more prudent nobles secretly offend in this matter by means of agents." Shipowning was a highly organised business ; Parisians, such as Hélie Fruit, Marie's jeweller, were engaged in it. The authority for the commerce of the period of Henry IV. is Ch. de la Roncière (*Revue des Questions Historiques*, 1904, p. 157).

which M. de la Rocheposay is instructed to place in pledge
with certain princes and states of Italy." Others were
pledged at a later date. Marie de Médicis took advantage
of the fact that the records dealing with these jewels were
so obscure to borrow for herself in Italy by sending thither
jewels which belonged to the King. The whole affair is
sordid. A distinction was then drawn between the
personal jewels of the Queen, which were her actual property and which she could give away or sell, and those of
the Crown which were inalienable. The matter concerned
the lists of these last, and the Chamber of Account, when
some heavy expenditure for the buying of a diamond was
brought before it in the Queen's accounts, had no scruples
in asking if the article bought had been entered on the list
of the crown jewels. Marie de Médicis naturally declared
in answer to this that she had purchased it with her own
money, for herself, and not for the profit of the State.

On her own behalf the Queen dealt with the Ruccellaï,
who had organised a firm of money lenders, and she confused her own business with that of the jewels already
pledged. At first it was carefully concealed from Sully,
but had eventually to be explained to him. There are
many urgent letters from Marie on this matter. To hide
what she had done, she urged Henry and his minister to
settle the whole matter at one stroke by redeeming all the
jewels on pledge in Italy, and Sully, in his *Economies
royales*, claims credit for this redemption. It was only
completed with difficulty. Henry IV., when his wife first
tried to bring it about, declared that he would not concern
himself with the matter. In her correspondence with the
Ruccellaï, the Queen urged them to agree to a composition,
reducing the sums which had to be paid ; but the difficulty
was to find the money. Eventually the King found that
the Queen had pledged the crown jewels, and after his first
natural burst of anger, determined to redeem them.

The negotiations were difficult. The Ruccellaï came to
Paris ; Marie de Médicis sent to Italy. The Government
of Henry IV. was resolved to supply the means of payment

by carrying through an edict which should exempt two persons in every parish from the payment of certain imposts, fees and dues, in return for a lump sum. Despite the resistance of the Parlements, which refused to register, a solution was reached in 1607. Nicolas Roger, one of the Queen's chamberlains and a goldsmith, went to Rome : the ambassador there, M. d'Alincourt, acted. The end of the business appears in the " Discharge given to Cardinal du Perron for the crown jewels which he brought back from Rome ; " the heirs of Horacio Ruccellaï handed over the jewels to him, and he returned with the valuable pledges in September 1607.

Marie de Médicis borrowed on all hands, and was well acquainted with the wretched lot of masters who are forced to depend for financial aid on the complaisance of their stewards. The unfortunate M. Florent d'Argouges had not only to undertake personal responsibility for those expenses which the captious Chamber of Account refused to sanction in the Queen's budget, but was also obliged to supply from his own pocket the means of gratifying the merest whim of the Princess. On one occasion, when she had conceived a passionate desire to purchase from the goldsmith de La Haye a diamond costing four thousand hundred crowns, as well as a dozen small gold buttons five valued at five hundred and thirty-eight livres, Marie, who was without a penny, offered to pay the merchant the amount from the King's winnings at the table—a curious source of revenue ! It appeared that the King had made some such promise, but, not unnaturally, the goldsmith declined the offer. M. Florent d'Argouges was then urgently " desired " to advance the necessary sum. Luckily for him, his control of the accounts enabled d'Argouges to evolve a method by which he could recover that which was owed to him whenever a profitable receipt came in. None the less, when he died in 1615, twenty-eight thousand two hundred and fifty-five livres were still due to him, though the fact that he was succeeded by his son indicates that his position was by no means without profit.

The embarrassment in which these complicated transactions involved Florent d'Argouges was so great that he was successfully prosecuted for debt, and all that the Queen could do was to secure proclamations from the Council of State "suspending the decree of the Parlement."

We have just spoken of Marie's bizarre proposal for paying a merchant, which, however, was but one of many similar devices, the direct outcome of extreme financial embarrassment. Thus, in order to satisfy the silver merchants Robin and Briant, she offered them whatever could be made out of mistakes in calculating the price of salt in the districts of Orléans and Moulins! The best of the story is that the wretched creditors, impressed by the letters patent professing to secure their rights, accepted the offer! On another occasion, when she had bought from M. de Monglat de Sain-Aubin four diamonds at the immense price of ninety-six thousand livres, she arranged for payment on the following terms: M. de Monglat was to receive six thousand livres in cash and for the rest was to have recourse to one Médéric Levasseur, " who had previously bought the right to farm the duty of thirty sous on every hogshead of wine entering the city and faubourg of Saint-Maixent." The farming dues for 1607 and 1608 were still owing, and the right was transferred to M. de Monglat, with the caution that he would take anything in excess of what was due to him " at his peril." The payment at least of interest on the sums due to them was demanded by those who would not agree to these extraordinary proposals, and so high was the rate of interest that it was said to be more like an annual penalty for delay in payment. Among others, Hélie Fruit and Mathieu Coulbes, jewellers, received for the space of several years four thousand livres as interest on thirty thousand livres due to them " for articles of jewellery sold and for each year of credit." The rate was over twelve per cent.

The difficulties in which the Queen of France found herself involved, and for which she was constantly trying to find a remedy in so many different ways, were, as we have said, to some extent the result of her relations with the Chamber of Account. Reorganised by Henry IV. in 1598, and strengthened by his action, the Chamber was full of zeal. Determined sticklers for form, its members demanded not only that all authorisations of expenditure on account of the Queen's household " should specify on what fund the expenses were to be charged," but also that all payments should be passed and audited by the Queen's Intendant General of Finance. When the intendant, M. d'Attichy, suffering from an illness which proved fatal, was unable to sign these quittances, M. Florent d'Argouges narrowly escaped ruin ! Failing these formalities, the Chamber refused its sanction : it was all illegal. Marie had to write a lengthy and detailed letter on the illness and death of d'Attichy.

On the day following Henry's assassination, Marie de Médicis sent an order for four hundred thousand livres to the Treasury, for the purpose of making good the deficit on the budgets of 1607 and 1608. She changed her mind when the money came, paying three hundred and twenty thousand four hundred and nineteen livres of debts, and causing Florent d'Argouges to set aside fifty thousand livres of the balance " to be used," as she said, " to meet our personal expenses." The Chamber authorised the withdrawal of four hundred thousand livres from the Treasury on her sole authority, and approved the payment of three hundred and twenty thousand livres of her debts ; but it struck out the fifty thousand livres from the accounts of the Comptroller, and left him to make good the loss, on the ground that " there was no receipt for the fifty thousand livres." It was in vain that d'Argouges pointed out that the sum was the balance in hand of the four hundred thousand livres ; he got nothing. He was compelled to wait for four or five years, until the emphatic commands of the Queen-regent induced the Court to give way.

The Treasurer sometimes waited nine or ten years for the definite settlement of trivial items in his accounts. In the budget of 1601 appear ninety livres to a certain doctor, M. Cappe ; in 1603, one hundred and ten livres ten sous to M. Arnauld, a councillor ; three hundred livres to M. de Bullion, and two hundred livres to M. de Rougemont, a clerk to the Council. The Chamber pointed out that M. Cappe was credited in the accounts with only ten livres ; that M. Arnauld, not having received his councillor's certificate until May 8, 1603, was not entitled to the entire year's salary ; that as to the other two, their names did not appear on the list of the household. It therefore said that a total of six hundred and sixty-three livres had been improperly paid away by the Treasurer General, and it disallowed this amount. For ten long years the Treasurer and the Queen pressed their claims, as the former had advanced the amount out of his own pocket, but it was not until 1612 that the Chamber gave way at the Regent's command, on receipt of a formal order to enter these six hundred and sixty-three livres.

There was no species of administrative chicanery to which the Chamber did not resort in order to find an excuse for refusing its sanction to items of expenditure. When the Queen gave a money present to any member whatsoever of her household, the document had to be countersigned by her private secretary, M. Phélippeaux de Villesavin. She once proposed to present M. Phélippeaux himself with a gift of one thousand two hundred livres, and he innocently countersigned the order. The results were most serious ! The Sovereign Court was extremely reluctant to pass these one thousand two hundred livres, on the ground that " the said Phélippeaux might not use his official position for his own advantage." Once more a royal mandate was required. It had been in vain that the Queen had explained that she had only one private secretary. One can have little conception of the innumerable objections raised by the Chamber on questions of trivial detail.

What ceaseless bickerings arose ! At one time the Chamber finds that the Queen has too many secretaries and masters of requests, poorly paid though they were, and Marie de Médicis, forced to defend herself, explains that the King appointed most of them, while at the same time she apologises and promises not to increase the total number and even to reduce it. At another time, the Court takes upon itself to exclude officials of the Queen's household from the privileges and exemptions enjoyed by those of the other royal households, of which privileges the most important was immunity from taxation. Perpetual chicanery was the result. We have seen what constant opposition was offered by the Court to the registration of edicts creating sources of revenue when they came before it, and it was a fortunate matter if this opposition was based only on irregularities in drafting, since it could then be overcome by a mere alteration in the wording of the edict. But the additional difficulties experienced by the sovereign in the management of her finances were without limit. Despite the fiction of unlimited power and the meaningless " such is our pleasure " with which royal proclamations concluded, the sovereigns were far from en- joying absolute executive authority. The ability of the different bodies to oppose was derived from no remnant of that spirit of disorder which had been the outcome of the troubles of the civil wars ; it was the effect of an adminis- trative tradition, bureaucratic in essence, narrowly formal and captious. It was this tradition which prevented the Queen after the death of Henry IV. from giving as free rein to her fancies as one might have expected. She could command more readily ; her ordinary revenues were in- creased ; but as her embarrassments increased with her expenses, Marie was reduced to still more extraordinary expedients. She met the demand of the Chamber of Account for modifications in her budget of 1609 with a declaration. The States-General of 1614 made a similar demand for the reduction of the expenses of the royal households.

As Regent of the kingdom, Marie de Médicis was unable to support her position without exceeding her original income, the four hundred thousand livres which she had still retained. First of all she had her dower in addition, and having examined the precedents, the officials of the Treasury decided that this dowry ought not to amount to more than one hundred and fifty thousand livres a year, a sum which was not very large considering the average annual deficit of the Queen. The letters patent of July 25, 1611, which named the total amount, named also the lands and lordships from which the Queen was to raise this sum. Yet the dowry was officially declared to be only the equivalent of the "interest on the marriage portion" of the sovereign. Indeed contemporary lawyers put forward involved theories as to the legal position in France of the personal property of the Queen in relation to the King, the Crown, and the nation at large. Henry IV. had discussed at length with Louise de Vaudemont, the widow of his predecessor Henry III., the question of the settlement of her dowry ; notes, drafts of agreements, and duplicate copies of the same had been exchanged between their representatives as to her marriage contract. It was not until three years after the death of Henry III., in October 1592, that his widow was able to secure the settlement of her financial position. She died at Moulins in 1601 at the age of forty or less.

Henry IV., in his marriage contract with Marie de Médicis, had settled the Queen's dower in advance at an annual income of twenty thousand gold crowns and a mortgage on the royal demesnes ; our information on this point is explicit. Letters patent of Louis XIII., fixing his mother's dower, were duly verified by the Chamber of Account. In the opinion of lawyers, the legal regulations as to the personal property of the Queen were precise, as appears from the case of Louise de Lorraine.

By letters patent of July 25, 1611, it was arranged that the Queen should begin to enjoy the proceeds of her dower on January 1, 1612 ; that is, a year and a half were necessary for the settlement of the matter. Marie claimed arrears from the date of her husband's death.

Fifteen districts were enumerated as making up the
dower lands ; the duchy of the Bourbonnais, the county of
La Marche, the duchy of Auvergne, the county of Auvergne
and Clermont, the barony of La Tour, the county of Forez,
the county of Nantes, the wardship of the castle of
Guérande, and so forth. Of these lands, the Queen was
" the lord," that is she received only the feudal and
seignorial dues, dues on the sale of lands held by feudal
tenure, succession duties on the property of aliens, fines of
justice, escheats, and dues payable for nomination to
offices and benefices. The duchy of the Bourbonnais,
which had already formed part of the dower of Louise de
Vaudmont and which appeared to be habitually assigned
for this purpose, brought in hardly four thousand three
hundred livres in all. Indeed, the apparent income was
in no sense realised ; year in, year out, in the opinion of
financiers, the total outcome of these revenues should
amount to one hundred and fifty thousand livres. The
income from each estate appears in the accounts of the
Queen, and it is evident that the total did not reach the
estimated sum.

Marie was following the bent of her inclination in
developing her demesne by the acquisition of lands in her
private capacity. For purchasing these lands, she relied
on the extraordinary sources of income which she found on
all sides owing to her authority as Queen-regent, and the
annual income thus went to her. It was in this way that,
as early as 1611, she bought the land and lordship of Saint-
Jean-des-Deux-Jumeaux, near her château of Montceaux ;
in 1612 the lands of Carentan and Saint-Lô from Marshal
de Matignon ; in 1613 the duchy of Alençon from a German
Prince, the Duke of Würtemberg. This last acquisition
was at once the most important and the most difficult. It
throws a flood of light upon the methods which Marie de
Médicis used and upon the financial conduct of contemporary princes.

During times of trouble, Henry III. and Henry IV. had
been alike constrained to borrow various sums from Duke

Frederic of Würtemberg, the total of which amounted to
three hundred and one thousand eight hundred and forty-
nine crowns, thirty-seven sous, twelve deniers, part of this
money bearing interest at the rate of five, and part at the
rate of eight and a third per cent. The total of the debts
due to the Duke of Würtemberg from Henry IV. which we
have given in crowns according to a proclamation of the
Council of State, is by another decree declared to be nine
hundred and sixty thousand and fifty-five livres, sixteen
sous, and six deniers. Duke Frederic died in 1608, and was
succeeded by his son John-Frederic, who reigned until 1628.

Henry IV. had undertaken to repay this debt in instal-
ments beginning in 1600, but afterwards, disheartened by
the amount of the total, suggested to the Duke that, in
order to compensate him, he should make over to him " as
a security, and with the perpetual right of re-emption, the
domains, mansions, lands and lordships of Alençon, Val-
ognes, Saint-Sauveur-Lendelin, Saint-Sauveur-le-Vicomte
and Néhou." The Duke accepted the proposal, which was
carried out under a contract of April 23, 1605, but the King
had some difficulty in persuading the Parlement of Normandy to verify the bill of sale.

As a result, these possessions, which were so far away
from him, were only an embarrassment and worry to the
Duke ; their administration was faulty, and there were
countless difficulties connected with them. When he
learnt in 1612 that Marie de Médicis was buying land, he
offered to sell back to her all that he owned in Basse-
Normandie : he promised that payment should be on the
easiest terms, that the Queen should use as her agent in the
matter the international bank of Lumagne and Sainctot,
which should transmit the stipulated price to the Duke at
the exchange of Frankfort-on-the-Main. M. d'Attichy,
and Léonora Galigaï, the Queen's confidant, strongly urged
the Regent to accept the offer, and in the spring of 1612
the business was arranged, the price being fixed at two
hundred thousand crowns, or six hundred thousand livres,
of which the first instalment was to be paid at Frankfort at

the next Easter fair. When that time arrived, Marie had not got the money. Deeply concerned about the affair in which she was engaged, and very anxious "to get the matter finished," she sent M. de Courson to Frankfort, with instructions to explain the compulsory delay in payment. She maintained that she wished to fulfil all her engagements, and she prayed the Duke to assist her "by agreeing to the times and places for payment and to the system of sureties which the said Courson will propose to you."

The date of settlement was postponed to the next fair, at which de Courson again appeared, and explained that the Queen had the amount ready to hand, but that the bankers Lumagne and Sainctot had been unable to arrange for its conveyance. He added that at the ensuing fair, she would, without fail, send the first third of the debt, and that the other two-thirds should be paid at the Easter and September markets of the following year. If the Duke would agree to it, the bankers would advance bills of exchange, bearing interest "at the rate of twenty deniers," and this would enable him to change them with the merchants of Germany. Meanwhile the duchy of Alençon should remain in pledge for the whole amount of the capital and for the interest, while at the same time the Duke was to hand over to the Queen the enjoyment of the Norman demesnes as soon as he should receive the first instalment. In order to assist the progress of these negotiations, Marie de Médicis wrote an extremely friendly letter to the steward of the Duke of Würtemberg's German property, M. de Beninghausen—"Beningose," as she called him—and accompanied the letter with "a mark and reminder of my good-will" in the shape of a beautiful gold chain and a medal. The German Prince agreed to these suggestions, all the details of which and of the other negotiations on the matter are to be found in the Queen's correspondence. She was clearly much concerned about the affair, and preferred rather to send to Frankfort than to write. "I do not mind the expense of the journey."

T

The next trouble was with the bankers. MM. Sainctot and Lumagne had little belief in the Queen ; they exacted very hard terms. In the end a contract was concluded with them on September 4, 1612, under which the Queen was to owe them not the six hundred thousand livres which had actually to be paid to the Duke, but seven hundred and twenty-one thousand livres. She further agreed to pay them interest at the rate of seven thousand livres a year on this amount, until the business was settled ; the bankers had demanded ten thousand livres, but the sum was reduced by the Council of State. They insisted that they had to bear the charge of " changing and re-changing the money," and the business was indeed very laborious. But it was the character of Marie de Médicis, the disorder of her finances, and the impossibility of securing prompt satisfaction from her owing to the insurmountable opposition of Courts and bureaus, that drove them to take precautions.

Punctually at the fast of Saint-Rémy, 1613, they carried through at Frankfort the transference of the first third, two hundred thousand livres, to the Duke ; and on the ensuing settling days they paid over the remainder. Five years later their loans had still not been repaid to them ; they demanded ten thousand livres interest, which was refused. They insisted on it as the yearly value of their capital, but the Parlement, the Chamber of Account, and the Court of Aids united in refusing this demand. It was Louis XIII., after the close of his mother's regency, and her departure from Paris, who by his letters patent of January 1618 put an end to the business. Even then it was completed only by means of royal mandates which Marie de Médicis' Council was forced to demand owing to the way in which the Sovereign Courts dealt with the matter in their proclamations.

By the union of her dowry and her personal property, Marie de Médicis managed to secure a total revenue which was twice that of which she had been possessed during the lifetime of Henry IV. It was soon discovered, from experience, that the dower lands were far from producing the expected one hundred and fifty thousand livres. We have mentioned that the duchy of the Bourbonnais only brought in four thousand three hundred livres, and from the statement of receipts for 1612 and 1613 we can construct the following estimate of the revenue of the Queen-regent. The duchy of Auvergne produced nine thousand two hundred and eighty livres, the county of Forez eight thousand, the county of Nantes three thousand seven hundred and seventy-two, and the other lands proportionate amounts ; the total came to sixty-four thousand livres, a deficiency of eighty-six thousand ! This deficiency was met by taking the amount needed from the general sum of the revenues of the kingdom. On the other hand, the lands of Montceaux and Saint-Jean-des-Deux-Jumeaux were farmed out and brought in revenue, but this was all spent on the upkeep of the château of Montceaux. The duchy of Alençon brought in thirty-six thousand livres, which was entirely the proceeds of seignorial dues ; Carentan and Saint-Lô, six thousand. Marie farmed out the isolated portions of her demesnes together to a certain Claude Largentier for sixty thousand livres. She retained in perpetuity an annual grant, which had been made to her by Henry IV. at some uncertain period, of one hundred thousand livres from the five great taxes, and seventy-two thousand livres on external and internal trade, as well as the four hundred thousand livres which constituted her normal budget. The total of her average yearly receipts thus reached eight hundred and twenty thousand livres.

As she constantly spent far more than the amount placed at her disposal, the Queen every year exceeded her resources. Her expenditure increased ; in 1611 it amounted to one million and five thousand four hundred livres, in 1617 to one million two hundred and twenty-five thousand eight hundred and eighteen livres, and in 1614 to one million eight hundred and eighteen thousand and fifty-seven livres, the deficit being a million livres ! One may ask what caused all this excess in expenditure ?

When she had become Regent, curiously enough, Marie de Médicis kept up a household which was no more elaborate than that which she had maintained in the lifetime of Henry IV. Her new rank was only indicated by the fact that a company of the bodyguards was specially attached to her service.[1] The maintenance of these guards formed a charge on her budget of twenty-eight thousand four hundred and sixty-three livres in 1610, increasing to fifty thousand in 1611 and to sixty-seven thousand eight hundred and eighty in 1616, while in the following year it disappeared, as the guards were disbanded on the conclusion of the Regency. Considering that her revenue had been increased by four hundred thousand livres, these fifty thousand livres were not in themselves an excessive burden. In other respects, the items of the budget in 1612 or 1613 were exactly the same as they had been in 1603 or 1604. There appear the same figures, sixty thousand livres, for the expenses of the stable ; the same seventy-two thousand three hundred and thirteen livres for the wages of the staff ; the same yearly credit of thirty-six thousand for the casual amusements of the Princess.

Extraordinary expenses, arising from different causes, some admitted and some concealed, furnish the explanation of the deficits. So large were these last, the secret expenses, that one can practically say that all the accounts

[1] Complete details as to the expenses of Marie de Medicis as Queen-regent are given in the budget statements of 1612 and 1613. As to the guards, the Queen had, during Henry's lifetime, ten life-guards commanded by an adjutant as her guard of honour. She presented each soldier with fifteen livres a month, and the officer with forty. The squadron was drawn from the company of *gardes du corps*, who shared with the *gardes françaises* the performance of daily duty at the Louvre. Letters patent of Louis XIII., May 24, 1610, gave to his mother as Queen-regent a special division of bodyguards, commanded by Captain de la Chataigneraie, Lieutenant de Presle, and the officers de Montbron and du Mont. Daily service at the Louvre was performed by the captain, one officer, and twenty-four "gentilshommes maîtres" or archers of the guard. The company was on the same footing as the other companies of royal bodyguards. Those who were on duty slept in the Louvre. We have details as to their rich uniforms, cloaks, helmets, and short mantles of velvet trimmed with gold and silver.

submitted to the Chamber were cooked, while at the same time the origins of the exceptional sources of income to which the Queen had recourse in order to meet her debts were concealed. The deficit of a million per annum was far surpassed.

Among the additional expenses which were admitted there were some which explained themselves. Such, for example, were those which touched the building of the Palace of the Luxembourg; for the buying of lands, the sending of the architect to Italy that he might study the Pitti Palace, the plans and designs of the architect Salomon de Brosse, the beginning of the actual work, and the planting in the gardens of elms brought from a great distance. The whole represented a variable annual outlay, which was frequently large, but never became very serious. The same remark applies to the repairs undertaken at Montceaux, an annual charge of thirty-two thousand livres.

On the other hand the gifts to various persons, the pensions granted from generosity or weakness from the budget, are almost innumerable. The doctor Montalto received six thousand livres ; Zoccoli, tailor, eight thousand ; the chambermaid Salvagia nine thousand ; M. de Thémines ten thousand ; the Cardinal de Gonzaga fifteen thousand ; M. de Sillery twenty thousand. Some expenditure for luxury was revealed, not to mention twelve thousand livres needed for the repair of the Queen's carriages, or fifty-one thousand assigned for the renewal of the Queen's furniture when she went out of full mourning in 1612. No economy appears in the bills of the goldsmith-jewellers ; in the accounts of the single year 1613 the merchant François le Prestre received one thousand two hundred livres, Peter Oliver six thousand, Martin Bachelier and Mathieu Coulbes eighteen thousand each, Nicolas Roger twenty-seven thousand three hundred and thirty-two, and Hélie Fruit thirty thousand three hundred. In all over one hundred thousand livres, an eighth of the budget, were spent in one year for jewellery, and this sum did not include all the money spent in this way.

But the amount of expenditure, which Marie de Médicis preferred not to explain, is still more astonishing. The Queen was constantly demanding ready money from her treasurer, M. Florent d'Argouges, and declared that the sums which he handed over to her were " for our pressing personal needs, which we do not care to describe or explain to you more fully." This vague expression, which permitted no further question, was used with increasing frequency as more and more objection was raised, and the payments thus accounted for absorbed an alarming proportion of the Queen's income. In 1611 Marie received in this way and under this head seventy-three thousand livres, in 1612 ninety-six thousand, in 1613 two hundred and fifty-three thousand, in 1614 seven hundred and eighty-two thousand, in 1615 three hundred and fifty-five thousand, in 1616 two hundred and fifty-nine thousand, and in 1617 six hundred thousand livres. Over and above her ordinary income then, she received a total of two million four hundred and eighteen thousand livres in the seven years of her regency, for which she gave no explanation. Whence came this money and where did it go ? How was it, that at a time when auditing was as careful as we have shown, such sums could be diverted ? Where could they be raised under the rigid system of the public finances ? And, above all, to what purpose did the Queen devote them, since the expenses of her pleasures, excessive as they were, do not seem to have been large enough to account for such extravagance ?

In order to secure money, the Queen at first adopted the same policy as had been pursued in the lifetime of Henry IV., and, as she had no longer to win the King's assent, she enforced the registration of edicts granting her special revenues. Yet, either from fear of the factious opposition of the Courts, or because she discovered simpler means for obtaining what she wanted, she did not abuse this method. At the most, she secured the assignment to her of twenty-four thousand crowns on the taxes of Languedoc ; or " of the sums which have been taken from the officers and councillors of the great and lesser Chanceries of the kingdom and from the secretaries of the same for the succession to their posts ; " or " from the dues resulting from the offices of advocates practising in the Courts dealing with taxes and the assessment of the salt-duties." Such a gift as that of the money " which might be derived from the demesne rights attaching to the King from free fiefs and newly added lands " brought in to her the appreciable amount of sixty thousand livres ; that of the income derived from the creation of treasurers for three years brought in one hundred thousand, and a similar sum was realised in respect of the due payable by all who held temporary offices. These particulars are preserved for us in the papers of the Queen, and it may be added that Marie at her accession to the regency caused Louis XIII. to create two masterships in each trade.

She also profited by her possession of sovereign power to exact pecuniary gifts, more or less substantial, from individuals or public bodies, and here we come to the realm of questionable receipts. Marie contended that the presents were voluntary, but there is ground for thinking that the public decision of the General Assembly of the clergy in 1616, by which homage in the shape of one hundred thousand livres " for her private purposes," that is not to the State but to the Queen's privy purse, was made to Marie, was inspired by the person most interested. It is not well to inquire too closely into the question as to the extent to which a similar gift agreed to by " the three estates of the country and duchy of Normandy in their General Assembly held at Rouen on September 15, 1613," was voluntary ; Marie took the precaution of securing the confirmation of this present by the King, her son.

Going still further, Marie de Médicis made use, frankly and on a large scale, of the custom of taking commissions. It would be an error to think that the public opinion of the period readily condoned such action. If, as a matter of fact, the phrase and the act have since acquired a peculiarly dishonourable meaning, they were already subject to clear disapproval. Marie de Médicis dared to arrange for the receipt of commissions openly, under the very convenient title of "the Queen's pin-money," and the persons or bodies which paid them did not protest against the principle of the custom. The revenge of the magistrates was taken in 1617, after the fall of the Regent, when they sternly rebuked Léonora Galigaï for certain questionable actions on her part. They asked her if the Queen-mother "had not received gifts from the fees payable by those holding office by royal appointment," and Léonora in her alarm could only transfer the blame to her fallen mistress. She professed that she did not interfere in the affairs of Her Majesty, but found means to make the Queen responsible for the commissions which she was charged with having received. Filled with respect for the royal family, the magistrates, intentionally or accidentally, had charged Léonora with actions which we know were the personal acts of the Queen, and now they suspended inquiry. But the character of the questions is in itself enough to indicate the opinion of the inquirers.

Something which can hardly escape the name of dishonesty marked the demand for, and the receipt of, these commissions. The Regent gave up the rights of the State in return for commissions which she received. In 1613 Brittany had some small dues to pay. The States of the province protested vigorously, and insistently demanded the suppression of these dues, which they declared to be illegal imposts. Marie de Médicis agreed to abandon them if she were given a personal present of sixty thousand livres for her private pleasures. By an edict of January 1603, Henry IV. had increased the number of tribunals for hearing questions as to taxation in Guienne, and therefore the number of officers of the finances, a kind of measure which—as we have said—resulted in reducing the value of similar positions in the rest of the province. The injured holders of these offices opposing the edict, the Regent suggested to them that it should be rescinded in return for the transference of one hundred and nine thousand livres to her coffers ; and to this they consented.

Similar agreements were concluded in respect of the less important nominations. On the death of M. Miron, civil lieutenant of Paris, his brother, President Miron, should have succeeded him in virtue of a legal assignment of his office which the dead man had placed in the hands of the President. But Marie de Médicis wanted the post for her own proctor, M. le Jay, who had promised her a present of seventy-five thousand livres, if he secured the place. It was in vain that the ministers insisted that the common usage, regulations and traditional customs should be observed; the Queen stood firm. "The Queen lets nothing slip," was the angry cry of the public. M. le Jay got his lieutenancy, and Marie her "pin-money." He paid fifty thousand crowns for the post in addition to his present to the Queen.

It may be remarked that every one, high and low alike, indulged in these exactions, at this period. The States-General of 1614 declared that the malversation in the public finances for three or four years involved a sum of one million eight hundred thousand livres, and as far back as 1604 Henry IV. had prosecuted persons suspected of embezzlement.

But the final and most important method by which Marie de Médicis made money was by the deliberate appropriation of the treasure of the Bastille, until it was exhausted. Thus vanished the treasure which Henry IV. and Sully had so laboriously collected since 1602 and so jealously kept intact. The savings amassed during eight years of economical rule had been stored there, with the determination, laid down in an edict, that they were only to be used in time of war. Behind the thick outer door of the Treasure Tower, of which the key was in the hands of M. de Vanssay, lieutenant of the fortress, and a second door secured by three locks, the keys of which remained, one in the hands of the King, one with the Superintendent of the Finances, and the third with the Comp-

troller General of the Finances, were accumulated almost
thirteen millions, contained in over eight thousand sacks,
four strong-boxes, and two hundred and seventy casks.
The preparation for the great war which Henry IV. had
been on the point of undertaking at the moment of his
death had greatly reduced the total, but at the accession of
Louis XIII. there remained five millions which had been
examined and checked on January 27, 1611, on the occasion of the disgrace and banishment of M. de Sully.

The Chamber of Account, financiers all, had secured the
re-enactment of the edicts which prohibited the use of this
money except for military purposes, and then only under
letters patent properly verified.   For three years Marie de
Médicis succeeded in restraining her greed.   But the crisis
of 1614, and the need for raising troops, furnished the first
excuse for passing the forbidden threshold.   On February
22, 1614, two million five hundred thousand livres were
taken ; in the following year Marie boldly decided to
appropriate a further one million two thousand livres, on
the ground, she said, of the marriage of the King and since
she had not a crown with which to meet the expenses resulting from this event.   As no war was in progress, the
Chamber of Account refused to accept the edict ; four
letters mandatory were in vain sent to the obstinate
Sovereign Court.   Marie de Médicis dispensed with its
assent.   A scene, remarkable for its solemnity, took place
on July 15, 1615, at the Bastille, when, at five o'clock in
the evening, the Queen went in great state to take the
money.   She caused the King, princes, dukes and peers,
the Crown officials, ministers, and intendants of the
finances, with the Swiss Guards, to accompany her.   M. de
Vanssay opened the first door at the command of the
Queen ; three keys were needed to open the second.   The
Queen had her own key, and M. Jeannin, Comptroller
General of Finance, and M. Phélippeaux, Treasurer of the
Exchequer, who had the other two and who were present,
were requested to hand over theirs.   They refused to do
so, declaring that the edicts had explicitly forbidden the

treasure to be used without letters patent verified by the Chamber of Account; that in the present case this condition had not been fulfilled ; and that if they assented to the appropriation of this money, the Chamber would hold them personally responsible for the sums taken. They therefore begged the Queen to attempt to gain the necessary verification by means of a fifth letter mandatory. Marie de Médicis replied that her own presence, her formal order drawn up in the presence of many witnesses, and those the most eminent of the kingdom, supplied, so far as they were concerned, a complete release from all responsibility ; she commanded them to give up their keys to M. de Tresmes, Captain of the Guards.

The two officers of the finances gave way as to superior force which compelled them to act. M. de Tresmes opened the door, and the chamber was entered. In the presence of the Queen, forty-one casks marked P.H., V.B., P.L., and one thousand two hundred sacks, which each contained a thousand livres in quarter crowns, or pieces of eighteen sous each, were taken away. Marie ordered the sacks to be taken to the house of M. Phélippeaux ; the doors were then again closed, the keys were returned, and the account of the transaction was drawn up in detail and in legal form, and attested by the signatures of the most distinguished witnesses.

A month later, on August 14, the Queen accomplished the removal of the remainder of the treasure, one million three hundred thousand livres, with the same display of authority. On this occasion, the Queen, feeling no scruples, did not even attempt to secure the registration of an edict from the Chamber of Account ; she proceeded by means of a simple proclamation of the Council, on the pretence first that she was pressed for time, as the King was about to go to Bordeaux, and then that the Chamber had made too many difficulties on the previous occasion. It was asserted that the whole action was necessitated by the expenses involved in the King's marriage.

Before the States-General of 1614, Jeannin had to explain what had happened to the treasure of Henry IV., as it was generally asserted that there had been maladministration of the finances since the retirement of Sully. He naturally defended the Queen, and Bassompierre also tries to show that Marie did not injure the financial position of the King. It is hardly necessary to point out how these details enlighten us on the extent of the power of the Crown in France at the beginning of the seventeenth century, on the theories of "assent to expenditure," which were so clearly maintained, and on the policy pursued between 1600 and 1700, from Henry IV. to Louis XIV.

If it is a comparatively easy matter to discover where Marie de Médicis found the money which she spent—five millions from the Bastille in two years—it is not so easy to say what was done with all this money, or at least to trace it in detail.

Speaking generally, the Regent undertook the payment of the debts which the Queen had owed on each of her budgets since her first arrival in France. She repaid the loans which she had had from her treasurers, simply giving an order to the Chamber of Account to pay M. Florent d'Argouges the sums named, without making any excuse, supplying any details, or giving any accounts. "For it is our pleasure," and the royal command was obeyed. Thus an order of December 25, 1611, instructed the Chamber of Account to pay d'Argouges a sum of nine hundred and sixty-seven thousand and ninety-six livres, nineteen sous, eleven deniers, and was issued by M. Doni d'Attichy, "intendent of our household and finances," without further explanation or any kind of justification.

Moreover Marie de Médicis gave many presents. Coming in conflict with the selfishness of the nobles, their ill-will, and their ardent ambition, she soothed quarrels and ended revolts with gifts of money. On December 14, 1613, at the end of three years of government, the total of her gifts reached as much as nine million six hundred thousand livres. This employment of money, as it was in the interests of the State as a whole, clearly concerned the Exchequer, the Treasury, and should not theoretically have affected the personal income of the Princess. The distinction between " the presents " of the Queen and the "grants of money " of the Regent was not, however, clear, and the necessity which the ruler had of giving undoubtedly involved her personal accounts. Despite the ordinance, signed by the ministers on behalf of Louis XIII. in 1610, when Henry IV. was hardly dead, in which the new King declared that in future no expenditure should be met if it were " hidden or confused with the money which is termed cash in hand "—a regulation which applied not only to the largess of the King of this kind, but also to the gifts made under the same name by " our most honoured lady mother, the Queen-regent "—despite the penalty assigned by this ordinance—which laid down that " if accidentally or otherwise any sum of money were entered as a payment on account, it should be disregarded and the sum paid erased and deleted from the statement of the accounts in which it appeared "—it is still certain that Marie de Médicis charged gifts for all purposes under this excuse. It is known that very great gifts were made by the Queen-regent. Between 1610 and January 31, 1612, she had distributed at the expense of the Exchequer three million livres, and, as we have said, by the 14th of December, 1613, the total of her gifts reached nine million six hundred thousand livres.

Finally, strange to relate, she saved money! This Princess, who took no forethought, who spent without thinking, and who appeared to be careless of the future, wished to invest money abroad ! Was she moved by the advice and example of the Concinis ? Did she feel that she was equally in danger, and think that the lot which awaited her might necessitate provision for leaving the kingdom ? It was afterwards alleged that the money sent to Italy in the Queen's name was really sent on the account of Léonora Galigaï ; her heirs even demanded the repayment of the money ; but the Government of Louis XIII., which also demanded and which eventually secured it, was able to prove that the sums had really been sent for the benefit of the Queen-regent. The account of the sending of this money, given by the banker himself at the trial of the Maréchale d'Ancre, leaves no doubt on the matter. The fact that the date of these foreign investments, the early months of 1617, coincides with the renewal of active and dangerous opposition to the Regent in general and to the Concinis in particular, and perhaps the receipt of some confidential information as to the *coup d'état* which was in preparation, as well as her sudden fear for her liberty if not for her life, are enough to explain Marie's resolve.

She carried it through with some haste. One morning, January 13, 1617, Marie ordered the banker, Jean-André-Lumagne, to come to the Louvre. He was a substantial man, fifty years of age, born in the neighbourhood of Ragusa, and ennobled in 1603. He had been a manufacturer, a merchant, a banker in all the countries of Europe, and in conjunction with the other bankers, Sainctot and Mascaragni, had become the agent for all international financial transactions.[1] The Queen explained to him that she had decided to place money in safety outside the limits of the kingdom, and that she wished to hand over to him the first instalment of this money. She asked him to undertake its conveyance across the Alps, for investment with the Italian money-lenders, who should place it wherever it might be invested under the best conditions, whether in Germany, the Low Countries, Cologne, Frankfort, or Antwerp. She then summoned the ladies in

[1] There were two Lumagnes, Jean-André and Charles, who were the chief bankers of Europe at this period. Jean-André, lord of Villiers and Saint-Loup, had a splendid house in the Rue Neuve-Saint-Merry, and a country house at Sannois, where he received Louis XIII. The letters of the Lumagnes and their partner Mascaragni are preserved. The bank had its chief house at Lyons, where the partner Mascaragni lived, as that city, being in direct communication with Italy, Germany, and Central Europe, was the chief commercial centre of France. All the trade in luxuries entered the kingdom by way of Lyons, where customs duties were levied on it. The merchants who attended the markets of Lyons were privileged by the King, and the banks in particular were very prosperous.

waiting, and in her presence they took from the Queen's strong-box two hundred thousand livres in pistoles, which were carefully counted and handed over to the banker in exchange for his receipt. The Regent protested that she was not making use of the money of the State, but of her own, and added that she was even thinking of sending six hundred thousand livres to Rome, and wished the money sent to that city to be placed in the hands of a Roman gentleman, Ferdinand Ruccellaï, with whom she had arranged for its investment so that it should bear interest at the rate " of twenty deniers."

The other amounts which M. Lumagne was at once to receive were to be handed over to the banker by different persons, as for example by the farmers of the five great taxes or by the Treasurer of the Dowry, M. Feydeau. M. Lumagne took the two hundred thousand livres and sent them at once to Lyons, to his partner, Paul Mascaragni, who sent them across the Alps to his agents. These details are revealed to us by the depositions of Lumagne at the trial of Léonora, which are extremely clear. Cardinal Borghese, Secretary of State to the Holy See, in a letter of September 16, 1617, instructed the nuncio Bentivoglio to warn the Government of Louis XIII. of the foreign investments of Marie de Médicis. Bentivoglio replied that it was generally reported that the money invested belonged to Léonora Galigaï, whereupon the Secretary retorted that there was no doubt that it was the property of the Queen-regent herself.

Three weeks later, on February 9, a further sum of one hundred and eighty thousand livres was sent, and on February 22 one hundred thousand livres, the proceeds of the Queen's dower, and these sums were handed over by M. Feydeau, as had been arranged. On March 14, one hundred and forty thousand livres were despatched.

All the evidence connected with these financial transactions was discovered shortly afterwards in the papers of the Maréchale d'Ancre, when she was arrested and her effects seized. The receipts were discovered in a small

casket, wrapped in some wearing apparel and labelled
Promesse di dinari della Maiesta della reina, which the
Maréchale had carried with her at the time of her arrest,
when an inventory of her papers was taken in the room in
which she was imprisoned in the Louvre. It is clear that
Cardinal Borghese had made no very important revela-
tions to the Government of Louis XIII.

The five great farmers of taxes had to account for
four hundred thousand livres, which were paid under
ambiguous conditions and in fact extorted. The farmers
of the taxes at Lyons, MM. Pierre Héroard, Jacques
Fagnier, Daniel Giovannini and Claude Buel, were informed that the King was in great and immediate need of
money ; that if they would not consent to hand over what
was demanded of them, they would find themselves in
difficulties, in lawsuits, and in troubles of all kinds, which
would culminate in the abrogation of their privileges. The
wretched men were compelled to obey. At the trial of
Léonora Galigaï, they made their angry complaints heard,
and whether in good faith or not, the victims of Marie de
Médicis attempted to recover their money by accusing the
Maréchale of the embezzlements of the Queen.

What was the sum total of these moneys sent to a safe
place ? The Queen declared to Santucci that she had sent
to Rome no more than one million two hundred thousand
livres ! It is not known what she sent to Germany, the
Low Countries and Holland. The sudden catastrophe of
April 24, 1617, which involved the murder of Concini, the
imprisonment of his wife, and the practical arrest of Marie
de Médicis, who was confined at first in her apartments in
the Louvre and then in the château of Blois, made these
precautions vain and useless. It is a curious end to the
royal life of an extravagant Regent, entirely given up to
careless expenditure and to thoughtless squandering, this
final impulse of bourgeois prudence, economy, and investment !

INDEX